The New Woman
and Her Sisters

The New Woman and her Sisters
Feminism and theatre 1850–1914

Edited by
VIVIEN GARDNER
and
SUSAN RUTHERFORD

9₂-16⁵⁴

Ann Arbor
The University of Michigan Press

Published in the United States of America by
The University of Michigan Press
1995 1994 1993 1992   4 3 2 1

Library of Congress Cataloguing-in-Publication Data

The New woman and her sisters : Feminism and theatre, 1850–1914 /
  edited by Vivien Gardner and Susan Rutherford.
      p.   cm.
   Includes bibliographical references and index.
   ISBN 0–472–10265–6 (cloth : alk. paper). — ISBN 0–472–08168–3
(pbk. : alk. paper)
      1. Feminism and theater—Great Britain.   2. Theater—Great
Britain—History—19th century.   3. Theater—Great Britain—
History—20th century.   I. Gardner, Vivien.   II. Rutherford,
Susan.
PN2582.W65N48   1992
792'.082—dc20   91–41480
                                                              CIP

To our mothers

Contents

Part III Women Singing

Part IV Venturesome Women

Part V Women Writing Women

Part VI Women in Control

List of Figures

Acknowledgements

Throughout this venture, we have benefited enormously from the unfailing support and generosity of our colleagues in the Department of Drama, Manchester University. We owe especial thanks to Professor Kenneth Richards, for kindly making the department facilities available to us; to Philip Cook, Paul Heritage, Michael Holt and George Taylor, for their sympathetic responses to our queries and problems; to Janet Jones and Claudette Williams for their invaluable secretarial services; and finally to Tony Jackson and David Mayer, whose initial course on the 'New Woman' in *fin-de-siècle* theatre was the true origin of this volume. The assistance of many kind friends made the staging of our conference on the 'New Woman' both possible and enjoyable: we are particularly grateful for the administrative and culinary skills of Chris Grimshaw; the warmth of the welcome we received at the Pankhurst Centre; the talents of a small but selfless band of actors (Jacqui Day, Simon Gleisner, Deborah McAndrew, Heather Phoenix and Katy Secombe); the informative exhibition mounted by Helen Day and David Mayer; the sterling aid given by students and former students too numerous to mention; and, of course, the interest of the conference participants themselves. The process of preparing the volume for publication has been made considerably easier by the tactful guidance of our editor, Jackie Jones. For permission to print copyright material we are glad to acknowledge the following: Mario Goetschel and David Mayer for the previously unpublished letters of Mary Garden; the Shakespeare Centre Library, Stratford-upon-Avon, for the photograph of Millicent Bandmann-Palmer; the Mander and Mitchenson Theatre Collection for the photograph of Julia Seaman; the Master and Fellows of Trinity College, Cambridge, for the photographs of Zazel and Leona Dare; and the courtesy of the Board of Trustees of the Victoria and Albert Museum for the photographs of Alice Marriot and Sarah Bernhardt. Our greatest debt, however, is to our contributors, whose commitment to this project has been truly generous and unstinting. Finally, although this volume is suitably dedicated to the first and most lasting female influences in our own lives, our mothers, we are equally conscious of the valuable support we have received from the much-loved men of our families: both from our fathers, and also from our partners, James and Jan, without whose constant encouragement, humour and understanding, we would be so very much the poorer.

Susan Rutherford
Viv Gardner

Notes on the Contributors

Zoë Aldrich taught film and television in the Department of Drama, Manchester University, from 1989 to 1990, and researched a documentary on early theatrical film. She is presently completing a postgraduate course in acting at the Webber Douglas Academy.

Elaine Aston is Lecturer in Drama at the University of Loughborough. Her essay in this volume is part of her Ph.D thesis entitled 'Outside the Doll's House: Images of Women in English and French theatre 1849–1914'. Her previous publications include essays for *New Theatre Quarterly*, and also *Sarah Bernhardt: A French actress on the English stage* (Oxford: Berg, 1989). With G. Savona, she has co-authored the volume *Theatre As Sign-System* (London: Routledge, 1991), and is also currently co-editing, with G. Griffin, *Herstory*, vols I and II, for the Women's Theatre Group.

J. S. Bratton is reader in Theatre and Cultural Studies at Royal Holloway and Bedford New College, University of London. Her many publications include *The Victorian Popular Ballad* (London: Macmillan, 1975), *The Impact of Victorian Children's Fiction* (London: Croom Helm, 1981), *King Lear: A stage history edition* (Bristol: Classical Press, 1987), *Coral Island* by R. M. Ballantyne (introduction to the Worlds Classics edition, Oxford: Oxford University Press, 1990), *Music Hall: Performance and style* (editor; Stony Stratford: Open University Press, 1986), and also essays in *Imperialism and Popular Culture* (Manchester: Manchester University Press, 1986), *Shakespeare and the Victorian Stage* (Cambridge: Cambridge University Press, 1986), the *Women's Review* and *Folk Music Journal*. Her forthcoming monographs and edited volumes include *Acts of Supremacy: The British Empire and the Stage* (Manchester: Manchester University Press, 1991), *Three Plays by Arthur Wing Pinero* (Worlds Classics edition, Oxford: Oxford University Press,

1991), *Cultural Politics and the Victorian Stage* (New Haven, Conn.: Yale University Press, 1992), *British Pantomimes* (Worlds Classics edition, Oxford: Oxford University Press, 1993) and *Women in the British Music Hall* (Cambridge: Polity Press, 1994).

Jill Davis is Lecturer in Drama at the University of Kent. She has edited *Lesbian Plays* (London: Methuen, 1987), *Lesbian Plays: Two* (London: Methuen, 1989); and published an essay entitled 'The lesbian drama of Mrs Havelock Ellis' in *Women: A Cultural Review*, vol. 1, no. 3, 1991. She is currently working on a book on lesbian theatre/drama from 1900 to 1990. She is a former member of the Arts Council Drama Panel and Chair of New Applications and Projects subcommittee.

Helen Day formerly lectured in Drama at both the Royal Holloway and Bedford New College, University of London, and Bangor College of the University of North Wales. She is currently a teacher/actor for *Between the Lines*, a TIE company based at the Pankhurst Centre which she founded in 1990, and which explores women's suffrage, equal opportunities and gender issues. She is co-author of *The Ticket O'Leave Man: 'A' Level study pack* (Manchester: Manchester University Drama Department, 1986).

Christine Dymkowski is Lecturer in Drama and Theatre Studies at the Royal Holloway and Bedford New College, University of London. She is the author of *Harley Granville Barker: A Preface to Modern Shakespeare* (London: Associated University Presses, 1986), and also of the introductions to three volumes of Eugene O'Neill's plays: *Long Day's Journey Into Night* (London: Nick Hern Books, 1991), *Strange Interlude* (London: Nick Hern Books, 1991) and *Anna Christie* and *The Emperor Jones* (London: Nick Hern Books, 1991). Futher introductions to O'Neill's *The Hairy Ape* and *All God's Chillun Got Wings*, *Desire Under the Elms* and *The Great God Brown*, *Mourning Becomes Electra, Ah! Wilderness, A Touch of the Poet, The Iceman Cometh,* and *A Moon for the Misbegotten* (London: Nick Hern Books, 1992–3) are also forthcoming, as are *The Tempest* (Plays in Performance series, Bristol: Classical Press) and *More than Miss La Trobe: A study of Edith Craig's Theatre Career* (London: Routledge).

Jill Edmonds is Senior Lecturer of the Department of Drama and Theatre Studies, Chester College of Higher Education, where she has taught since 1969. She is currently researching female actor–managers of the Victorian theatre.

Lesley Ferris is Director of Theatre at the Department of Theatre and Communications Arts at Memphis State University, and directed there the American première of Hélène Cixous's *Portrait of Dora* in November 1990.

Her book, *Acting Women: Images of women in theatre* was published by Macmillan (London) in 1990.

Linda Fitzsimmons is Lecturer in Drama, Theatre, Film and Television Studies, at the University of Bristol. She has edited *File on Churchill* (London: Methuen, 1991), and is co-editor, with Arthur McDonald, of *The Yorkshire Stage, 1766–1803* (Metuchen, New Jersey and London: Scarecrow Press, 1989) and, with Viv Gardner, of *New Women Plays* (London: Methuen, 1991).

Viv Gardner is Lecturer in Drama, at the University of Manchester. She is the editor of *Sketches from the Actresses' Franchise League* (Nottingham Play Texts, 1985) and, with Linda Fitzsimmons, co-editor of *New Woman Plays* (London: Methuen, 1991).

Geraldine Harris is Lecturer in Theatre Studies at the University of Lancaster. Her primary research interests are in women and the avant-garde, and her previous publications include articles for *Theatre File* and *New Theatre Quarterly*.

Susan Rutherford was Special Lecturer in Perfomance Studies at the Department of Drama, University of Manchester from 1986 to 1989. She is currently completing a Ph.D thesis on women and nineteenth-century opera.

Sheila Stowell is a lecturer in the Theatre Department of the University of British Columbia. Her publications include *A Stage of Their Own: Feminist Playwrights in the Suffrage Era* (Manchester: Manchester University Press, 1991) and, with Joel H. Kaplan, *Drama, Fashion, Society 1890–1914* (Cambridge: Cambridge University Press, forthcoming).

A Select Chronology, 1850–1918

	Social and political	Cultural	Theatrical
1850	North London Collegiate established.		
1851		Harriet Taylor, *Enfranchisement of Women*.	Charlotte Cushman plays Hamlet
1852		First wearing of Bloomer costume.	
1853			
1854	Cheltenham Ladies' College established.		
1855		Caroline Norton, *Letter to the Queen*.	
1856		Barbara Bodichon, *Women and Work*.	
1857	Matrimonial Causes Act: divorce reform act enabling men to divorce wives on grounds of adultery alone; women to divorce husbands for adultery plus cruelty, desertion, incest, rape (of another woman), sodomy or bestiality.		
1858		Dinah Craik, *A Woman's Thoughts About Women*.	
1859		Arthur Mumby begins writing his diary — continues until 1889. Mrs Henry Wood, *East Lynne. Englishwoman's Journal*.	Lotta Crabtree, aged 8, begins performing in the mining camps of California.

	Social and political	Cultural	Theatrical
1860	Society for Promoting Employment of Women. Nightingale Nurse Training School set up.		
1861			Madame Genevieve (Celina Young) crosses Thames on a high-wire. Alice Marriott as Hamlet at the Marylebone Theatre, London.
1862		Mary Braddon, *Lady Audley's Secret*.	First recorded performance of Tayleure's adaptation of *East Lynne*, at the Brooklyn Academy of Music, New York.
1863	Cambridge Local Examinations opened to girls.		Hazlewood's adaptation of *Lady Audley's Secret* opens at Royal Victoria Theatre, London.
1864	1st Contagious Diseases Act.		Marie Wilton takes over the Queen's Theatre, Tottenham Court Road, renaming it the Prince of Wales.
1865	Elizabeth Garrett Anderson granted medical licence.		Julia Seaman plays Hamlet.
1866	2nd Contagious Diseases Act. First petition to British Parliament for female suffrage.	Emily Davies, *The Higher Education of Women*.	
1867	National Association for Women's Suffrage formed. N. England Council for Promoting Higher Education of Women.		Sarah Thorne takes over management of Margate Theatre Royal—until her death in 1899.
1868	Ladies National Association against Contagious Diseases Acts.	Francis Paget, *Lucretia, or the Heroines of the Nineteenth Century* (parody of sensational novels). Eliza Lynn Linton, *The Girl of the Period*.	
1869	3rd Contagious Diseases Act.	Josephine Butler, *Women's Work and Culture*. John Stuart Mill, *The Subjection of Women*.	
1870	Married Women's Property Act: wives allowed to keep £200 of own earnings.		
1871		Josephine Butler, *Constitution Violated*. George Eliot, *Armgart*.	First recorded performance of Leona Dare at Hooley's Opera House in Brooklyn, New York.

1872			
1873	Custody of Infants Act: giving women custody of children up to age of seven. Girton College founded.		
1874	London School of Medicine for Women founded.		
1875	Newnham College founded.		
1876			
1877			Zazel first performs in London.
1878	National and Union Training School. London University admits women.		Dare appears in London at Oxford Music Hall. Henrik Ibsen, *A Doll's House*.
1879	Somerville College and Lady Margaret Hall founded.	Bebel, *Women and Socialism*.	Zazel appears in New York with Barnum's Circus. Dare performs balloon act at Alexander Palace – MP introduces bill to suppress dangerous performances. First London performance of Bizet's *Carmen*. Lotta Crabtree hires David Belasco to play Foxy Joe in her San Francisco production of *Little Nell and the Marchioness*.
1880			First performance of Ibsen in England – *Quicksands* or *Pillars of Society*. Emma Cons takes over management of the Victoria Theatre, renaming it the Victoria Coffee Music Hall.
1881	Cambridge degrees open to women, but not graduation.	Amy Fay, *Music Study in Germany*	
1882	Married Women's Property Act: women allowed to own and administer their own property.		
1883	Women's Co-operative Guild.	Olive Schreiner, *Story of an African Farm*.	
1884	Married Women's Property Act: woman no longer considered her husband's 'chattel' but separate and independent person. Fabian Society established.	Frederick Engels, *Origin of the Family*.	

	Social and political	Cultural	Theatrical
1885			Opening of Sarah Thorne's School of Acting. Dare banned from repeating her balloon act in Paris.
1886	Invention of the 'safety' bicycle.	Eleanor Marx and Edward Aveling, *The Woman Question*.	
1887	Agnata Ramsey heads 1st Class Hons in Classics at Cambridge but cannot graduate.	Rational Dress campaign.	
1888	Women's Trade Union League.		
1889			*A Doll's House*, Achurch/Charrington management. *Pillars of Society*, Mrs Oscar Beringer management – first appearance of Elizabeth Robins in Ibsen.
1890			
1891		Hughes le Roux, *Acrobats and Mountebanks*.	Independent Theatre founded by J. T. Grein – opens with *Ghosts*. *Rosmersholm*, Florence Farr. *A Doll's House*, Marie Fraser. *Hedda Gabler*, Lea–Robins management. Lotta Crabtree retires from the stage.
1892		Emily Massingberd opens the Pioneer Club for women of advanced views to meet and debate.	Millicent Bandmann-Palmer manages own company, touring the northern circuit.
1893	Independent Labour Party established.	George Egerton (Mary Chavelita Dunne), *Keynotes*. Sarah Grand, *The Heavenly Twins*. George Gissing, *The Odd Women*.	*The MasterBuilder*, Robins–Waring management. Independent Theatre Ibsen season – Grein–Robins. Beginning of Mrs Ormiston Chant's campaign against Empire Music Hall. Shaw writes *Mrs Warren's Profession*. Florence Bell and Elizabeth Robins, *Alan's Wife*.
1894	New Zealand Women's Suffrage Act. Local Government Act: women allowed to vote in local government elections.	George Egerton, *Discords*. Havelock Ellis, *Man and Woman*.	Yvette Guilbert gives first British performance at Empire Music Hall. Florence Farr produces experimental season at the Avenue Theatre, secretly financed by Annie Horniman. Sydney Grundy, *The New Woman*, at Comedy Theatre. Manchester Independent Theatre Society Ibsen season – Robins.

1895		Grant Allen, *The Woman Who Did.*	Emmaline Ethardo performs juggling/contortion act at Palace Theatre, London. Pinero, *The Notorious Mrs Ebbsmith*, at the Garrick Theatre. Marie Lloyd song, *Salute My Bicycle.*
1896			Guilbert tours America with 'coster' singer, Albert Chevalier. *Little Eyolf*, Robins–Foss management with Mrs Patrick Campbell and Janet Achurch.
1897	National Union of Women's Suffrage Societies formed under Millicent Garrett Fawcett.		*John Gabriel Borkman*, New Century Theatre, Robins–Archer.
1898		Sarah Grand, *The Beth Book.* Charlotte Perkins Gilman, *Women and Economics.*	Olga Nethersole takes over management of Her Majesty's Theatre.
1899			Sarah Bernhardt plays Hamlet at the Adelphi Theatre, London. The Stage Society set up to 'pioneer theatre of ideas'.
1900			
1901	Death of Queen Victoria.		'La Femme Nouvelle' discussed in *La Revue d'art dramatique.*
1902			First film version of *East Lynne* (Harrison, UK). First production of *Mrs Warren's Profession* at New Lyric Club. Shaw, *Man and Superman.* Olga Nethersole manages Adelphi Theatre.
1903	Women's Social and Political Union formed by the Pankhursts.		
1904			Dolly Shepherd performs parachute act. Barker–Vedrenne management of Court Theatre – until 1907. Olga Nethersole manages Shaftesbury Theatre. J. M. Barrie, *Peter Pan*, opens in London.
1905	First militant action by WSPU at Free Trade Hall, Manchester.		Belasco, *Girl of the Golden West*, opens in New York.

Year	Social and political	Cultural	Theatrical
1906	Women's Freedom League formed. Labour Party founded.		Guilbert and Chevalier appear at Duke of York's Theatre, London. First film version of *Lady Audley's Secret* (Walturdaw, UK).
1907	Qualification of Women Act: County and Borough Councils open to women.	WSPU newspaper, *Votes for Women*, set up. Artists' Suffrage League formed. Elizabeth Robins, *The Convert* – novel version of play, *Votes for Women*.	Elizabeth Robins, *Votes for Women*, at the Court Theatre. Opening season of Gaiety Theatre, Manchester, under Annie Horniman. Lena Ashwell takes over management of Kingsway Theatre. Music Hall Artists' strike.
1908	Women's National Anti-Suffrage League formed. Fabian Women's Group established.	Actresses' Franchise League and Women Writers' Suffrage League formed. Alexandra Kollantai, *Social Basis of the Woman Question*.	Actresses' Franchise League and Women Writers' Suffrage League formed. Cicely Hamilton, *Diana of Dobson's*, at the Kingsway Theatre. Shaw, *Getting Married*. Suffragette film, *When Women Rule* (Hepworth, UK).
1909	First hunger strikes by suffragettes. Forcible feeding policy implemented.	Cicely Hamilton, *Marriage as a Trade*. H. G. Wells, *Ann Veronica*. WSPU, *The Women's Exhibition*, at the Prince's Skating Rink, Knightsbridge, London.	Elizabeth Baker, *Chains*, at the Court Theatre. Ellen Terry and others appear in Cicely Hamilton's *Pageant of Great Women* for AFL and WWSL, directed by Edy Craig.
1910		Gertrude Atherton, *Tower of Ivory*.	First London performance of Strauss's *Salome*. Elizabeth Baker, *Miss Tassey*. Gertrude Kingston establishes Little Theatre, John Street.
1911	Escalation of militant tactics by WSPU following failure of Conciliation Bill.	Olive Schreiner, *Women and Labour*. Gertrude Collmore, *Suffragette Sally*.	Edy Craig founds the Pioneer Players; first production at Kingsway Theatre, 8 May. Lillah McCarthy takes over management of Little Theatre. Cicely Hamilton, *Just To Get Married*, at Little Theatre.

1912			Stanley Houghton, *Hindle Wakes*; Gaiety Theatre production opens in London, moves to Manchester then tours USA. Githa Sowerby, *Rutherford and Son*, at the Court Theatre. Elizabeth Baker, *Edith*. First Royal Command Performance. American National Women's Suffrage Movement and Reliance Films collaborate to make film, *Votes for Women*. Lilian Baylis takes over Old Vic.
1913	'Cat and Mouse' Act. Death of Emily Wilding Davison at the Derby.	Christabel Pankhurst, *The Great Scourge*.	Woman's Theatre Season at Coronet Theatre.
1914	First World War. Cessation of militant suffrage activities.		Guilbert condemns violence against British suffragettes. Film, *A Busy Day – a Militant Suffragette* (Chaplin–Keystone production). Film, *Girl of the Golden West* (Cecil B. de Mille).
1915		Clementina Black, *Married Women's Work*. Willa Cather, *Song of the Lark*.	
1916			Guilbert speaks at American Congressional Union for Women's Suffrage. Elizabeth Baker, *Partnership*. Elizabeth Baker, *Miss Tassey*.
1917			
1918	End of War. Woman Suffrage Act: property-owning women over age of thirty given vote. Countess Markievicz first woman elected to British Parliament – does not take up seat because member of Sinn Fein and in Holloway Prison at time.	Marie Stopes, *Married Love*.	

Introduction

VIV GARDNER

> The New Woman, this obsessing phantom of which everyone speaks and which so few have seen. [1]

This volume of essays started life as an idea for a book on the New Woman and the stage, in the context of what might loosely be called 'feminism' in British theatre in the 1890s. It soon became clear, however, that the concept of the New Woman alone was a complex one, and that it would be impossible to limit just to the 1890s any examination of the ways in which women have used the stage to challenge and subvert the prevailing male hegemony, or to confine the discussion to the 'legitimate' stage.

The result was that a conference was held by Manchester University Drama Department which brought together scholars working in many areas of theatre history. Whilst the conference had at its centre the original idea of the so-called New Woman and the ways in which she had been depicted on the stage, most of the contributors found much wider evidence of subversion of the female norm in diverse areas of nineteenth-century theatrical activity. Some of the papers looked outside England – providing a frustrating glimpse of parallel movements in Europe and America that the conference had no time to explore – while the parameters of the subject were extended to include the music hall and circus, opera, *café concert* and film. It was also necessary to start before 1890 in order to understand fully the radical nature of female performance in the nineteenth and early twentieth century.

This book, then, following the shape of the conference, examines the

1

relationship between the 'Woman Question' and the theatre of the end of the nineteenth century, looking backwards to the elder sisters of the New Woman, and forward into the twentieth century to some of her daughters. It is necessary, by the way of introduction, to look at the New Woman herself and at what she represented to the 1890s and the ways in which female performers of that *fin-de-siècle* era projected both positive and negative feminist images in their lives and work.

Latchkeys and cigarettes: The image of the New Woman

Sydney Grundy's play, *The New Woman*, opened at the Comedy Theatre on 1 September 1894. The poster for the performance shows a rather severe young woman in black, pince-nez perched on her nose. On the wall behind her in a cabinet is a large latchkey, in the margins of the poster a smouldering cigarette. This image of the New Woman was instantly recognisable to the public at large in 1894 – the latchkey and cigarette already infamous tokens of her 'advanced' nature. Grundy was capitalising on a potent and apparently fast-growing phenomenon.

The New Woman of the play's title is Mrs Sylvester, a married female of progressive views and conduct, who is author of a volume entitled *Aspirations after a Higher Morality*. While spending her time with the play's hero, Gerald Cazenove, collaborating on another work of radical, sexual philosophy, Mrs Sylvester wilfully neglects her husband – feeding him on cold mutton two days running and thus driving him to his club and the delights of the notorious Empire Music Hall.[2] Three other members of the New Woman sisterhood are regular visitors to Gerald's house, with devastating consequences for his masculinity. The opening stage directions describe Gerald's chambers as: 'A sitting-room, somewhat effeminately decorated. The furniture of the boudoir type, several antimacassars and a profusion of photographs and flowers.'[3] These three women are variously referred to as 'Frankensteins', 'of a new gender' and 'badly in need of a husband'. Like Mrs Sylvester, they are authors of advanced literature: *Man the Betrayer: a study of the sexes*, *Ye Foolish Virgins: a remonstrance* and *Naked and Unashamed: a few plain facts and figures*. They smoke 'on principle', argue about whether men too should be allowed latchkeys and become coy in the presence of any male. They are clearly dismissed by the author as objects of ridicule, but Mrs Sylvester is not. She is shown to be dangerous and her assault on the hero is not confined to his mind and décor; she soon drops any pretence of aspirations to a 'Higher Morality' in her relationship with Gerald and actively seeks to break up his marriage to 'a woman who is a woman'. This New Woman is an active threat to conventional male–female relationships.

Grundy's successful comedy presented its audience with two versions of

the New Woman; the caricature that borders on the grotesque and a more
serious figure. All four characters are drawn with something more than
general satirical intent. The play demonstrates an underlying hostility to the
whole notion of the New Woman.

There is profound irony in this. The women who played these roles were
themselves, in many ways, New Women. Simply by working they were
transgressing the social boundaries that required middle-class women to be
dependent on either father, husband or brother. To be working on the stage
doubled the offence and alienated these women from 'normal' female society:
'Doesn't one have to be [a strange girl] to want to go and exhibit one's self to a
loathsome crowd, on a platform, with trumpets and a big drum, for money –
to parade one's body and one's soul?'[4] At least two of the female cast of *The
New Woman* had gone further and had been associated with radical theatre
experiments of the day. Alma Murray, who played Mrs Sylvester, was a well-
established actress. She came from a theatrical family and had played Portia
with Irving at the Lyceum. More interestingly, in 1886 she had been involved
with the Shelley Society's production of Shelley's banned play, *The Cenci*,
which 'Shaw and every other person in London who regarded themselves as
cultivated, attended'.[5] Murray became an associate of Shaw and played Raina
in the première of *Arms and the Man* in Florence Farr's experimental theatre
season at the Avenue in 1894 – the same year that she created Mrs Sylvester.
Another member of the *New Woman* cast, Gertrude Warden, who played
Victoria Vivash as '*a garçon manqué*, who smokes and wears her hair short',[6]
was Mrs Linden in the first British production of *A Doll's House*. The part of
Gerald's wife, the 'real woman', was taken by Winifred Emery, who was later
to become a member of the Actresses' Franchise League. These actresses
were conspicuously independent, creative women involved with politically
and artistically progressive ventures, playing roles diametrically opposed to
the reality of their own lives, roles that denigrated women who crossed
conventional boundaries, in a play that upheld as the ideal the woman who
remained 'what Nature has made her . . . the companion and lover of a man,
the mistress of the home'.[7]

The paradoxical position of the actress beside, a further dichotomy existed.
In the beginning, the New Woman, although apparently omnipresent, was
elusive in the extreme. As Olive Schreiner wrote:

> Much is said at the present day on the subject of the 'New Woman': . . . It
> cannot truly be said that her attitude finds a lack of social attention. On every
> hand she is examined, praised, blamed, mistaken for her counterfeit, ridiculed
> or deified – but nowhere can it be said, that the phenomenon of her existence is
> overlooked.[8]

Not overlooked, immediately identifiable but somehow unknown, the New
Woman was first named, it is claimed, by the radical novelist, Sarah Grand,
in the *North American Review* in May 1894. Thereafter and with great rapidity

the New Woman was dissected in the pages of *Punch* and the *Yellow Book*, spawned a genre of novels and was much discussed in ladies' magazines. She was to be found on stage in the plays of Grundy, Shaw, Pinero, Jones, Barker and others, part of a decade that produced societies, journals and even cafés called the New Era, the New Dawn, the New Age, that looked forward to the new century as a beginning but also saw itself as morbid, neurotic, decadent and degenerate.[9] Inevitably, perhaps, because she was a female phenomenon, she was the subject of special denigration: 'Life has taken on a strange unloveliness, and the least beautiful thing therein is "the New Woman"', wrote Mrs Roy Devereux in 1895.[10]

The popular image of the New Woman is best exemplified by one of the *Punch* cartoons from 1894 entitled 'Donna Quixote'. She sits, plain and bespectacled, in an armchair, in her sensible, 'hygienic' or 'rational' dress, book in one hand and latchkey held aloft in the other. She is surrounded by images of the 'disorderly notions' that crowd her imagination and the source of those notions – the works of Mona Caird, Tolstoi, Ibsen and the *Yellow Book*. Behind her there is the Amazon holding aloft the flag of the divided skirt, another fighting the dragon of Decorum and a third tilting at the windmill of Marriage Laws. The decapitated head of 'Tyrant Man' sits by one foot, her new 'Mrs Cerberus, with the three heads of Mrs Grundy, Chaperone and Mamma, 'keeping the portals of that Home Elysian/ That cranks now call a Hades', by the other. The accompanying poem has her cry:

> In spite of babies, bonnets, tea,
> Creation's Heir, I must, I will be – Free!
> . . .
> Nay, 'tis a gaol to those who long to roam,
> Unchaperoned, emancipated, and free,
> With the large Liberty of the Latch-key![11]

The poet then warns Donna that despite the *'Doll's House* delirium that sets your nerves a-thrill' she should ignore all 'the cants of culture's cranks' for these will never produce true emancipation, and is exhorted by Punch:

> . . . dear Donna Quixote, be not stupid,
> Fight not with Hymen and war not with Cupid.
> Run not amuck 'gainst Mother Nature's plan.
> Nor make a monster of your mate, poor Man,
> Or like La Mancha's cracked, though noble knight.
> You'll find blank failure in mistaken fight.[12]

The New Woman, then, was seen typically as young, middle class and single on principle. She eschewed the fripperies of fashion in favour of more masculine dress and severe coiffure. She had probably been educated to a standard unknown to previous generations of women and was certainly a devotee of Ibsen and given to reading 'advanced' books. She was financially independent of father or husband, often through earning her own living in one of the careers opening up to women at the time, like journalism and teaching. She affected emancipated habits, like smoking, riding a bicycle, using bold language and taking the omnibus or train unescorted. She belonged to all-female clubs, like

Figure 1 Donna Quixote (*Punch* cartoon)

Mrs Massingberd's Pioneer Club, or societies where like-minded individuals
met and ideas and sexes mixed freely. She sought freedom from, and equality
with, men. In the process she was prepared to overturn all convention and all
accepted notions of femininity.

This is the New Woman of Grundy's play and the *Punch* cartoons – a fiction
clearly, the creation of a largely unsympathetic press for whom there was 'no
more insulting epithet [to hurl] at any girl or woman than to call her a New
Woman'.[13] And yet in many ways this New Woman did exist in the 1890s and
1900s. She is a composite product of the accelerating woman's movement, a
forerunner to the – equally frequently caricatured – suffragette. The New
Woman was 'essentially the old, non-parasitic woman from the remote past,
preparing to draw on her twentieth century garb'.[14]

One of the most important bequests to the New Woman of the turn of the
century was the changing attitude to education and work – the former opening
up opportunities for the latter. The fruits of earlier improvements in girls'
education were maturing by the 1890s. Since Miss Buss had established the
first girls' day or 'high' school, the North London Collegiate, in 1850, the day
school and girls' public school movement had expanded rapidly. Over ninety
girls' schools alone were created under the 1869 Endowed School Act. Access
to Higher Education was also well established by the 1890s – though not to all
faculties and not always to degree level.

In the field of work, too, things were changing. When Schreiner first wrote
her 'Musings on Women and Labour' in the 1890s, her clarion call for the
right of women to their share of useful human toil echoed one of the most
significant demands in the decade.[15] In her book she inveighed against the
parasitical state that the majority of women are reduced to in the ideal world
of the late nineteenth century. Work would redeem women from the cultural
stasis in which they found themselves.

> The past material conditions of life have gone for ever; no will of man can recall
> them; but *this* is our demand: We demand that, in that strange new world that
> is arising alike upon the man and the woman, where nothing is as it was, and all
> things are assuming new shapes and relations, that in this new world we also
> have our share of honoured and socially useful human toil, our full half of the
> labour of the Children of Woman. We demand nothing more than this, and we
> will take nothing less. *This is our* 'WOMAN'S RIGHT!'[16]

There was a small, but significant rise in the number of women employed in
the United Kingdom in the period 1890–1914, the rise being concentrated
amongst the middle classes, with a concomitant fall amongst female working-
class employment. Between 1881 and 1911 there was an increase from
12.6 per cent to 23.7 per cent in the number of middle-class women in the
total female workforce.[17] By 1890 there was a generation of reasonably
educated young women who looked for some continuing fulfilment through
work. These New Women were to become a visible endorsement of Schreiner's

demand for women's right to work. Many went into teaching, some into journalism, typewriting and other 'white-collar' occupations; some looking for a 'creative' outlet went into that highly visible profession, the theatre.

The New Woman and the theatre

Another cartoon, from the early twentieth century, shows yet one more New Woman.[18] Again she is young and middle class, wears rational dress unadorned by anything except her latchkey. She is trampling on the figures of a conventional young man and woman and appears to have flung down a book on etiquette. Behind her stand her concerned parents, the father stern and frowning, the mother, aspidistra at her side, worriedly clutching a sampler that reads 'God Bless Our Home'. In the iconography of the New Woman all she lacks is a cigarette. Above the girl's head in the clouds are three angels with the heads of Shaw, Ibsen and Wells, clutching their 'Bibles' – *Mrs Warren's Profession*, *The Doll's House* (sic), and *Ann Veronica*. Significantly, all the New Women's 'guardian angels' are shown as male and two of them are dramatists. In the latter part of the nineteenth century the theatre was seen to be a radical and influential place. Its gurus might be male but its disciples were often female.

Since the Restoration the theatre in England had offered women a career, mainly as performers, but also as writers and even managers. The tradition on the Continent went back even further. Whilst the theatre was not deemed a respectable place for a woman to be on either side of the curtain, as we have seen in the case of the actresses involved in *The New Woman*, it had long offered those in it a degree of independence. Some women achieved a measure of equality with men in the theatre, even superiority, but the structure remained male-dominated. Overall, the theatre was a problematic domain. In a society which, particularly since the mid-eighteenth century, had excluded its females from public discourse, the theatre was anathema. It not only placed its women on public view but often put them in positions of physical and emotional intimacy with men not their fathers or husbands. The ambiguous position of the actress was further compromised by any association with the New Woman and her philosophy of sexual self-determination.

The second half of the nineteenth century saw a serious attempt to raise the status of theatre and to create a 'legitimate' and respectable stage divorced from the world of variety and music hall. (The music hall was to experience its own 'cleaning up' process at the end of the century culminating in the first Royal Command Performance of 1912). It is interesting that one of the most important contributors to this movement was a woman, as socially women had the most to gain from such improvements. The actress–manager, Marie Wilton, not only undertook the transformation of the old Queen's Theatre

on Tottenham Court Road into a theatre that would attract the professional
classes – renaming it the Prince of Wales Theatre – but did so in a recognisably 'feminine' style. She described the alterations she had made to the
auditorium:

> The house looked very pretty, and although everything was done inexpensively,
> had a bright and bonnie appearance, and I felt proud of it. The curtains and
> carpets were of a cheap kind, but in good taste. The stalls were light blue, with
> lace antimacassars over them.[19]

She presented the decoration of the Prince of Wales Theatre as she might her
own drawing-room, bringing the discourse of the domestic, the female, into
the theatre.

By the end of the century there were signs that the 'campaign' was having
some effect. The gradual shift in public attitude was best exemplified by the
knighting of Henry Irving in 1895 but can also be seen elsewhere. Figures
taken from the census returns between 1841 and 1891 show that there was a
steady increase in the number of people employed in the theatre, indicating
that more people considered it as a possible career. More significantly the
ratio of actresses to actors – or rather performers, as these figures included
people working in all branches of the industry – had increased. In 1841 there
were about three actors to each actress, two to one in 1851 and by 1891
actresses were just in the majority.[20] Many of the new entrants to the
profession in the 1880s and the 1890s came not from the theatrical families
but from the educated middle classes. It was still true that few of the women
who entered did so with the unconditional blessing of their families, nevertheless, in moving into that 'nether world' where they were certain 'to lose
caste',[21] they were to achieve a degree of autonomy in their lives and an
opportunity for creative fulfilment, and the very lack of conventionality that
was still part of the image of the stage may have been part of the attraction.
Further, whilst there is little evidence that many actresses began their careers
with a radical view of the repertoire, it is clear that some were radicalised by
the frustrations of playing parts that were not only far from representing their –
or any other woman's – experience of life but also presented images of women
that ran counter to their personal politics. As we have seen, the irony was that
this 'unconventional' world was the purveyor of some of the most conventional
– not to say reactionary – attitudes towards women in the period.

It comes as no surprise that a writer of popular West End comedies like
Sydney Grundy should reproduce the antagonistic iconography of the dominant
ideology. Similarly antipathetic portraits are to be found in other plays from
the decade, including Pinero's *The Amazons* and Henry Arthur Jones's *The
Case of Rebellious Susan*. But it is paradoxical that many of the male
dramatists, sympathetic to the Woman Question, produced work that, whilst
not overtly hostile to the New Woman, did not seem able to allow her or her
philosophies to prevail. Mrs Patrick Campbell wrote of Pinero's New Woman

drama from 1895, *The Notorious Mrs Ebbsmith*, in which she played Agnes Ebbsmith:

> The role of Agnes Ebbsmith and the first three acts of the play filled me with ecstacy . . . but the last act broke my heart. I knew that such an Agnes in life could not have drifted into the Bible-reading inertia of the woman she became in the last act. . . . To me Agnes was a finer woman. In those days, not so long ago, she was a new and daring type, the woman agitator, the pessimist with original independent ideas – in revolt against sham morals.[22]

Agnes Ebbsmith begins the play a quintessential New Woman. Photographs of Mrs Patrick Campbell in the part show her in a dark dress 'plain to the verge of coarseness; her face which has little colour, is at first glance almost wholly unattractive',[23] with a chatelaine at her belt and no other ornamentation. By the fourth act, Agnes has put on a luxurious evening gown, repudiated her ideals and agreed to self-imposed exile living in darkest Yorkshire with a curate and his widowed sister. As Agnes herself says: 'My sex has found me out!'[24] In her memoirs, Mrs Pat wondered whether 'Sir Arthur Pinero missed an opportunity or was the time not yet ripe? The suffragette, with her hammer in her muff, had not yet risen above the horizon'.[25] This may have been so, but the evidence is that none of the male writers of the period dealt adequately with the New Woman figure, condemning her either to a metaphorical suicide, as with Agnes Ebbsmith, or to an actual suicide, like Constance Denham in John Todhunter's *The Black Cat*. Some, like Shaw and Barker, created idealised, independent, self-determining women – Vivie Warren in *Mrs Warren's Profession* and Marion Yates in *The Madras House* – but denied them any sort of three-dimensional reality.

It remained for the women writers who emerged in the period up to the First World War to combine the new ideas and ideology of the Woman Question with a grasp of the reality of the lives of contemporary women. Whilst there were a number of women writing successfully for the commercial stage by the end of the century, there were also some who wrote almost exclusively in the area of the New Drama and chose to prioritise women's experience – dramatists like Elizabeth Baker, Florence Bell, Cicely Hamilton, George Paston, Margaret Nevinson, Elizabeth Robins, Christopher St John and Githa Sowerby.[26] One telling example of the difference in approach between the male and female playwrights in dealing with feminist issues of the day can be found in the published edition of Florence Bell and Elizabeth Robins's play, *Alan's Wife*. In a lengthy introduction William Archer defends the play against its critics but also undermines the authors' handling of the subject matter – infanticide. Had he written the piece (he claims with becoming modesty), he would have turned the play into a polemic – a eugenic defence of the killing of the handicapped – and would have created 'a subtle piece of intellectual as opposed to merely emotional, drama'.[27] The emotional truth of the heroine's infanticidal act was something that the male rationalist and ideologist, Archer, would not and could not come to grips with. This rational and idealised attitude permeates many of the plays about women written by the male writers of the period and accompanies a lack of comprehension of reality as experienced by women.

In the wake of a more aggressive suffrage campaign, the birth of the suffragette Women's Social and Political Union in 1903 and the founding of the Actresses' Franchise League in 1908, women dramatists also began to engage more directly with political issues in their drama. Suffrage meetings gave women dramatists an exclusive platform, and performers, that had hitherto been denied them. Actresses seized the opportunities offered by these plays but, overall, these opportunities were too few to offer any real hope of permanent employment in a 'woman-orientated' theatre.

The problem for dramatists and performers alike lay in the institution of theatre itself. The majority of theatres of the day were not interested in the Woman Question, neither the commercial managements nor the experimental theatres that followed in the wake of J. T. Grein's Independent Theatre. The latter, like Archer's New Century Theatre and Court Theatre ventures, had a general commitment to the promotion of the New Drama, but no specific commitment to women's work. But although commercial and experimental theatre managements were dominated by men, they were not exclusively so. In fact, a surprising number of incursions had already been made by women into the power structures of the theatre.

Whilst the actress–manager was never a significant rival *numerically* to the actor–manager in the nineteenth century, she did constitute a significant challenge to the traditional notions of a woman's place. For the actress, as for the actor, the best way to exercise control over her work was through management, and for those who did achieve it, it was far more than just a token. Women like Eliza Vestris and Fanny Kemble in the earlier part of the century were equal to their male contemporaries in popularity and the management of their business affairs. Marie Wilton, as we have seen, was one of the most influential London managers of her day. Outside London women could also be found in positions of power. The tradition for whole families to be in the same company (sometimes to be the whole company!) was particularly strong in the provinces. This made it easier, and logical, for women to share managerial responsibility. Many assumed control on the death of a spouse. Sarah Baker, one of the most successful provincial managers of either sex at the beginning of the nineteenth century, was daughter of a show-woman, married one of her mother's company and, in quick succession, was left a young widow with three children and became manager of the Canterbury Circuit. When she retired after nearly thirty years, she had amassed herself a small fortune. Later in the century Millicent Bandmann-Palmer successfully toured the north of England with her own company for several decades, and Sarah Thorne not only ran the Margate Theatre Royal almost continuously between 1867 and her death in 1899, but also founded a much-respected school for the 'Ladies and Gentlemen wishing to enter the theatrical profession'.[28] These women were not unique.

Not all the women who effectively managed theatres or music halls, though, felt able to acknowledge this publicly, preferring to allow male colleagues to be the public face of the management. The move towards greater acceptability in the theatre may, paradoxically, have encouraged this self-effacement amongst theatrical women and forced them into assuming a more conventional role. Adelaide Stoll, it is said, when left a widow, took over the running of her husband's Liverpool music hall but used her teenage son, Oswald, to 'front' for her in many business dealings. Mary Moore, a prominent suffragist and the business brains behind the Wyndhams' management,[29] maintained a decorous secondary role to Charles Wyndham before and after their marriage.

A contrary movement beginning in the 1880s and 1890s saw a new and different initiative amongst actress–managers. The Free Theatre movement that had originated on the Continent, began in England with performances of Ibsen's plays. The attraction of Ibsen for the actresses has been well documented,[30] and it is not surprising that many of the private performances of Ibsen plays were undertaken by women. The most notable were Janet Achurch and Charles Charrington's *A Doll's House* (1889) and *Hedda Gabler* (1891), Florence Farr's production of *Rosmersholm* (1891) and Elizabeth Robins's productions of Ibsen throughout the 1890s. It may not be a coincidence that one of Robins's fellow managers, Marion Lea, was one of Sarah Thorne's students at the Margate Academy. Women's contribution to the experimental stage was not confined to the works of Ibsen. Florence Farr ran an experimental season of plays at the Avenue Theatre in 1894, including plays by Todhunter, Shaw and Yeats. The venture was financed secretly by one of the most important theatre managers of the period, Annie Horniman, who went on to fund the Abbey Theatre in Dublin and create and run Britain's first provincial repertory theatre, the Gaiety in Manchester. Dorothy Leighton, a dramatist, was part of the management of the Independent Theatre, and Elizabeth Robins's role in the running of the New Century Theatre has been consistently undervalued.

The early twentieth century saw several women engaged in what became known as the Little Theatre movement, producing a more serious and adventurous repertoire than was possible in the West End. Amongst them was Lena Ashwell, who took over the Kingsway Theatre in 1907, successfully premièring Cicely Hamilton's *Diana of Dobson's*, amongst other plays. Olga Nethersole, Lillah McCarthy and Gertrude Kingston – the latter yet another student of Sarah Thorne – were but three of the actresses known to have been involved in the women's movement at this time, who also ran 'Little Theatres' before the First World War. There were also the 'odd' women like Emma Cons, who had no obvious connection with theatre but who managed the Old Vic, producing 'cheap and decent amusement along temperance lines' and, followed by her niece, Lilian Baylis, brought a new audience to drama, ballet and opera.

There is, however, little consistency in the pattern of women managers. Both commercial and experimental theatre work – but particularly the latter – was financially unstable. Many women managers, like Elizabeth Robins, were eventually forced out of management and back into performing or other related activities, because of the uncertainty of income from experimental theatre work. The most consistent feminist work emerged, for a little period, from the founding of the Actresses' Franchise League in 1908, with its policy of performances in support of the campaign for votes for women. Out of the Actresses' Franchise League's work came Inez Bensusan's successful Woman's Theatre season at the Coronet Theatre in 1913 – a second season was prevented by the outbreak of war – and Edy Craig's Pioneer Players, which lasted into the 1920s. Craig's company, set up in 1911, though not exclusively female, was dominated by women in all areas of production and adminstration and was committed to experimental work, including, naturally, that by women.

It is clear, then, that as performers, dramatists and managers, women in the theatre had anticipated the challenge of the New Woman to the establishment. Whilst the feminist movement of the 1890s brought new momentum and focus to the Woman Question, these theatrical women had already subverted normal expectations of female behaviour – often at the expense of their own reputation and social position – and many were ready to grasp the opportunities offered by the New Woman movement for more substantial freedoms. These moves towards greater emancipation were, however, constantly mediated and undercut by the conventional forces at work within the institutions. The most successful subversions came only when the women went outside the existing structures and created, however temporarily, their own theatre.

The New Woman Papers

The esays in this volume cover many aspects of the New Woman problem in relation to theatre but are by no means exhaustive of the topic. They examine the ways in which the image of the New Woman and her sisters was appropriated and circumscribed by male theatrical and cinematic texts (Jill Davis, 'The New Woman and the New Life', Lesley Ferris, 'The Golden Girl', and Zoë Aldrich, 'The adventuress: *Lady Audley's Secret*') and the various strategies that women used, consciously or unconsciously, to confront and circumvent the limitations imposed on their sex by nineteenth-century society. The New Woman's challenge to physical and metaphorical corsetting in the adoption of 'rational dress' (or even Ellen Terry's kimonos) finds an echo in the physical freedom of the circus performer (Helen Day, 'Female Daredevils') and vocal freedom of the singer (Susan Rutherford, 'The Voice of Freedom' and Geraldine Harris, 'Yvette Guilbert: *La Femme Moderne*'), and in the assumption of 'masculinity' through cross-dressing (Jill Edmonds, 'Princess Hamlet', and J. S. Bratton, 'Irrational Dress') found in both the music hall and 'straight' theatre. The distance that women had to travel in their struggle for emancipation is discussed through the work of just two of the female dramatists of the period – Cicely Hamilton and Elizabeth Baker (Sheila Stowell, 'Drama as a Trade: Cicely Hamilton's *Diana of Dobson's*', and Linda Fitzsimmons, 'Typewriters Enchained: The work of Elizabeth Baker') – both of whom show clearly the importance of work as a route to independence. The volume concludes with an examination of two women who publicly and consistently espoused the feminist cause in the 1890s and 1900s, both in their life and their work and who were able through the assumption of power in the form of theatre management to empower other women (Elaine Aston, 'The "New Woman" at Manchester's Gaiety Theatre', on the work of Annie Horniman and Christine Dymkowski, 'Entertaining ideas: Edy Craig and the Pioneer Players').

Not all the women under consideration in this volume can, strictly speaking, be described as New Women, but each does represent facets of the New Woman's fight for self-determination as manifested in the theatre of the nineteenth and early twentieth centuries.

Notes

1. A. Filon, *The English Stage: Being on account of the Victorian Drama* (London: John Milne, 1897), p. 231.
2. The Empire Music Hall was particularly notorious in the early 1890s and was the subject of a clean-up campaign lead by W. A. Coote and Mrs Ormiston Chant. The Empire was under attack for its improprieties both on and off stage. See J. Stokes, 'Prudes on the prowl', in his *In the Nineties* (Hemel Hempstead: Harvester Wheatsheaf, 1989).
3. S. Grundy, *The New Woman* (London: Chiswick Press, 1894), p. 8.
4. H. James, *The Tragic Muse* (1890; London: Penguin, 1978), p. 113.
5. J. Briggs, *A Woman of Passion: the Life of E. Nesbit* (London: Penguin, 1989), p. 85.
6. Filon, *The English Stage, op. cit.*, p. 230.
7. V. Jozé, 'Le Féminisme et le bon sens', *La Plume*, 154 (September 1895), pp. 391–2; cited in E. Showalter, *Sexual Anarchy: Gender and Culture at the Fin de Siècle* (London: Bloomsbury, 1991), p. 40.
8. O. Schreiner, *Women and Labour* (1911; London: Virago, 1978), pp. 252–3.
9. The ambiguous nature of *fin-de-siècle* culture is discussed in Showalter, *Sexual Anarchy, op. cit.*
10. Mrs R. Devereux, 'The feminine potential', *Saturday Review*, 22 June 1895, pp. 824–5.
11. 'Donna Quixote', *Punch*, 28 April 1894, p. 195.
12. *ibid.*, p. 195.
13. H. Friederichs, 'The "old" woman and the "new"', *Young Woman*, 3 (1895), p. 202.

14. Schreiner, *Women and Labour*, *op. cit.*, pp. 252–3.
15. Schreiner first wrote *Women and Labour* in the 1890s, but the manuscript was destroyed, rewritten and finally published in 1911.
16. Schreiner, *Women and Labour*, *op. cit.*, p. 68.
17. A. L. Bowley, *Wages and Income in the United Kingdom since 1860* (Cambridge: Cambridge University Press, 1937); cited in David Rubinstein, *Before the Suffragettes* (Brighton: Harvester Press, 1986), p. 70.
18. From *The Graphic*, Christmas number, 1929, reproducing an earlier cartoon erroneously dated 1905.
19. M. Bancroft and S. Bancroft, *The Bancrofts: Recollections of Sixty Years* (London: Nelson, 1909), p. 80.
20. Figures taken from M. Baker, *The Rise of the Victorian Actor* (London: Croom Helm, 1978), p. 225.
21. L. Ashwell, *Myself a Player* (London: Michael Joseph, 1936), p. 46.
22. Mrs P. Campbell, *My Life and Some Letters* (London: Hutchinson, 1922), pp. 98–9.
23. A. W. Pinero, *The Notorious Mrs Ebbsmith* (London: Heinemann, 1895), p. 14.
24. *ibid.*, p. 156.
25. Mrs P. Campbell, *My Life and Some Letters*, *op. cit.*, pp. 99–100.
26. Many women writers at this time still adopted male pseudonyms. Christopher St John was Christabel Marshal and George Paston was Emily Morse Symonds. Cicely Hamilton wrote in her autobiography about the warning she had received in 1908 that 'it was advisable to conceal the sex of the author . . . as plays that were known to be written by women were apt to get a bad press' (C. Hamilton, *Life Errant* (London: Dent, 1935), p. 60).
27. W. Archer, Introduction to F. Bell and E. Robins, *Alan's Wife* (London: Henry, 1893), p. xv.
28. M. Morley, *Margate and its Theatres* (London: Museum Press, 1966), p. 109.
29. 'Mary Moore . . . had a fine brain for finance, was worldly wise, and had a strong sense of "what people will say". . . . It was largely due to her practical commonsense and forethought that even when the Criterion Theatre was financially booming they built the two new theatres, the New and Wyndham's' (Ashwell, *Myself a Player*, *op. cit.*, p. 117).
30. For example, E. Robins, *Ibsen and the Actress* (London: Hogarth Press, 1928), and Tracy C. Davis 'Acting in Ibsen', *Theatre Notebook*, vol. xxxix, no. 3 (1985), pp. 113–23.

PART I

Women Defined

1   The New Woman and the New Life

JILL DAVIS

> It is possible that society is evolving in the direction of a family supported by
> the earnings of both parents, the children being cared for meanwhile and the
> work of the house being performed by trained experts. To me personally that
> solution seems more in harmony with the general lines of our social develop-
> ment than does any which would relegate all women to the care of children
> combined with the care of households.[1]

Clementina Black's early-century vision is today the developing pattern of
family life in Britain, as much of the change – material, legislative, fiscal –
which her socialist–feminist contemporaries saw as the path to sex equality
has occurred. None the less, a problem remains:

> The main problem for the present-day women's rights movement is that in many
> parts of the world the enemy has gone underground. At least when women are
> kept in their subordinate position by laws and institutions no one can pretend
> these do not exist. But when these formal devices go, the residual pressures
> which still push the sexes towards the old familiar spheres are often so subtle
> that even the well-intentioned may deny they exist at all.[2]

The relation between these two feminist statements is one of the focuses of
this essay. In exploring late-nineteenth-early-twentieth-century responses to
the challenge posed by the New Woman, the independent feminist, and her
aspirations I hope to provide some explanation of those 'residual pressures'.
My focus will be on dramatic representations of the New Woman, but I want
to look first at the responses to feminism in the radical intellectual circles

which produced the progressive drama of the period. In doing so, I want to challenge a still-held assumption that the representations of women made by early-century socialists and liberals, whether in dramatic form or in political or scientific writing, were necessarily and unambiguously pro-feminist.[3]

The world of the New Drama: Feminism and socialism 1880–1914

The New Drama was the cultural product of the radical and millenarian movements of the late nineteenth and early twentieth centuries. Drama entered into that arena through the interest of radicals in the work of Ibsen; and from the early 1890s play-producing societies and independent repertory seasons provided this milieu with 'advanced' British and European drama which reflected its own social concerns.[4]

The New British Drama was particularly associated with Fabian socialism. The Stage Society was an offshoot of the Fabian Society; the Court Theatre was co-managed by Granville Barker, a member of the Fabian Society from 1901 and of its executive from 1907 to 1912, and Shaw, a major Fabian figure, was effectively the Court's resident dramatist.[5] The Fabian Society's political allegiance was to non-revolutionary socialism: in Sidney Webb's famous phrase, to 'the inevitability of gradualness'. It was not a political party; its preferred strategy was to urge existing institutions towards their ultimate socialist form. But if it has been common to regard the Fabian Society as merely a debating society for middle-class intellectuals, Fabianism did, none the less, come to affect the material and ideological reality of the later twentieth century through its influence on the early Labour Party (founded in 1906).[6] The New Drama, likewise, should be regarded less as simply an avant-garde theatre for middle-class intellectuals than as one of the fields in which emergent social ideas were being explored in representation.

One of those ideas, the one which concerns us here, was 'the Woman Question'. The increasing activism and vociferousness of feminism in this period demanded response, and where conservative forces could act to repress, progressives and socialists were bound to engage positively with it. But the engagement of socialism with feminism – in the Fabian Society as in the socialist movement in general – was not an unproblematic one. It took place across the contest between the two major theoretical explanations of human history produced in the nineteenth century: Marxism and Darwinism. The former, in key texts such as those by Bebel and Engels, offered a historical-materialist account of women's oppression, locating it in the development of capitalism (specifically in the exclusion of women from the economy as the productive household became the private family) and proposed that women's freedom would result from their economic liberation within a transformed economic and social system.[7]

A similarly materialist – if evolutionary rather than revolutionary – position underpinned the practical agenda of the Fabian Women's Group, founded in 1908, and explains its opposition to the notion of the 'family wage', its insistence on the right of all women to paid work and its support for the state endowment of mothers and schemes for communal home maintenance and child-care.

In spite of the marxist orthodoxy of such demands, they were not un-contested within the socialist movement; for example, the newly formed Labour Party saw economic independence for women as offering capitalism an increased pool of labour and thereby threatening working men's wages.[8] The resistance offered to feminist ideas was, ostensibly, because class issues took precedence, but gender relations clearly formed a subtext to policy debates. In a discussion of state endowment of mothers, for example, 'one Labour MP, a Mr. Roberts, even argued that "to insist on the money being paid to the woman was an insult to the working man."'[9] In confining, as it did for a long time, its policies on women to enhancing the conditions for wife- and motherhood, and only hesitantly considering policies which would bring women outside the family, the Labour Party was protecting not just the working class but masculinity, as signified by power over women and children.[10]

Charlotte Shaw, a member of the Fabian Women's Group and wife of G. B. Shaw, spelt out the dangers of this for women:

> a great school of socialists holds that when security and a good wage shall have been brought within the reach of every head of a family the case of the dependent woman and children in each household can be left to the head to deal with. Such a state of things amounts to Socialism for men, but for most women would involve the subordination of the patriarchal family.[11]

The Fabian Women's Group was careful, therefore, to accompany its own support of women as mothers by insistence that

> it was crucially important to discuss maternity pensions in conjunction with schemes providing for women's return to the labour market, otherwise feminists might unwittingly find their arguments taken up by those conservative thinkers and eugenicists who saw the state endowment of motherhood as a way of encouraging women to accept that 'their real place' was in the home.[12]

But it was not just conservatives who held such views, nor was the Labour Party the only part of British socialism to replace marxist theory with social-darwinist ideas at the point where women/gender relations appeared on the agenda. The Fabian Society itself subscribed to eugenic ideas. Sidney Webb's arguments are well known,[13] and Henry Harben's argument for the endow-ment of motherhood was significantly premised on a vision of an ideal socialist state in which 'all babies would have the best chance of growing up into *perfect men made in God's image*, where all mothers would have pleasure in the beauty of their motherhood and receive the meed of care and reward which is their due' (my emphasis). [14]

It is in eugenics that we see the specific form in which darwinist ideas came to contest marxist and feminist ideas about women's social role. Eugenics – part of the social-darwinist attempt to enhance human evolution by rational intervention into it – is concerned with control of human reproduction. While it is clearly a social project concerned with change, it is predicated upon the reduction of people to their sexual and reproductive roles. Whereas in marxist thought it is the (alterable) role of human beings in production which determines their being, in social-darwinism it is their roles in relation to reproduction, and these are biologically fixed. Eugenic thinking therefore holds particular dangers for women: indeed I would argue its capture of social thinking in this period defeated much of the potential of early-twentieth-century feminism, for its terms reassert the binary opposition of man/woman, mind/body, civilisation/nature which feminism was struggling to deconstruct.

The eugenics movement of the early twentieth century grew in response to late-nineteenth-century fears about the 'decline' in the birthrate and a growing anxiety that the major imperial nation on earth was 'degenerating'. [15] That the fear was not one of species but of class and race extinction on the part of the English bourgeoisie is clear even in Sidney Webb's writing:

> In Great Britain at this moment, when half, or perhaps two thirds, of all the married people are regulating their families, children are being freely born to the Irish Roman Catholics and the Polish, Russian and German Jews, on the one hand, and to the thriftless and irresponsible – largely the casual labourers and other denizens of the one-roomed tenements of our great cities on the other. [16]

Fabian socialists did not espouse crude strategies of 'counter-breeding' as a solution. They were committed to the material improvement of social conditions, the eradication of the 'one-roomed tenements'. None the less, their position, in espousing eugenic theories, was, as far as women were concerned, a conservative one and took its place in re-inscribing rather than rejecting the Victorian idea of woman. She might now be fecund, and thus sexual, rather than a bodiless angel, but she was still the object of male de-/ prescription and harnessed to a patriarchal project of social control.

Eugenics inevitably implied a scrutiny of sexual behaviour, a scrutiny with particularly repressive consequences for feminism. Again, this was not the product of conservative anti-feminist reaction, but was taking place within the progressive Ibsenite milieu itself. It was Havelock Ellis, part of that milieu and a utopian socialist, who was the major British contributor to the new 'science' of sexology. [17] While the Fabians were debating tenements and taxation systems, Ellis saw the key to the New Age as a freer and more enlightened attitude to sexual relations and intended his major project, the seven-volume *Studies in the Psychology of Sex*, as a contribution to that. But

Ellis, too, proved unable to contemplate gender and sexuality outside Darwinian biological and evolutionary models. [18] So, although his personal stance on the Woman Question was a supportive one, his essentialist assumptions and growing attraction to eugenics brought him to conclusions in his work which were to be conservative and negative for women. Whereas in 1894 in *Man and Woman*, the preamble to his *Studies*, he had written

> Any reader who has turned to this book for facts or arguments on the everlasting discussion regarding the alleged 'inferiority of women' and who has followed me so far, will already have gathered the natural conclusion we reach on this point. We may regard all such discussion as absolutely futile and foolish. [19]

by 1912, in *The Task of Social Hygiene*, Ellis was writing far more prescriptively about women and from a specifically eugenic perspective. While he continued to support 'the new culture of women', he was critical of the militant feminist activism of this period and asserted:

> The breeding of men lies largely in the hands of women. That is why the question of Eugenics is to a large extent at one with the woman question. The realisation of eugenics in our own social life can only be attained with the realisation of the woman movement in its latest and completest phase as an enlightened culture of motherhood, in all that motherhood involves alike on the physical and psychic sides. [20]

Ellis's formulation provides a clear example of the way in which feminism in this period was appropriated and reorganised by male discourse. Feminism is here reduced to a movement dedicated to achieving the best conditions for 'breeding men'.

Ellis's work on sex was to be immensely influential throughout the English-speaking world for much of the twentieth century. Clearly influenced by eugenic theory, his particular contribution to it was to produce the 'scientific' evidence for the innateness of procreative heterosexuality in women. His descriptions of the 'normal' woman re-intensified the incitement of women towards marriage and motherhood, and his diagnoses of 'abnormal' women were to have particularly devastating consequences for feminist aspirations to female autonomy. As the figures of the 'frustrated' spinster, the 'selfish' barren wife and the 'predatory' lesbian were picked up and proliferated through popular culture they came to act as guarantors of women's compliance with patriarchal prescription for female behaviour. Sheila Jeffreys's book, *The Spinster and her Enemies*, offers some spine-chilling examples of the ways in which such representations threatened feminism. Who would not fear celibacy after reading this in *The Freewoman*? 'I write of the High Priestess of Society. Not of the mother of sons, but of her barren sister, the withered tree, the acidulous vestal under whose pale shadow we chill and whiten, of the Spinster I write.' [21] Or feminism itself, as the view was popularised that 'the "Women's Question" is mainly the question of the destiny of the virile homosexual woman'?[22]

In a double sense these figures are the real 'New Women' of the period: representations of the feminist offered back in forms which denied her and controlled her. It is not surprising, then, that, although individual feminists did contest them, eugenic and sexological ideas were so pervasive that much of the feminist movement itself came to frame its demands within their terms.[23] Even Mabel Atkinson, a key figure in the Fabian Women's Group, asserted that 'the married woman who is leading a normal and healthy life is likely to do better work and be a more satisfactory person than the spinster.'[24]

What I have tried to suggest in this very brief introduction is that two related features marked the response of progressive/socialist men to feminism in this period: firstly, a retreat from materialist into essentialist ways of thinking when faced with the 'Woman Question'; and secondly, an associated (and successful) appropriation and reorganisation of the terms of feminism. These responses signify, I think, an attempt to deny those aspects of feminism which offered potential disruption to gender relations as a power system which privileges masculinity. I want now to turn to a theatrical enactment of that process of denial and to explore the way in which the New Woman was made, in the New Drama, to speak 'her master's voice'.

My examples in the limited space of this essay will be three plays by G. B. Shaw covering the period 1890–1910. Shaw was at the centre of the New Drama movement: as critic and theorist, as promoter of Ibsen, as its most prolific and popular playwright and as its financial mainstay. His political authority was of equal magnitude; as one of the major Fabian theorists he was at the centre of the progressive politics of the day. It is in his plays that we see most clearly – but not atypically – the way in which progressive ideas and patriarchal reaction combined to produce ambiguous representations of the New Woman.

Shaw and the New Woman

Mrs Warren's Profession (1894)

In Mrs Warren's Profession Shaw signals his radical intentions by bringing together the two most disturbing female figures of nineteenth-century representation: the Prostitute (Mrs Warren) and the New Woman (Vivie Warren). In a parody of the melodramatic revelation scene, Vivie's bourgeois prudishness melts into sentimental forgiveness as her mother, 'in the dialect of a woman of the people', relates her escape from destitution and death into the 'economic independence' of prostitution.[25] But Shaw's purpose is greater than merely bringing plain speech to the topic of prostitution. When Sir

George Crofts reveals to Vivie (to punish her for refusing to marry him) that her mother continues in the prostitution business as managing-director of a European chain of high-class brothels, that he has a financial stake in this business and that his brother's endowment of the Crofts scholarship has, with her mother's money, allowed Vivie her Cambridge education, the play discloses its twin arguments about prostitution. Not only is the audience to understand that its origin is an economic one – all intelligent working-class women, Shaw implies, would choose prostitution over other forms of sex slavery – but, more importantly, that prostitution is a paradigm of capitalism. As all the characters in the play are shown to depend upon prostitution so the audience is intended to learn that there are no 'clean hands' in a capitalist society.

Shaw hoped thus to bring Ibsenite realism to the West End drama's erotic fascination with the 'fallen woman', by emphasising not sex but money. None the less, sex remains a potent issue in this play and the source of a representation of women which operates in opposition to the progressive arguments of the play.

Shaw's characterisation of Mrs Warren, for example, is in conventional terms. She is 'decidedly vulgar', dresses 'showily'[26] and, as Ian Clarke points out, 'Her flirtation with Frank [Vivie's "little boy" friend] suggests that she has a taste for the trade, and Shaw exploits the frisson of a possible sexual encounter between an older experienced woman and a younger, inexperienced man.'[27] Equally significant is Shaw's relative lack of scrutiny of male sexuality as a feature of prostitution. The Reverend Gardner, Frank's father, has been a former client of Mrs Warren (Frank may therefore be Vivie's half-brother), but he is naive and incompetent. By contrast, the powerful George Crofts may have been Mrs Warren's lover but never her client. Her sarcasm when he offers her money to allow him to marry Vivie – 'so it's come to that with you, George, like all the other worn-out old creatures'[28] – and her other reference to a prostitute's clients – 'some half-drunken fool'[29] – imply that only the 'unmanly' resort to prostitutes: the young, the drunk, the fool, the old. Shaw's radical argument may locate prostitution in economic circumstance but it is subverted by a representation which ascribes prostitution to the power of female sexuality over weak men.

A similar ambiguity surrounds the figure of the New Woman. Since her real-life counterparts were part of Shaw's milieu one might expect a positive representation, but Shaw's portrait has more in common with the parodies of the New Woman (of which Viv Gardner writes in the Introduction to this volume) to be found in West End dramas. Vivie Warren – 'plain business-like dress . . . a chatelaine at her belt, with a fountain pen and a paper knife'[30] – is, the title of the play notwithstanding, its main character. Interestingly, then, her role in the Fabian argument of the drama is a passive one: it is through her, as listener rather than speaker, that the audience learns the play's arguments. Her own situation within those arguments is a negative one.

As she sits, in the play's final image, at her desk, in her office, undertaking work (actuarial accountancy) which is for profit not for benefit, the New Woman's economic independence signifies the continuation of capitalism. For this she has rejected family and marriage: 'I am still my mother's daughter. I am like you. I must make more money than I spend. But my work is not your work, and my way is not your way.'[31]

It may be that Shaw intended by such an ambiguous representation to pose the same question to bourgeois feminism as Caryl Churchill was to do a century later in *Top Girls*: are women to be liberated only to collude in other systems of oppression? But Vivie is at the centre of a cluster of images which are so in excess of this role that they demand further explanation.

Her 'masculinity' is constantly stressed. Her education has been in an abstract discipline, mathematics; she is achieved and ambitious in male fields; her behaviour – from her firm handshake to her preference for intellectual and physical exercise over 'beauty and romance' – is 'mannish'. But Shaw also associates Vivie with the opposite of mannishness/power; with childlikeness/powerlessness, principally through her relationship with Frank, a pre-sexual relationship of 'babes in the wood':

> *Vivie* (*rhythmically, rocking him like a nurse*): Fast asleep, hand in hand, under the trees.
> *Frank*: The wise little girl with her silly little boy.
> *Vivie*: The dear little boy with his dowdy little girl.[32]

Through these images – mannishness and childlikeness – Shaw constructs Vivie as doubly outside, and resisting, adult female sexuality; and opposes her to the only other female character, the prostitute mother.

Michael Holroyd locates this sexual ambiguity, in Freudian terms, in Shaw's own 'sexual ambivalence' and in his 'doubts about his parenthood and ambiguous feelings for his mother'.[33] Read in these terms, but from a feminist perspective, what we see in this play is that the female characters are not 'representations of women', but cyphers of a psychic struggle for male sexual identity. The ambiguities in the character of Vivie Warren derive from the fact that a very complex representation is taking place through her. The story of Vivie in this play is at one level a representation of Shaw's oedipal struggle: to move from pre-oedipal child to gendered adult 'she' must distance 'herself' from the sexual body of the mother. But Vivie also represents the adult Shaw's conflicting views of the a(nti)-sexual New Woman, who offers him a (welcome) release from the pressure to be virile, but also threatens to dissolve his masculine gender identity by withdrawing the female 'other' by which that identity is guaranteed. Vivie is not, then, as Jan McDonald describes her, 'a woman pretending to be a man', but a man 'pretending' to be a woman.[34]

But in a theatrical context that statement is impossible. In performance Vivie is undeniably, bodily, a woman. What is crucial is the effect of that inscription onto a female body of male gender problematic: acutely so when the 'woman' represents a troublesome social figure, the feminist/New Woman. One such effect is indicated by Grace Matchett's suggestion, taken up by Jan McDonald, that Vivie's 'mother's capitalist exploitation of the sexual drive has brought about in her a disgust with physical intercourse between men and women . . . which may lead her to pursue lesbian relationships in the future.'[35] This is particularly interesting in its replication in the late twentieth century of a response to the New Woman which evolved in the sexological discourse of the early century. I do not think Shaw intended Vivie Warren to be a representation of 'the lesbian'. Although sexological ideas were certainly in the process of theorisation as *Mrs Warren's Profession* was being written, and Shaw did know women who were homosexual (for example Edith Lees, who later married Havelock Ellis, and Kate Salt, wife of the Fabian Henry Salt, who were known to Shaw as part of the Ibsenite milieu[36]), the social 'persona' of the lesbian had not yet issued from the discourse of sexology into cultural reality and could not therefore be 'represented'. There is, none the less, a relationship between the ambiguous characterisation of Vivie Warren and the sexological description of the lesbian. The one does not derive from the other, but both issue, I think, from the negotiation in progressive men in this period between conscious desires, which led them to support women's emancipation, and unconscious fears of that as a threat to masculine gender identity. Havelock Ellis's response was the pathologisation of the self-sufficient New Woman into the lesbian:

> The brusque energetic movements, the attitude of the arms, the direct speech, the inflexions of the voice, the masculine straight-forwardness and sense of honour and especially the attitude towards men, free from any suggestion either of shyness or audacity, will often suggest the underlying psychic abnormality to a keen observer.[37]

Shaw created in Vivie Warren a theatrical parody of the New Woman which, in emphasising exactly these characteristics, acted to similar effect in placing the woman who refuses masculine prescription beyond recognition as female. That female, feminist critics at the end of the twentieth century should read Vivie Warren in the same terms indicates the degree to which such male resistance to the New Woman achieved success in circumscribing twentieth-century women's ways of seeing themselves.

Man and Superman (1901/2)

By the turn of the century Shaw had temporarily lost faith with materialism. His experiences in the realities of municipal government, and a sense that Fabianism had been marginalised in the establishment of the first parliamentary socialist party (the Independent Labour Party) led him to a diagnosis of despair: that democracy 'cannot rise above the level of human material of which its voters are made'.[38] His solution was a social-darwinist one, the breeding of new human material, 'a Democracy of Supermen'.

The new race of Supermen would, of course, issue from women's wombs, so in *Man and Superman* women are again the object of description. Here the 'New' Woman is not the feminist but the woman freed of all artificial restrictions – enforced chastity being the most threatening – so that the 'Life Force', the drive to procreation, may operate through her. The agent of that 'Life Force' is the 'formidable' Ann Whitefield. Formidable indeed for Shaw, because the drive to procreation takes the form of a powerful female sexual desire. *Man and Superman* then, ostensibly a social 'philosophy', is again an enactment of male sexual anxiety.

The reversal which Shaw has made to conventional comic structure signifies this: instead of a 'love chase' of heroine by hero, there we see a flight of hero from heroine. So, too, do the verbal images of entrapment – 'snares, traps and pitfalls', 'spiders' webs' – which occur throughout the multiple texts of *Man and Superman*. Ann is a 'boa constrictor' with 'ensnaring eyes', even a vampire who 'gobbles up' and 'swallows'.[39] She is less the woman of Shaw's philosophy, from whose body a better future will issue, than the one of his unconscious, whose body threatens to engulf and extinguish the male gen(i)us.

As in *Mrs Warren's Profession*, male sexual desire is denied. The men are variously romantic, dull and uxurious, and, in the case of John Tanner, the hero, intellectual and political. Sex and masculine behaviour are woman's fault:

> *Tanner*: They accuse us of treating them as a mere means to our pleasure; but how can so feeble and transient a folly as man's selfish pleasure enslave a woman as the whole purpose of Nature embodied in a woman can enslave a man?[40]

> *Tanner*: I wanted to brag to you, to make myself interesting. And I found myself doing all sorts of mischievous things simply to have something to tell you about. I fought with boys I didn't hate; I lied about things I might just as well have told the truth about; I stole things I didn't want; I kissed girls I didn't care for.[41]

Patriarchy is biologically inevitable:

> *Don Juan*: This superfluous energy has gone to his brain and muscle. He has become too strong to be controlled by her bodily, and too imaginative and mentally vigorous to be content with mere self-reproduction. He has created civilisation without her, taking her domestic labour for granted as the foundation of it.[42]

As the comedy of *Man and Superman* is built on sex antagonism – 'no man is a match for a woman, except with a poker and a pair of hobnailed boots' – so is the philosophy.[43] Nature's Will can only be achieved through conflict between men, the possessors of mind, and women, the possessors of sexual/procreative drive.

Sex antagonism was precisely what contemporary feminism was attempting to deconstruct. So, although Shaw's rational arguments in *Man and Superman* for freer choice of marriage partners, freer divorce, the separation of sex from domesticity, imply what we take to be benefits for women, these are the accidental contents of arguments which are profoundly misogynistic. They derive from a male problematic about female sexuality and their intention is not women's autonomy but its opposite: circumscription of women's sphere of operation. Those, then, who have chosen to disregard this, not least because of the apparently self-conscious irony with which Shaw writes, and to read the play as feminist, at least in its representation of woman as actively sexual, should note Shaw's dismissals both of recreative rather than procreative sex, and of contraception:

> it will prevail with those degenerates only in whom the instinct for fertility has faded to a mere itching for pleasure. The modern devices for combining pleasure with sterility, now universally known and accessible, enable these persons to weed themselves out of the race.[44]

Similarly, Shaw does not argue for closer and more equal relations between men and women, but, on the contrary, for greater distance between them. For Nature prescribes for men – at least the geniuses amongst them – the task of developing 'Life's incessant aspiration to higher organisation, wider, deeper, intenser self-consciousness and clearer self-understanding'.[45] Man, Tanner asserts, 'creates new mind'; woman's function is only to create 'new men'.[46]

The reaffirmation in *Man and Superman* of male and female gender roles along the polarities of mind/body, productive/reproductive, evolving/repeating, is the antithesis of feminism and in the play all those women who may represent it are marginalised. The spinster Miss Ramsden represents 'sexual-purity' views which will hold back the fecundity of women; women who 'go about in rational dress are insulted and get into all sorts of hot water'[47] and the New Woman is just 'some unusually old-fashioned female'.[48]

Getting Married (1908)

In *Getting Married* Shaw returned to Fabian pragmatism to debate the practical implementation of Creative Evolution. In more apparently pro-feminist terms, he argued that the contemporary form of marriage and the 'sex slavery' of women it depended upon must give way to companionate marriage, divorce and serial monogamy, economic independence for women, state endowment of motherhood and, crucially, the right of unmarried women to bear children.

But, once more, social arguments are a mode of containing personal anxieties. Shaw objects to modern marriage primarily because it entails men being 'shut up in one room' for eight hours a day with that dangerous figure, the mother/wife:[49]

> A wife entirely occupied by her affection for her children may be all very well in a book . . . but in actual life she is a nuisance. Husbands may escape from her when their business compels them to be away from home all day, but young children may be, and quite often are, killed by her cuddling and coddling and preaching.[50]

A homosexual environment is preferable:

> the result of withdrawing children from [home life] completely at an early age,
> and sending them to a public school and then to a university, does, in spite of
> the fact that these institutions are class-warped . . . produce sociabler men.
> Women, too, are improved by the escape from home provided by women's
> colleges; but as very few of them are fortunate enough to enjoy the advantage,
> women are so thoroughly home-bred as to be unfit for human society.[51]

Even for a socialist it is better for a boy to be 'class-warped' than sex-warped
because the effect of domestic life on men is their inadequacy as 'electors
governing an empire'.[52] Supermen born of 'improved' women are needed. But
that very process of improvement – education and independence – is making
women less 'able or willing' to produce 'more. . . than three or four children'.[53]
Another problem, a falling birth-rate, is the result.

All Shaw's powers of argument are needed in the prefaces to *Getting
Married* as he attempts to reconcile personal and social anxieties. How to end
the declining birth-rate whilst allowing for women's 'improvement'? How to
allow women's improvement whilst not surrendering male power? How to
increase the status of the mother whilst avoiding emasculation? A reference
earlier in his argument to the sexual economy of bees is a signifier of Shaw's
concerns:

> a queen bee [produces] 4000 eggs a day whilst the other females lose their sex
> altogether and become workers supporting the males in idleness and luxury
> until the queen has found her mate, when the queen kills him and the quondam
> females kill all the rest.[54]

This is Shaw's unconscious contemplation of female emancipation and a
fully socialised system of reproduction. It is from its threats that he retreats
immediately into devising a human model in which women will not, like
worker bees, become fatally desexed as they become economically independent. The New Woman must be resexed by an 'absolute right to sexual
experience' and all women, regardless of marriage, 'permitted' to bear a
child. This is what women want, Shaw's 'own experience of discussing this
problem' allows him to assert:

> One point on which all women are in furious rebellion against the existing law
> is the saddling of the right to a child with the obligation to become the servant
> of a man. Adoption . . . of another woman's child is no remedy: it does not
> provide the supreme experience of bearing the child.[55]

As to those women who may refuse such description, Shaw refers his readers
'who are curious about the psychopathy of . . . spinsterhood to the monu-
mental work of my friend Havelock Ellis'.[56]
This is a clear attempt by Shaw to reorganise feminist arguments to

masculinist ends; and that this was a conscious response to feminist threats to male sexuality is quite clear: 'The political emancipation of women is likely to lead to a comparatively stringent enforcement of law by sexual morality [that is why so many of us dread it].'[57] Only thus having recontained woman within a reactionary and patriarchal prescription is Shaw free to be radical and socialist: 'The child is a vital part of the nation, the nation cannot afford to leave it at the irresponsible disposal of any individual or couple of individuals as a mere small parcel of private property.'[58]

Like other Fabians, he draws the line at the full implication of this – wholly socialised child-care – preferring a 'system of simply requiring certain results' of the private family. Since in none of the arguments is a new role for fathers explored (the 'couple' as parents seems somewhat of an afterthought in his formulation), the object of scrutiny will be woman. The responsibilities of paternity, but not of maternity, are to be transferred from the individual to the state, and woman 'freed' from control by one man, only to be passed into the control of the many, the patriarchy.

Dramatically, *Getting Married* is slight. It is an animated version of its Preface: 'There will be nothing but talk, talk, talk, talk, talk – Shaw's talk. The characters will seem to the critics nothing but a row of Shaws, all arguing with one another.'[59] The action of the play centres around three potential marriages and discussion of a New Marriage contract. Shaw arranges the three 'brides' in a hierarchy of preferred types. Edith, whose marriage to Cecil is the occasion of the play, is a New Woman whose demand is for 'self-respect and independence' and who is 'engaged in social work of all sorts: organising shop assistants and sweated work girls and all that', not unlike those in the process of forming the Fabian Women's Group.[60] But when Edith appears on stage it is as

the typical spoilt child of a clerical household: almost as terrible a product as the spoilt child of a bohemian household: that is, all her childish affectations of conscientious scruple and religious impulse have been applauded and deferred to until she has become an ethical snob of the first water.[61]

Shaw again offers an anti-feminist representation of the New Woman: not woman but child, motivated not by principle but by affectation, not a feminist but simply an 'ethical snob'.

Leo is the 'old' woman – the 'womanly woman' – and no less disapprobated by Shaw. Her name signifies the lion and her 'restlessness is much less lovable than the kittenishness which comes from a rich and fresh vitality'.[62] Her 'restlessness' is signified by polyandrous desires. In the process of divorcing her husband Rejjy and engaged to Sinjon Hotchkiss, she would like a New Marriage to allow her to 'marry them both' (and others, if possible).[63] Of all the 'row of Shaws' Sinjon (like Shaw known as Sonny 'in the bosom of my family'[64]) is Shaw's psychosexual self. So, as Leo is not the appealing and tameable kitten but the cat with claws, not the woman-as-mother who prefers her offspring to her mate but the man-eater, she must be displaced from Shaw's universe. Sinjon breaks off the engagement, claiming that he was bullied into it, and Leo returns to Rejji, the idle bourgeois.

Having disposed of the old and the New woman, Shaw introduces his ideal New Woman: Lesbia Grantham, a 'tall, handsome, slender lady in her prime . . . sure of herself'. It is she who is the object of the play's argument, the 'superfluous woman' who wants neither marriage nor sex but does want children.[65] 'I ought to have children. I should be a good mother to children. I believe it would pay the country well to pay ME to have children.'[66]

Lesbia's name is undoubtedly significant. The audience's attention is drawn to it by General Bridgenorth (who wants to marry her):

> *Mrs Bridgenorth*: Why do you always call Lesbia my sister? Don't you know it annoys her . . . ?
> *The General*: . . . She knows her name sticks in my throat. Better call her your sister than try to call her L— (*he almost breaks down*) L— well, call her by her name and make a fool of myself by crying.[67]

The joke depends upon the audience's familiarity with the sexological description of the lesbian and it is likely that a Fabian audience would by this period have been familiar with Havelock Ellis's work on sexual inversion. Shaw is thus enabled to complete the joke by bringing on stage a woman who does not fulfil the audience's expectations. Lesbia is not 'mannish' and she refuses neither men nor womanhood, only the idiocies of marriage. Shaw thus conjures up the lesbian only to deny her female autonomy by subsuming her in his argument – all women are innately heterosexual and maternal and only prevented from fulfilling their destiny by absurd social laws. In this play Shaw does not have to tell a homosexual woman that 'what she really needed were children', he constructs her so that she can say it 'herself'.

Edith, Leo and even Lesbia are thinly drawn stereotypes. When the ideas they represent have been debated they are dismissed from the scene. But the play does not end there. It is in the scenes between Sinjon and Mrs George – 'in language whose excess imparts the power they feel so well' – that Shaw re-enacts the psychic conflict which forms the subtext of, I think, all of his representations of women.[68]

Mrs George is between forty and fifty, with eyes which are 'alive, haunting, arresting'. She is married, but has had a life of passionate affairs. Since her name is a clear reference to both Shaw's wife and his mother, her explanation that 'George and I are good friends. George belongs to me. Other men may come and go; but George goes on for ever', has multiple meanings.[69]

Sinjon is terrified of this 'harpy . . . siren . . . mermaid . . . vampire'. They have met before: 'I felt in her presence an extraordinary sensation of unrest, of emotion, of unsatisfied need.' Then he had fled into the all-male world of the army; now his desire is again for 'flight, instant precipitate flight'.[70] But Mrs George catches up with him and the love/hate ('It's the same thing') battle begins again. Mrs George refuses to give in to his – and her – passion and proposes a decorous relationship. He may become to her and her husband what Shaw had been (in his eyes, at least) to couples in his milieu: a guarantor of their marriage as romancer of the wife and protector of the husband. But sexual desire must be negotiated before such domestic order can prevail. Sinjon kisses Mrs George: she pushes him away. He retaliates, proposing to see her husband and 'defeat and humiliate him. . . . Sooner than expose him to that, you would suffer a thousand stolen kisses, wouldn't you?'. He seizes her. His fear of her can only be met by sexual conquest of her: 'You are stronger than me in every way but this. Do you think I will give up my one advantage?'[71]

That this is an enactment of the oedipal struggle of the male child to possess the mother and displace the father is transparent. And in Shaw's psychodrama Mrs George almost submits to her desire. It is the entry of Bishop Bridgenorth which saves them both. Of the 'row of Shaws' in the play, the Bishop is Shaw's representation of his rational self; it is he who articulates the Fabian arguments in the play. When he enters the scene Mrs George immediately submits to him and reveals herself to be the author of anonymous love letters the Bishop has been receiving. Shaw, the child refused by the mother thus becomes Shaw, the adult who is, as 'Father', both the object and the controller of woman's desire. Male gender identity has been painfully but finally achieved. Its corollary is the defeat of female power and this is enacted in a scene, excessive to both narrative and argument, in which the Bishop urges Mrs George to tempt his curate ('Anthony') from his vow of chastity. As Mrs George goes into a trance she dissolves from the powerful Ashtoreth into Everywoman, Universal Victim.

> We spent eternity together; and you ask me for a little lifetime more. We possessed all the universe together and you ask me to give you my scanty wages as well. I have given you the greatest of all things; and you ask me to give you little things. I gave you your own soul: you ask me for my body as a plaything. Was it not enough? Was it not enough?[72]

Just as in the prefatory argument, only when female sexual power has been replaced by powerless supplication does male power dare to attend to woman's 'scanty wages' – the 'little things'.

Conclusion

Shaw's representations, dramatic and discursive, of women – including the New Woman – are deeply ambiguous and, I have argued, are not representations of women, but cyphers for a psychic strategy to achieve and protect masculinity. There is in Shaw's writing both 'that which *insists* on being spoken [and] what is *allowed* to be said'.[73] It contains both a text which issues from Shaw's unconscious and a text which is produced by conscious rationalism. The latter is a Fabian, pro-feminist text, the former is a struggle for male gender identity which depends upon subduing the power of the female other. Crucially, however, the subconscious text – in its images of domination of one gender class by the other – operates to recuperate the radical proposals of the conscious arguments, which are predicated upon notions of the equality of persons.

But a psychoanalytic explanation of Shaw's work must not be allowed to desocialise or dehistoricise it. Shaw's struggle for gender identity was particular, but it was articulated through available conventions for representing women. His images of woman as threat, whether as voracious consumer or sexual refuser of the male, have a long cultural history and his own re-representations reissued those myths back into radical culture by insinuating them into a socialist discourse. Crucially, in his theatrical representations this was effected by inscribing them literally on to the bodies of women, as actresses brought 'authenticity' to his female roles.

Neither was Shaw, however personal his demonology, unique in resisting and recontaining the threat posed by the nineteenth-early-twentieth-century New Woman. This process, I have argued, was taking place in a variety of forms in socialist, as in conservative, circles. Historically, I think, male gender identity was everywhere made more difficult to sustain in this period by a challenge from women, collectively and individually, to the social effects of masculinity. Men's response to that challenge, collectively and individually, and crucially in their unique access to discourse and representation, was to recontain women within a definition which sustained hard-won masculine identity. But that redefinition of woman – its crucial insertion of the importance of active (male-directed) sexuality, its injunctions against 'man-likeness', its insistence on the primacy of the maternal urge – in turn created a further problematic for the achievement of gender identity in women.

The mothers of many of the feminists of the 1960s were among the first women whose gender identities were constructed across popular cultural representations of this idea of woman in the 1920s. Modern feminism may thus be the inheritance psychically as well as materially of the contest of discourses around earlier-century feminism. As women of the later twentieth century began to live the consequences of the rights to education, work, political activity won by early-century feminist and socialist activism, so the psychic struggle to maintain that female gender identity became intensified. The discontinuity between female identity as m/other of the penis/phallus, and material reality – entry into male domains which confers an illusion of phallic power – is the contradiction which modern women live.

It is in this field of contradiction, I think, that the 'residual pressures' I earlier referred to reside. While the pressure of restrictive 'laws and institutions' has eased, the pressure never to act in excess of male de-prescription of what is properly female remains intense – a definition which, if it was not created, was certainly discursively and representationally re-intensified in this period in response to threats from women to claim the right to self-determination.

Notes

My thanks to Jan McDonald for allowing me to read her manuscript of 'New Women in the New Drama', and to Kate and to Norma for bearing patiently with me.

1. C. Black, *Married Women's Work* (London: Bell, 1915), the published results of a survey carried out by the Women's Industrial Council in 1909/10 (London: Virago reissue, 1983, with introduction by E. Mappen), p. 14.

2. J. Radcliffe, *The Weekend Guardian*, 18/19 November 1989.

3. See B. Bellow Watson, 'The New Woman and the New Comedy', and S. Lorichs, 'The "unwomanly woman" in Shaw's drama', both in R. Weintraub (ed.), *Fabian Feminist: Bernard Shaw and woman* (Pennsylvania: Pennsylvania State University, 1977), pp. 114–29 and 99–111. See also J. McDonald, 'New Women in the New Drama', *New Theatre Quarterly*, vol. VI, no. 21 (Feb. 1990), pp. 31–42.

4. Edith Lees, Havelock Ellis's wife, recalled her impression of the Achurch/Charrington production of *A Doll's House*:

   > how well I remember after the first performance of Ibsen's drama in London . . . a few of us collected outside the theatre breathless with excitement. Schreiner was there and Dolly Radford, the poetess . . . Honor Brooke . . . and Eleanor Marx. We were restive and almost savage in our arguments. What did it mean. . . . Was it life or death for women . . . Was it joy or sorrow for men? (quoted in J. Walkowitz, 'Science, feminism and romance: The men and women's club 1885–1889', *History Workshop Journal* 21 (Spring 1986), p. 54)

   For accounts of Ibsen and this milieu see Y. Kapp, *Eleanor Marx*, vol. 1: *Family Life* (London: Lawrence and Wishart, 1972) and vol. 2: *The Crowded Years* (London: Lawrence and Wishart, 1976); and J. Stokes, *Resistible Theatres* (London: Paul Elek, 1972).

5. I. Britain, *Fabianism and Culture* (Cambridge: Cambridge University Press, 1982), pp. 173–4.

6.
   > With the publication of . . . the 1918 Constitution . . . the link was made between the Fabian Society and the Labour Party. . . . The Labour Party, founded rather by the ILP than the Fabians, had come by 1918 more under Fabian than ILP influence . . . the Labour Party had accepted Fabianism as its doctrinal basis. (A. M. Briar, *Fabian Socialism and English Politics 1884–1918* (Cambridge: Cambridge University Press, 1962), p. 344).

7. A. Bebel, *Women in the Past, Present and Future* (London: Modern Press, 1885); F. Engels, *The Origin of the Family, Private Property and the State* (Zurich: Hottingen, 1884; Chicago: C. H. Kerr & Co, 1902).

8 For a full account see C. Rowan, '"Mothers, vote labour!": The state, the Labour movement and working class mothers 1900–1918', in R. Brunt and C. Rowan, *Feminism, Culture and Politics* (London: Lawrence and Wishart, 1982), pp. 59–84; and C. Rowan, 'Women in the Labour Party 1906–1920', *Feminist Review*, 12 (Oct. 1982), pp. 74–81.

9. Rowan, 'Women in the Labour Party', *op. cit.*, p. 80.

10. 'The Day Nursery is, of course, from the labour point of view, a necessity of the moment, but not an ideal of the future, for its main purpose is to provide for children whose mothers go out to work' (*Labour Woman*, Jan. 1920, quoted in Rowan, 'Women

in the Labour Party', *op. cit.*, p. 84. It should be stressed that this did represent the aspirations of working-class women, who sought liberation from oppression as wage labourers in improved conditions for family life. In this their interests were opposed to those of bourgeois women who sought freedom, not from poverty and labour, but from 'parasitism' and uselessness.

11. Quoted in C. Dyhouse, *Feminism and the Family in England 1880–1939* (Oxford: Blackwell, 1989), p. 58.

12. *ibid.*, p. 93.

13.   To the vast majority of women, and especially those of the fine type, the rearing of children would be the most attractive occupation, if it offered economic advantages equal to those of, say, school teaching or service in the post office. . . . Once the production of healthy, moral and intelligent citizens is revered as a social service and made the subject of deliberate praise and encouragement on the part of the government, it will, we may be sure, attract the best and most patriotic of citizens. (S. Webb, *The Decline of the Birthrate*, Fabian Tract 131 (London: Fabian Society, 1907 and 1913), p. 19)

14. H. Harben, *The Endowment of Motherhood*, Fabian Tract 149 (London: Fabian Society, 1910), p. 3.

15.   As the National Birth Rate Commission . . . pointed out, amongst the upper and middle class there were around 119 births per 1,000 married males under 35, while for the skilled workmen the figure was 153, and the unskilled 213. The result, Karl Pearson argued, was that 25 per cent of the population threatened to produce 50 per cent of the next generation. Consequently, the racial mixture of the population was undergoing a fundamental change: the worst stock were reproducing busily, while the best were dying out. (J. Weeks, *Sex, Politics and Society* (London: Longman, 1981 and 1989), p. 125)

16. S. Webb, *Decline of the Birthrate, op. cit.*, p. 17.

17. He was a member of the Fellowship of the New Life, founded in 1883, from which the Fabian Society was born. For accounts of Ellis's life and work see P. Grosskurth, *Havelock Ellis* (New York: Knopf, 1980); and S. Rowbotham and J. Weeks, *Socialism and the New Life: The personal and sexual politics of Edward Carpenter and Havelock Ellis* (London: Pluto, 1977).

18. Although Ellis maintained a long correspondence with Freud, and each acknowledged the importance of the other's work, Ellis resisted Freud's theory of the polymorphous nature of sexuality and of gender as an achieved state.

19. H. Ellis, *Man and Woman* (London: Walter Scott, 1894; rev. edn, London 1914), pp. 520–1 in the revised edition.

20. H. Ellis, *The Task of Social Hygiene* (London: Constable, 1912), p. 87.

21. S. Jeffreys, *The Spinster and Her Enemies* (London: Pandora, 1985), p. 95.

22. I. Bloch, 1908, quoted in Jeffreys, *Spinster, op. cit.*, p. 108.

23. One such resister was the Fabian feminist Emma Brooke:

    The assumption of this strong Desire in Women for Children – so strong that it can only be compared to the mighty impulse of men towards women – is a *most* important one; because if such an imperial Desire exists there is an end to the Sex-question; what remains is a population question. (Emma Brooke, 'Notes on a man's view of the Woman's Question', quoted in R. Brandon, *The New Women and The Old Men: Love, sex and the Woman Question* (London: Secker and Warburg, 1990), p. 52)

24. *The Economic Foundations of the Women's Movement*, Fabian Society, 1914), p. 19. B. L. Hutchins's hesitancy is also clear:

    The present paper does not attempt to discuss what is in theory the highest life for women; whether the majority of women can ever realise their fullest life outside the family, or whether an intelligent wife and mother has not, on the whole, other things equal, more scope for the development of her personality than any single woman can possibly have. (*The Working Life of Women*, Fabian Women's Group Series 1, Fabian Tract 157 (London: Fabian Society, 1911), p. 3)

25. *Mrs Warren's Profession*, Act II, p. 245. All references are to *Plays Unpleasant* (London: Penguin, 1946).
26. *ibid.*, Act I, p. 220.
27. I. Clarke, *Edwardian Drama* (London: Faber, 1989), p. 108.
28. *Mrs Warren's Profession*, Act II, p. 240.
29. *ibid.*, Act II, p. 245.
30. *ibid.*, Act I, p. 214.
31. *ibid.*, Act IV, p. 284.
32. *ibid.*, Act III, p. 259.
33. M. Holroyd, *Bernard Shaw*, vol. 1: *The Search for Love* (London: Chatto and Windus, 1988), p. 295.
34. J. McDonald, 'New Women', *op. cit.*, p. 34.
35. G. Matchett, 'The parent/child relationship in the English domestic plays of George Bernard Shaw' unpublished Ph.D thesis, University of Glasgow. Referred to in McDonald, 'New Women', *op. cit.*, p. 34.
36. Shaw's attitude to lesbianism was anyway to deny it:

> Though Kate would not sleep with Salt she was always falling in love with some woman. . . . Such escapades were bad for her, as what she really needed were children; and I told her to get a job in a factory to bring her to her senses. (G. B. Shaw, Preface to S. Winsten, *Salt and His Circle* (London: Hutchinson, 1951), p. 10)

37. H. Ellis, 'Sexual inversion in women', *Alienist and Neurologist* XVI (1895), quoted in C. Smith-Rosenberg, *Disorderly Conduct: Visions of gender in Victorian America* (New York and Oxford: Oxford University Press, 1986), p. 280.
38. *Man and Superman* (all references are to the Penguin edition, London, 1946), *The Revolutionist's Handbook*, V: The Political Need for the Superman, p. 227.
39. *ibid.*, Epistle Dedicatory, p. 19 and p. 20; Act I, p. 49 and p. 54; Act IV, p. 203.
40. *ibid.*, Act I, p. 61.
41. *ibid.*, Act I, p. 70.
42. *ibid.*, Act III, p. 148.
43. *ibid.*, Act IV, p. 198.
44. *ibid.*, *The Revolutionist's Handbook*, IV: Man's Objection to His Own Improvement, p. 225.
45. *ibid.*, Act III, p. 165.
46. *ibid.*, Act I, p. 62.
47. *ibid.*, Act IV, p. 204.
48. *ibid.*, Act II, p. 89.
49. *Getting Married*, Preface: A Forgotten Conference of Married Men, p. 22 (all references are to Penguin edition, London, 1986).
50. *ibid.*, Preface: Too Much of a Good Thing, p. 29.
51. *ibid.*, Preface: Hearth and Home, p. 26.
52. *ibid.*, Preface: A Forgotten Conference of Married Men, p. 23.
53. *ibid.*, Preface: The Question of Population, p. 43.
54. *ibid.*
55. *ibid.*, Preface: The Right to Motherhood, p. 44.
56. *ibid.*, Preface: Male Economic Slavery and the Rights of Bachelors, p. 87.
57. *ibid.*, Preface: A Probable Effect of Giving Women the Vote, p. 69.
58. *ibid.*, Preface: What is to Become of the Children?, p. 100.
59. Interview with himself drafted by Shaw for *The Daily Telegraph*, 7 May 1908, The Bodley Head Bernard Shaw, vol. 3 (London, 1971), p. 665 (not included in Penguin edition).
60. *Getting Married*, p. 148.
61. *ibid.*, p. 149.

62. *ibid.*, p. 126.
63. *ibid.*, p. 132.
64. *ibid.*, p. 215.
65. *ibid.*, p. 116.
66. *ibid.*, pp. 121, 119.
67. *ibid.*, p. 111.
68. *ibid.*, p. 216.
69. *ibid.*, p. 189.
70. *ibid.*, p. 186.
71. *ibid.*, pp. 196–8.
72. *ibid.*, p. 205.
73. J. Rose, *Sexuality in the Field of Vision* (London: Verso, 1986), p. 86.

2

The Golden Girl

LESLEY FERRIS

> Men, indeed, appear to act in a very unphilosophical manner when they try
> to secure the good conduct of women by attempting to keep them always in a
> state of childhood.[1]

> Her eye of light is the diamond bright,
> Her innocence the pearl.
> And these are ever the bridal gems
> That are worn by the American girl.[2]

David Belasco, known in his later theatrical career as the Bishop of Broadway,
claimed that he had created a new and unique type of American heroine when
he wrote and produced his melodrama *The Girl of the Golden West*. Belasco's
formal innovation, his *Girl*, is a particularly and specifically American image:
energetic, cheerful, apparently independent, unconventional, vivacious and,
as he describes her, 'a child of nature, spontaneous and untrammelled by the
dictates of society, and normally and healthily at home in the company of the
opposite sex'.[3]

If Belasco's claims are justified, then he spawned a particularly vibrant
image when his production opened with great success in New York in 1905.
Belasco's sense of his own generative powers must have profoundly increased
when the long-running production was targeted by Giacomo Puccini in 1907
as a fitting subject for an opera. The world première of *La fanciulla del west*,
the first grand opera with a specifically American theme, took place in New
York in 1910 with incredible celebration and media attention. Enrico Caruso

sang the central male role and the orchestra was conducted by Toscanini. Belasco himself served as stage manager for this lavish production.

What I hope to demonstrate in the course of this article is that David Belasco's claims are partially unfounded and ultimately simplistic. Belasco's sense of his own creativity is inextricably linked to the social and ideological mores of his era, just as is the activity of theatrical image-making itself. Daniel Gerould, in his essay on American melodrama that accompanies the republication of Belasco's script, describes the Girl as a specifically American version of the New Woman.[4] Unlike her sophisticated urban counterpart who brandishes cigarettes and latchkeys, the Golden Girl wields a pistol and mounts a horse. Part of her attraction for the American audiences was the opportunity it gave them to acknowledge publicly a vital and particular American image. Her presence and popularity served to vindicate and reaffirm America's image of itself; self-reliant, fearless, optimistic and independent. Old-world Europeans, accustomed to a more complex, intricate urban world view, found the Girl's lack of inhibitions and unconventional behaviour refreshing and amusing in the face of the stale ideals of female submissiveness.

I hope, then, not only to dismantle Belasco's singular view of his own creative powers but also, more importantly, to suggest a complex and multi-faceted way in which the process of image-making has often – to our detriment – lost or discarded the very people it claimed to serve and elevate. The Golden Girl image, exemplified and perhaps codified by Belasco's script, developed from a variety of sources: the late-nineteenth-century focus on the New Woman, the lived reality of the pioneer woman who helped to settle the American West, the ideologically promoted myth of the 'cult of True Womanhood' and the popular child performers who themselves were part of a larger 'cult of childhood'. In particular, one child performer – Lotta Crabtree – embodies all the aspects of the 'Golden Girl', and in the final section of this essay she appears, if not the initiator, then certainly a primary inspiration behind the image.

The cult of the child

Historians of art and literature, as well as social historians, seem to agree that it is in the nineteenth century that the image of the child develops a cultural significance unparalleled in previous epochs. Philippe Ariés, in his study *Centuries of Childhood*, states: 'In the tenth century, artists were unable to depict a child except as a man on a smaller scale. How did we come from that ignorance of childhood to the centering of the family around the child in the nineteenth century?'[5] Rousseau's proscriptive campaign for a return to nature in the late eighteenth century focused on the child as the ultimate natural being untainted, as yet, by the confining and artificial world of adults. Wordsworth's celebration of himself as subject matter for his own poetry infused his literary world with a nostalgic longing for his lost child self. Rousseau's call for child liberation from the constraints of adulthood found visual confirmation in Philip Otto Runge's paintings and drawings, which demonstrate 'the full scale discovery of children, both as empirical realities and lofty symbols'.[6] And it was in the late eighteenth century that a concern with childhood as a category of human development became clearly distinguished from adulthood. In Hanover in 1798 the work of the doctor Christian August Struve was published with the title *On the Rearing and Treatment of Children in Their First Years of Life: A handbook for all mothers who care in their hearts for their children's health.* The popularity of this book prompted a speedy translation into English.[7] In 1882 the Italian historian of art, Corrado Ricci, published *The Art of Children*, in which hundreds of children's drawings were analysed both for their subject matter and their techniques.[8] James Sully's 1895 work, *Studies of Childhood*, includes a chapter entitled 'The child as artist', in which the author compares children's drawings with those of 'primitive man'.[9]

In 1894, when the English painter Thomas Gotch had completed his painting, entitled *The Child Enthroned*, of his young daughter in a majestical Madonna-like pose, another facet of the child-conscious century was signalled. The child becomes gender specific: the child is a girl. This particular focus on the girl child became manifest in both the literary and the theatrical world of the late nineteenth century. A variety of well-known literary figures celebrated their fascination with young girls through their work; perhaps the best known is Lewis Carroll (Charles Dogdson). Other figures include Robert Louis Stevenson, John Ruskin, William Ernest Henley, George Meredith, G. F. Watts and Ernest Dowson.[10] The biographer Longaker, in discussing Dowson's poetry, describes the cult of little girls at Oxford during the 1880s:

> The students . . . were in the habit of taking professors' small daughters on the River and inviting them to tea. Little girls were the mascots, they appeared at student rituals and celebrations, and they were generally held in an esteem which Oxford knew neither before nor since.[11]

Dowson demonstrates his own fascination with girlhood in his sequence of eight poems entitled 'Sonnets of a little girl'.

The child actor

In 1890 the *Lady's Pictorial*, in surveying the current theatrical trends, declared: 'Whether artistic or inartistic, boding good or evil to the state, the craze for child actors is a widespread one and must be reckoned with.'[12] In his research on the image of childhood on the British theatrical stage Brian Crozier identifies two major periods which focused on the child. From 1887 to 1891 the craze for child stars was in full swing and the vehicles to showcase these children were plays like Burnett's theatrical adaptations of her stories *Little Lord Fauntleroy* and *Editha's Burglar*. In both these works the image of the child is essentially a sentimental stereotype which views the innocent child as a moral and benevolent influence on the adult world. From 1898 to 1905, Crozier defines the child theatrical cult as evolving to one of 'fairyland as a metaphor for the world of the child's imagination', a world that ultimately and permanently excludes adults. The fullest development of this theme is J. M. Barrie's *Peter Pan*, which capitalises on the child as determining hero of the play's action.[13]

Importantly for our purposes here, this cult of the theatrical child is also gender-specifically female. Even in the male roles of Cedric in *Little Lord Fauntleroy* and the eponymous hero in *Peter Pan* girls or young women took the roles. The majority of child stars were genuine girls or diminutive adult actresses who became known for their portrayals of children during this period. The titles of the plays themselves suggest this gendered focus: Boucicault's *My Little Girl* (1882), Jones's *The Dancing Girl* (1891), Garrick's *The Country Girl* (1894), Hilliard's *The Littlest Girl* (1896), and other titles included *The Shop Girl* (1895), *That Girl* (1890), *Four Little Girls* (1897) and *A Gaiety Girl* (1893).[14]

This fascination with the child actor was not limited to the British stage. Throughout the latter half of the nineteenth century 'child wonders' were a staple of theatrical fare in America. Nowhere did they get a more riotous welcome than on the West Coast, where the male members of the audience vastly outnumbered the women. In northwest California the discovery of gold in 1847 had attracted a large male population to mine or pan for gold. Many of these Argonauts, as they had become known, had left wives and children in the east. As George MacMinn says in *The Theater of the Golden Era in California*, 'A child actor was therefore no mere curiosity. From the first stride and the first sprouted line, little Anna Maria Quinn was bound to be a darling to every person of any parental sensibility.'[15] Miss Anna Maria Quinn performed an impressive and unsettling performance of *Hamlet* in 1854 at the Metropolitan in San Francisco. Miss Quinn's *Hamlet* vaulted her into a brief but stellar career as 'the greatest curiosity, and prodigy of the age'.[16] This precocious success was followed by numerous other child stars, the majority of whom were girls. A staggering number of child performers, who were often given the epithet 'Petite', toured the mining towns and entertained theatre-goers in the city: La Petite Clorinda, La Petite Soledad, La Petite Lizzie, La Petite Cerito and La Petite Susan clambered on the stages with an eclectic array of performance styles and speciality numbers.

At times, these numerous yet individual child performers were supplanted by entire companies of children. One of the most impressive was the Marsh Juvenile Comedians, ranging in age from five to fifteen years, which featured a troupe of twenty-six girls and four boys.[17]

A plethora of girl children dominated the stage at the very moment in theatrical history when other, more revolutionary images of women were being forged. In 1882 the first English-speaking production of Ibsen's *A Doll's House* was produced in the United States. It was adapted – a new happy ending having been grudgingly provided by Ibsen – and produced with the title *The Child Wife*. By 1889 the original ending as well as the title was restored and the play toured all the major American cities. *Ghosts* followed in 1894 and *Hedda Gabler* in 1898. American enthusiasm increased for this writer of complex, three-dimensional roles for women, and many of the major actresses of the day eagerly embraced his female characters. While George Bernard Shaw championed Ibsen and actresses on both sides of the Atlantic were playing Nora, Hedda, Mrs Alving and Rebecca West, plays such as *Editha's Burglar*, featuring a precocious seven-year-old girl, were also playing in New York and London. The dolls in Nora's house outnumbered her considerably.

New Woman: True Woman

By the time the theatrical imaginings of Ibsen's women and the New Drama with its New Woman aesthetics appeared on the stage for the first time in America, the well-worn pieties and selfless virtues of True Womanhood were already firmly and decidedly in place. Between 1820 and 1860 a range of printed material – now widely and cheaply available for the first time – promoted and prescribed the cult of True Womanhood. As Barbara Welter has pointed out:

> The attributes of True Womanhood, by which a woman judged herself and was judged by her husband, her neighbors and society could be divided into four cardinal virtues – piety, purity, submissiveness and domesticity. Put them all together and they spelled mother, daughter, sister, wife – woman. Without them, no matter whether there was fame, achievement or wealth, all was ashes. With them she was promised happiness and power.[18]

The rise of this 'cult' shows a determined effort to stabilise the domestic sphere by instilling feminine ideals through public lectures and sermons as well as a prodigious amount of prescriptive literature such as child-rearing books, etiquette manuals, women's magazines and marriage guidance books. The titles of such works are in themselves a telling encapsulation of the literature of female moral guidance: *The Ladies' Parlor Companion*, *The Young Lady's Book*, *Whisper to a Bride*, *Women of Worth: A book for girls*, *The Mother's Assistant and Young Lady's Friend*. One of the significant elements of this particular American ideology was apparently to 'democratise' woman's place in the world. No longer was woman a servile inferior, a lesser being, a subordinate baby machine to ensure the continuity of the male line; woman's place was necessarily separate, ensuring the continuity of civilisation, as this excerpt from Henry C. Wright's 1870 tract *The Empire of the Mother Over the Character and Destiny of the Race* demonstrates:

> The influence of woman is not circumscribed by the narrow limits of the domestic circle. She controls the destiny of every community. The character of society depends as much on the fiat of woman as the temperature of the country on the influence of the sun.[19]

The True Woman might be a hostage in her own home, but she had been elevated to a tempting centrality. Sun-like, she was its warm, life-giving centre; she reigned supreme. Her domestic perfection guaranteed her an apparent active role in the 'destiny of her race' as a keeper of civilisation, protecting the community and safeguarding the social order.

As a national icon, the True Woman had no difficulty in infusing herself into the social and cultural lives of men and women who lived a predominantly urban, leisure-class existence. But how can such an image be maintained in the face of a radically different reality – that of the pioneering women of the West? The pioneer woman took an active and often hazardous role in settling the West; she fought adversity, physical hardship and extreme deprivation in a hostile, unknown terrain. The daily realities of Western women's lives were shaped by hard work both in and outside the home. Although separate work roles were for the most part maintained – men tended livestock, ploughed, planted and harvested and women took care of the household, cared for children and the sick – they were permeable. Women were often, for a variety of different reasons, left alone with the full responsibility for managing their families' economic fortunes.[20] Despite the predominance of the True Womanhood ideology, the practical reality was that women often pioneered their way west on an equal footing with the men and out of sheer necessity discarded any pretence of 'femininity'. One of the many examples is that of Kate White, who left a refined middle-class existence in Virginia to travel west, riding a horse, using a six-shooter and winning a reputation for being 'as big and broad and capable as a strong man'.[21]

Such pioneer women who broke with conventional codes of womanhood to travel west and establish a home life could not simply be ignored. Despite attempts to corral these autonomous, self-possessed women into the 'True Woman' camp as 'mothers of civilisation', and so maintain the ideology of 'separate spheres', some recognition of women's active role developed. In 1869 Wyoming gave women the right to vote; in 1893 Colorado followed suit; by 1914 eleven states had given women the right to vote and ten of these were west of the Mississippi.[22] The woman's suffrage movement was launched in 1848 by Lucretia Mott and Elizabeth Cady Stanton at the Seneca Falls Convention in New York. But this apparent 'early start' (compared to a much later date in Britain) did little to prevent Susan B. Anthony from being fined $100 when, in 1893, against the state law in Rochester, New York, she voted. Anthony's sisters in Colorado, however, were voting legally.

Belasco's Girl

The Girl – Belasco's unadorned and highly significant name for his heroine –
lives in the Sierra Mountains in a small cabin with her companion and
servant, Wowkle, an Indian squaw. The play's setting at the height of the
'gold fever' in a mining camp in California, finds the Girl running the Polka
Saloon, inhabited by miners with characteristically colourful names of the
American West: Sonora Slim, Trinidad Joe, Happy Halliday, Handsome
Charlie. Jack Rance, the sheriff of the camp, wants to marry the Girl; he calls
a toast in her absence at the beginning of the play: 'Gentlemen, the Girl! The
only girl in the Camp – the girl I mean to make Mrs. Jack Rance!'[23] Belasco
establishes the male-dominated tone of the camp through several short scenes
in which men gamble, sing with the local banjo player, fight, argue and finally
provoke Sheriff Rance to pull his gun – violence that is only prevented by
the bartender's warning that the Girl approaches. This ends the quarrel and
the men drink to each other in apparent friendship. Belasco gives time and
descriptive detail to the Girl's first appearance:

> The character of the Girl is rather complex. Her utter frankness takes away all
> suggestion of vice – showing her to be unsmirched, happy, careless, untouched
> by the life about her. Yet she has a thorough knowledge of what the men of her
> world generally want. She is used to flattery – knows exactly how to deal with
> men – is very shrewd – but quite capable of being a good friend to the camp
> boys.[24]

Belasco's description astutely and deliberately qualifies the moral position of
the Girl: the stereotype of the Western woman who worked in a saloon was
that she was a 'bad woman', possibly a 'good-hearted prostitute', but a 'bad
woman' nevertheless. Belasco is clearly aware that by placing his independent heroine in an all-male camp as proprietor of the Polka Saloon, he must
dispel the conventional assumptions about such a woman. He immediately
specifies, therefore, that she is free from 'vice'. However, he creates in her an
odd mixture of apparent contradictions: 'untouched by life about her', at the
same time she possesses a 'thorough knowledge' of what these tough, Western
miners want.

When Rance continues to pester her about marriage she fearlessly and
forthrightly talks back to him:

> Look here, Jack: let's have it right now. I run this Polka alone because I like it.
> My father taught me the business, and – well, don't worry about me – I can look
> after myself. I carry my little wepping [weapon] – (*touching her pocket to show
> that she has a pistol*). I'm independent – I'm happy – the Polka's paying an' –
> ha! – it's all bully! Say, what the devil do you mean proposin' to me with a wife
> in Noo Orleans? Now, this is a respectable saloon – an' I don't want no more of
> that talk.[25]

Despite this articulated display of strength and determination, her status as 'the Girl' in the midst of the miners continually undermines any autonomy she might have, and with the entry of Dick Johnson, a fashionable gentleman from Sacramento, the Girl is smitten. They dance together, she invites him to her cabin for a midnight supper. But in reality Johnson is the road-agent and bandit Ramerrez, hunted by Sheriff Rance and the Wells Fargo posse with a $5,000 reward on his head. Johnson, who knows that his fellow road-agents are awaiting his signal to rob the Polka Saloon, agrees against his better judgement to the Girl's rendezvous; and when he discovers that the Girl runs the Polka he decides to abandon his plans to rob it.

During their meeting they talk intimately, slowly revealing their love for one another, interrupted by the sound of distant gun shots which the distracted Girl takes to mean that the sheriff has tracked down Ramerrez. When Sheriff Rance knocks on the Girl's cabin, she hides Johnson (at his insistence) so her late night assignation with him will not compromise her. Sheriff Rance innocently reveals to her that Johnson is Ramerrez, and after the sheriff's departure, the Girl angrily accuses Johnson/Ramerrez of deception. He readily admits to his deceit, refusing to defend himself and with feeling articulates the transforming power of the Girl: 'But, so help me God, from the moment I kissed you to-night, I meant to change, I meant to change.'[26]

As the changed Johnson/Ramerrez leaves the Girl's cabin Sheriff Rance shoots and wounds him. The Girl audaciously hides him in her attic but his blood dripping through the attic floor from his wound reveals his hiding place. Rance prepares to hand over the wounded, unconscious road-agent to the Wells Fargo posse for 'shooting or the tree'; but the Girl, always at the ready to redeem her man, pulls her pistol on Rance, and says to him:

> I live on chance money – drink money – card money – saloon money. We're gamblers – we're all gamblers. . . . You asked me to-night if my answer to you was final. Now's your chance. I'll play you a game – straight poker. . . . If you're lucky, you git him an' me; but if you lose, this man setting' between us is mine – mine to do with as I please – an' you shut up and lose like a gentleman.[27]

In the amazing archetypal gambling scene that follows, the Girl deftly and expertly plays poker for Johnson/Ramerrez. Belasco exploits her pure virgin–siren image – she feigns fainting in order to pull cards from her stocking and so saves the wounded, unconscious Johnson from Sheriff Rance by cheating, only to see him caught again on his recovery: this time the men of the camp, totally committed to the Girl's wishes and loyally sympathetic to the Girl's great love, trick the Wells Fargo agent and free the road bandit. As the bartender of the saloon says after Ramerrez's escape, 'The Polka won't never be the same, boys – the Girl's gone.'[28]

The final act of the play creates a scenic panorama which displays 'The boundless prairies of the West', against which the Girl and Johnson return

east to begin their new life. As they view the sunrise the Girl closes the play
with these final lines:

> A new life. (*Putting her hands in his.*) Oh, my mountains – I'm leaving you –
> Oh, my California, I'm leaving you – Oh, my lovely West – my Sierras! – I'm
> leaving you! – Oh my – (*Turning to Johnson, going to him and resting in his
> arms.*) – my home.[29]

Belasco's authorial naming (and by implication ownership) of 'the Girl' sets
up a mirror image within the narrative of his script. The absence of a first,
or Christian, name throughout the text continually emphasises the generic
quality of the character known as 'the Girl'; but the repeated use of the
adjective 'the' gives this generic name a specificity which sets her both apart
and within the community. She is the one and only *girl*, the unique and
special other, the odd-'man'-out in this male landscape of rough-and-ready
miners. The miners take great pleasure in talking about her, discussing her
attributes, speaking her name with tenderness. Indeed, there is a sense that
they cannot stop speaking her name. Before her entrance in the first act, for
example, eventually all the male characters within a short ten-line sequence
speak her name:

> Rance: (*Accepting a glass.*) Gentlemen, the Girl! The only girl in the Camp – the
>   girl I mean to make Mrs. Jack Rance! . . . .
> Nick: (*Seeing the Girl coming in through the dance-hall.*) The Girl . . .
> Rance: Ha! Ha! Ha! Once more friends, – the Girl!
> All: The Girl![30]

As Valerie Walkerdine has pointed out, it is not uncommon for men to give
nicknames or baby names to women or girls within their families or social
domains.[31] This infantilised naming provides the namer with a fantasy of
male strength and protection. By creating names which invoke smallness, the
need for protection and a sense of adoration, male desire and passion is
displaced and hidden in favour of the safer and socially acceptable masculine
position of the big man, paternal defender, moral guardian.[32]

Furthermore, this desire to infantilise through naming offers a sense of
omnipotent power to the male namer by stopping the passage of time. Belasco
freezes his creation in our dramatic memory as forever 'the Girl'; a heroine
who has the capacity to make choices, to control her own fate, but whose very
name undermines and trivialises this capacity.

Belasco's script underscores the significance of names and naming in other
ways as well. The men of the mining camp are singularly specific with their
colourful, double names and serve as a stark contrast to the generic singularity
of 'the Girl': Trinidad Joe, Sonora Slim, Sidney Duck, Happy Halliday. In the
cast list 'The Girl' appears first with no adjectival description characteristic of
the other major characters: for example, 'Dick Johnson, a stranger', 'Jack

Rance, gambler and sheriff'. It is something of a surprise, then, to find that
the Girl does have a name, though it is used only a few times in the text. The
first use is in the first act when Sheriff Rance proposes to the Girl:

> *Rance*: Say, Minnie –
> *Girl*: (*Polishing glasses*) H'm?
> *Rance*: Will you marry me?
> *Girl*: Nop.[33]

As in the three other instances of using her name, Rance cuts off his sentence.
As the sheriff continues to pursue the Girl in his marriage request, she
continually answers him with 'Nop'. In exasperation, he says, 'Now, see here,
Min –.'[34] The Girl herself cuts him off, severing her name in half.

The next time her name is heard the scene has shifted to the interior of her
one-room cabin on Cloudy Mountain. The Girl and Johnson are alone, the fire
burns in the hearth, a storm rages outside, causing the lamp to flicker and
the curtains to flap gently. The Girl and Johnson, however, are completely
oblivious of their surroundings: he has just embraced her for the first time with
an ecstatic declaration of love. Following this moment of quiet intimacy,
Johnson asks the Girl her name:

> *Johnson*: What's your name, Girl – your real name?
> *Girl*: Min – Minnie. My father's name was Smith.
> *Johnson*: Oh, Minnie Sm –
> *Girl*: But 'twasn't his right name.
> *Johnson*: No?
> *Girl*: His right name was Falconer –
> *Johnson*: Minnie Falconer. That's a pretty name. (*He kisses her hand.*)
> *Girl*: I think that was it, – I ain't sure. That's what he said it was. I ain't sure of
> anything – only – jest you.[35]

Again, Belasco with deliberation graphically breaks the lines of spoken text
as if he, as author, finds difficulty in writing the Girl's 'real' name. As if to
underscore the ambiguous nature of her name, the Girl herself can barely
speak it and even claims not to be sure of her last name. So the Girl does have
a specific name, a name with which she is clearly uncomfortable, a name
which can only be rarely and haltingly spoken, a name with which she is
ultimately confused and unclear.

When Dick Johnson appears for the first time at the Polka Saloon, Sheriff
Rance approaches him and says, 'I haven't heard your name, young man.' The
Girl responds with a laugh: 'Oh! Names out here!'[36] Yes, out here in the West,
names exist in a particularly protean state, unstable, slippery, capricious. For
the men of the camp, their colourful names are not conventionally patronymic;
instead, they have earned them as part of their active exploits in the male
community of the mining camps. Handsome Charlie is 'a big picturesque
miner' and Sonora Slim 'a tall, lanky miner with an emphatic manner'.[37]

Dick Johnson's name is Anglo-Saxon, East Coast respectable; but he is also Ramerrez, Spanish–Western road-agent, outlaw. The Girl's double naming contrasts considerably with Johnson/Ramerrez. His is clear, delineated, specific. Hers is confused, hidden, unknown and utterly generic.

Ann K. Clark's fascinating essay entitled 'The Girl: A rhetoric of desire' analyses the current practice of using the Girl image as a rhetorical device in the advertising world of corporate capitalism. Clark's uncanny perceptions sound convincingly like an astute critique of Belasco's Girl until we must remind ourselves that Clark wrote the essay in 1987 not in reference to any theatrical text, but as a personal reflection on both understanding and exorcising the female image that is replicated endlessly on billboards, in magazines and in television commercials: Helen Curtis, Swiss Formula, L'Oreal, the American Dairy Association, Schick, Coca Cola, Harvey's Bristol Cream, Pierre Cardin.

Clark describes how one of the generating principles of the Girl resides in the way she appears deceptively as a source of freedom while simultaneously existing out of context, without a past, without history: '[The Girl] promises that it is possible to be anyone. She has the freedom of 'no-history' which enables her, being formless, to be any form; enables her, without prejudgement, to choose anything. She is infinitely free.'[38] Looking at Belasco's Girl, her 'real' name is lost to history, lost in a cloudy memory of her dead parents. She thrives in her formless, generic Girlhood, a magic state with an aura of personal freedom and independence, where her 'girlishness' keeps her at enjoyably safe distance from the male miners.

Clark's vision of a product-orientated Girl representing the desires of consumer capitalism demonstrates the enduring quality of this image. In some sense, Belasco's Girl, arriving at the end of one dramatic era and the beginning of another, has perfect theatrical timing. She is an image which will have a warm commercial welcome in the early film industry as well as the musical theatre. Later, her generic attributes celebrate a conflicting duality – she is both formless and formed, as Clark has pointed out – as she is exploited, replicated and refined in endless advertising campaigns.

Importantly, the theatrical image of Belasco's Girl ends on the golden threshold to a new, married life. Her sexual innocence is about to vanish: we never see her after it has – or, perhaps more significantly, after she has been integrated in an Eastern society where her Western independence and self-reliance will not be valued. Moreover, in her new life with Johnson, she can hardly carry on as 'the Girl'; she will be named at last, and her name will finally be specific and stable: Mrs Dick Johnson.

Lotta Crabtree: 'The most perpetual gamin on the American stage'

The life and career of Lotta Crabtree deserve a detailed consideration in their own right for the way in which, first, she affected the fortunes of American theatre in the late nineteenth century and, secondly, the way in which the narrative of her life dramatises the contradictions and the paradoxes faced by women actresses in her time.[39]

Charlotte Crabtree was born in 1847 in New York; at the age of six she went with her mother to search for a wayward father who had temporarily vacated family life for the lure of California gold; by the age of eight she was touring the mining camps and performing solo song-and-dance numbers to a pleasure-starved rowdy male audience. Her mother, Mary Ann, was a dominant woman who, faced with impending poverty and an unpredictable husband, quickly realised the potential of her daughter's stage career; when Mary Ann and Lotta arrived in San Francisco they would have opportunely noticed the popularity of Kate and Ellen Bateman, aged eleven and nine years, who toured the West Coast with their miniaturised renditions of *Hamlet*, *Richard III*, and *Merchant of Venice*.

We have already seen how child performers flooded the West like gold-diggers: El Dorado County was no exception, with its chorus of tiny girls known as the 'Fairy Minstrels'. The mining camp of Grass Valley, where Mary Ann Crabtree settled with her daughters, boasted a troupe of child performers, and proudly supported a theatre company, a number of saloons with stages offering evening entertainment and a playhouse. The popular female performer in a sense solved the demand for women in the all-male mining camps by allowing a group of males collectively to share one woman. As one biographer of Lotta Crabtree observed:

> The prizes were going to women. In this new world composed preponderantly of men, women were rising to a singular eminence. For months all the drift of interest on stage had been toward women, Caroline Chapman, Lola Montez, Matilda Heron, Laura Keene, Catherine Sinclair. . . . If the stage in California was still a gusty affair, full of dangerous, sudden changes, it offered an un-paralleled opportunity for feminine initiative.[40]

Lotta's theatrical apprenticeship took her on extensive tours of the mining camps and both her own and her mother's perseverance in such a harsh, rigorous, often dangerous environment led to eventual star billing in the legitimate theatres in San Francisco, where between 1859 and 1864 she became a popular, successful performer known as 'Miss Lotta, the San Francisco Favorite'.[41] Lotta's speciality did not lie in the serious Shake-spearean drama of so many of her competitors, but rather in comedy that included music, dance, burlesques of serious plays, farce and minstrel-show routines. This Shirley Temple of the mining camps danced and sang her way into the hearts of these brutalised, childless miners and made the image of orphanhood into a personal triumph. Young boy rascals and saucy, gamin-like waifs figured among her popular characters.

Even before Lotta took the essential road to national fame in New York City she had inspired numerous imitators, and once well established in the East she became all the rage: her fans, now from coast to coast, danced the 'Lotta Polka' and the 'Lotta Gallop'.[42]

Lotta was forty-five when, in 1891, an injury during performance forced her to retire from a career where, one could say, her entire fame and fortune derived from playing versions of her eight-year-old self for over nearly forty years. It is difficult not to recognise this 'perpetual gamin' as Belasco's unacknowledged source for 'The Girl'. David Belasco must have known of Charlotte Crabtree from his earliest memories. He was born in California to a theatrical family in 1859, the very year that twelve-year-old Lotta made the necessary move from mining-camp tours to an engagement before an adoring public at Tom Maguire's 1,700-seat Opera House in San Francisco. Lotta was an established, popular star when Belasco himself performed as a child in the role of the Duke of York to Charles Kean's Richard III on Kean's farewell tour. Later, as a member of the stock company of the San Francisco Theatre, he played with a variety of established actors when they toured the West. Belasco's most important theatrical apprenticeship before he moved to New York was as secretary, actor, writer and stage manager to Tom Maguire, the city's leading theatre entrepreneur.

In 1867 Lotta's first major New York success was in John Brougham's stage adaptation of *The Old Curiosity Shop*. The piece had been retitled *Little Nell and the Marchioness* to signify the delightful double roles Lotta was able to play with speed and alacrity, stunning her audience with the pathos of Little Nell one moment, returning to the stage in a matter of minutes as the comic, ludicrous Marchioness. This production, to which Lotta added a range of musical material, perhaps featured her most famous performing roles and she kept it in her repertoire for twenty-five years. When Lotta toured *Little Nell and the Marchioness* to London some years later a London critic delighted in her comic talent:

> Lotta's Marchioness is a performance *sui generis*. It is the quaintest, oddest conception in the world . . . her breakdown is the funniest thing ever done in comic dancing. . . . Lotta's face as she sits on the kitchen table, eyeing the dreadful mutton-bone, haunts me. No words can describe the fantastic tricks of this actress.[43]

Billed as 'The Peerless and Ever-Welcome Lotta', she returned to San Francisco in 1879 with several productions, including her now famous *Little Nell and the Marchioness*. A young David Belasco performed with her in the role of Foxey Joe in this production while supervising a revival of his own dramatisation of Zola's *L'Assommoir*.[44]

Brougham's adaptation of *The Old Curiosity Shop* for Lotta was one of many commissions she made to a variety of established playwrights. When the mania for equestrian performance was the rage, Edmund Falconer adapted *Under Two Flags* for her with the new title of *Firefly*. Besides her usual singing and dancing Lotta led a regiment and rode a horse speedily across the desert. Falconer also wrote *Heartsease* for her and it became her major production throughout 1870. The play is unusual in that, unlike the majority of Lotta's other scripts, it has a primarily American locale and theme. *Heartsease* has been described as one of the earliest uses of the American frontier theme in a substantial script as opposed to short sketches and musical numbers. Comer describes Lotta's role as May Wydlerose, who experiences life in the California mining camps, as a pistol-packin' girl with more than a strong resemblance to Annie in *Annie Get Your Gun*.[45]

David Belasco was among the various writers Lotta commissioned for her plays. For *Pawn Ticket 210*, written by Belasco in collaboration with Clay Greene, Lotta had promised $5,000 dollars for the script of which $1,000 was a down-payment. Both authors travelled to the opening in Chicago in September 1887. When Belasco saw the devastating reviews, he felt so embarrassed at seeing Lotta the next morning after the opening that he was prepared to forgo the commission balance. To his astonishment a cheerful Lotta greeted him with the assuring words, 'Don't pay any attention to the criticism. None of my plays has ever received good notices, but the public comes. We have a great big success in this piece.'[46]

The central character that Belasco created for Lotta was a diminutive girl, Mag, whom her poverty-stricken mother had pawned in a desperate need for ready money. While locked in the pawn shop, along with the watches, rings and jewels, Mag takes advantage of the pawned musical instruments to play the banjo, sing and dance. Uncle Harris, the pawn-shop owner, grows very fond of her and plans to adopt her when her pawn-ticket redemption period has expired. The precocious child is suddenly and mysteriously claimed by a shady businessman. Installed in his home, she cleverly detects and foils a crime and is miraculously reunited with her long-suffering mother.

The theme and plot of *Pawn Ticket 210* sound much like a hackneyed version of *Editha's Burglar* by Frances Hodgson-Burnett. While Burnett's own dramatised version of her short story was playing in London, a pirated version directed by David Belasco opened in New York in September 1887, the same month of Lotta's *Pawn Ticket 210* première in Chicago. As we have seen in the previous discussion on the child actor, *Editha's Burglar*, along with Burnett's equally popular *Little Lord Fauntleroy*, represents the dramatic narratives of children as benevolent influences on the adult world. Just as Mag charms the crotchety Uncle Harris and then prevents a crime from taking place, so the child Editha, on discovering a threatening burglar in her home,

charms him into taking only her own unimportant items from her impoverished household while she cleverly protects her sick mother in the next room.

In the light of such evidence, Belasco opportunely had first-hand knowledge of the public enthusiasm for this theatrical image of 'the girl'. By the
time Lotta ended her enterprising and productive career in 1891, she retired
as possibly the wealthiest single woman ever to generate her own fortune. She
left over $2 million to charity when she died in 1924 at the age of seventy-six;
she was indeed a 'golden girl'.

David Belasco was also accumulating considerable wealth as one of the
leading directors of the American stage. In New York he completely rebuilt a
theatre and renamed it the Belasco. Whereas his previous work had been
primarily stage management and play doctoring, his distinguishing trade-
mark was to become his dazzling scenic effects. He specialised in manufac-
turing the snowstorm that brewed outside the Cloudy Mountain cabin as
Johnson and the Girl exchanged their first intimacies. The Californian sunrise
over the Sierra Nevadas that closes *The Girl of the Golden West* took him over
three months to perfect. Belasco, alone, served as the single motivating force
in his theatre: he both wrote or selected his scripts, hand-picked his performers
in order to reinforce his theatrical style and produced and directed the plays
on a massive scale using the latest developments in stagecraft and technology.

Belasco's theatrical creativity extended beyond play-writing and scenic
effects to the very performers he featured in his plays. The press often took
him to task as a tyrannical director who achieved his brilliant *mise-en-scene*
through a demanding and tortuous torment of his leading performers. As
Marker says in her study of the autocratic director:

> Belasco himself admitted . . . that he would 'coax and cajole, or bulldoze and
> torment' his actors, according to the temperament with which he had to deal.
> His unique personal capacity for developing and reinforcing the distinctive
> abilities of his actors constitutes a keystone of his theatrical success.[47]

In particular, he became known for his Svengali-like relationships with his
actresses. His first real breakthrough as an independent producer occurred
with his sensational production of *The Heart of Maryland*, an auspicious
event as it also established the first of his personally created stars, Mrs Leslie
Carter. Mrs Carter, whom the director coached and trained for two years,
became celebrated in Belasco's roles for her ability to play a variety of emotionally charged, feverish roles. Belasco was attuned to typing his actresses to
the familiar female stereotypes of the day: Mrs Carter served him well as a
passionate melodramatic heroine. Blanche Bates, on the other hand, with her
vibrant girlish innocence and trustful, ingenuous style was the antithesis of
Mrs Carter. Her hair coiffured in childish braids, Blanche Bates originated
the role of 'the Girl'.

There was no significant Svengali male figure in Lotta's life except for the
shaping forces of patriarchal culture itself. Indeed, if anything, the males in

Lotta's life were conspicuously absent. Her father had forsaken the young family on his trip West for gold and though Mary Ann Crabtree relocated him, he never contributed anything substantial to his daughter's career. Her wayward, unreliable brothers followed her father's footsteps with a variety of failed business ventures (all underwritten by Lotta) and constant need for financial support.

Though would-be male suitors were in abundance, Mary Ann Crabtree monitored every possible attachment. For the most part, Lotta herself referred to the senders of endless letters, gifts and declarations of undying love as her 'idiotic admirers', and she once told an interviewer, 'I do wish that a man of a little sense would admire me for once.'[48] For a few years Lotta was actually engaged to a young man from a respectable Philadelphian family. She seemed genuinely attracted to him and seriously mourned his unexpected death in 1872. But even he had gambled away large sums of Lotta's money.

The tight reins on Lotta's personal life, held by her overprotective mother, were not totally lost on her adoring, indulgent public. 'Lotta the Unapproachable' was to become one of her familiar epithets.[49] Mary Ann Crabtree safeguarded her daughter with a determination bordering on obsession. Once, when Mary Ann parted briefly from her daughter, who was then in middle age, a female member of staff was required to accompany her whenever she left her rooms. On the stage Lotta's exuberant, comical child roles earned her a string of adjectives from her numerous critics: 'saucy, pert, gamey, devilish, mischievous, unpredictable, impulsive, rattle-brained, teasing, piquant, and rollicking'.[50] But in her own cloistered child-life these characteristics seem strangely muted and out of kilter with her mother's watchful precautions. Mary Ann Crabtree's comments on her daughter are particularly revealing in this aspect:

> Lotta is a veritable child who never has done things like older women. She has been sheltered, cared for and has no idea of the value of money nor what it will buy. I have kept her that way and never consult her in regard to business outside the theater.[51]

Lotta's stage narratives – especially those she commissioned herself from *Heartsease* in 1870 to *Pawn Ticket 210* in 1887 – uncannily parallel her own life. The theme of the resourceful, enterprising waif separated from her rightful parent, and in some cases unaware of her own identity, served as a central motif. In the tradition of the matriarchal pieties of melodrama, the happy ending lies not in marriage but in newly discovered wealth and identity through the reuniting of mother and child. The mother–daughter bond reasserts itself as the central autonomous relationship without the conventional necessity for male intervention or protection.

This lack of a male presence finds further illumination in Lotta's name. Early in her career, both she and her mother decided to drop 'Crabtree' and use a shortened version of her first name. This disregard for the patronymic protocol was also used by Belasco, as we have seen, with his 'Girl' who fumblingly tries to remember her real last name. But for Belasco, his Girl, who, unlike Lotta, is utterly unique in a landscape full of men, gloriously finds a last name in her marriage to Johnson.

David Belasco opened his wildly romantic Western melodrama starring Blanche Bates as 'the Girl' in November 1905. Charles Frohman, one of Belasco's leading competitors, had opened Barrie's *Peter Pan* a week earlier with Maude Adams, known for her child roles and her elfin persona, in the title role. Both plays were fantastically successful, spawning numerous revivals, films and musical versions. In November 1905 both Frohman and Belasco were like sparring partners in a boxing match, trying to outdo each other with their own theatricalised girls: Belasco's lived and worked in a male community, riding horses, swearing and shooting; Frohman's lived inside a boy's costume and a fantasy world where growing up was not only impossible but undesirable. Belasco's obsession with his own self-promoted Pygmalion-like powers exploded in resentment and anger when critics dared to attack the mechanics of his plot. The offended playwright claimed nothing short of total artistic creativity and 'truth' with his comment: 'I know the period of Forty-nine as I know my alphabet, and there are things in my *The Girl of the Golden West* truer than many of the incidents in Bret Harte.'[52]

In that same year of 1905, when Mary Ann Crabtree died, a virtually forgotten Lotta had been retired from the stage for fourteen years. Lotta, who greatly mourned the much-loved companion of her child life, began to age at last. When in 1924 Lotta herself passed away, one commentator who recalled her star status exclaimed with the characteristic enthusiasm of her admirers: 'What a Peter Pan she would have made!'[53] Unlike her theatrical girl images, which could be played again and again located in a repertoire of Never Never Land, Charlotte Crabtree lived the reality of a desexualised, innocent female whose unacknowledged artistic creation was her own theatricalised girl-self.

Notes

1. Mary Wollstonecroft, *A Vindication of the Rights of Women* (Harmondsworth: Penguin, 1985), p. 101.
2. Sigourney, *et al.*, 'The American Girl', *The Young Lady's Offering; or Gems of Prose and Poetry* (Boston: Phillips and Simpson, 1848).
3. D. Gerould, 'The Americanization of melodrama', in D. Gerould (ed.), *American Melodrama* (New York: Performing Arts Journal, 1983), p. 25.
4. *ibid.*, p. 26.
5. P. Ariés, *Centuries of Childhood* (London: Jonathan Cape, 1962), p. 10.
6. R. Rosenblum, *The Romantic Child from Runge to Sendak* (New York: Thames and Hudson, 1988), p. 18.
7. *ibid.*, p. 18.
8. G. Boas, *The Cult of Childhood* (London: University of London, 1966), p. 81.
9. ibid., p. 83.

10. M. Longaker, *Ernest Dowson* (Philadelphia: University of Pennsylvania, 1967), p. 27.
11. *ibid.*
12. B. Crozier, 'Notions of childhood in London theatre 1880–1905', unpublished Ph.D thesis, Cambridge University, 1981, p. 170.
13. *ibid.*, p. 238.
14. *ibid.*, p. 266.
15. G. R. MacMinn, *The Theater of the Golden Era in California* (Caldwell, Idaho: Caxton Printers, 1941), p. 446.
16. *ibid.*, p. 448.
17. E. Gagey, *The San Francisco Stage: A history* (New York: Columbia University, 1950), p. 96.
18. B. Welter, 'The cult of True Womanhood 1820–1860', in M. Gordon (ed.), *The American Family in Social-Historical Perspective* (New York: St Martin's Press, 1973), p. 225.
19. Quoted in M. P. Ryan, *Womanhood in America: From colonial times to the present* (New York: New Viewpoints, 1975), p. 14.
20. E. Jameson, 'Women as workers, women as civilizers: True Womanhood in the American West,' *Frontiers*, vol. VII, no. 3 (1984), p. 4.
21. Ryan, *Womanhood in America*, *op. cit.*, p. 140.
22. Jameson, 'Women as Workers', *op. cit.*, p. 2.
23. D. Belasco, *The Girl of the Golden West* in *American Melodrama*, ed. D. Gerould (New York: Performing Arts Journal, 1983), p. 194. All quotes from Belasco's script are from this source.
24. *ibid.*, p. 194.
25. *ibid.*, p. 198.
26. *ibid.*, p. 225.
27. *ibid.*, p. 245.
28. *ibid.*
29. *ibid.*, p. 247.
30. *ibid.*, p. 194.
31. V. Walkerdine, 'Video Replay: Families, film and fantasy', in V. Burgin, J. Donald and C. Caplan (eds), *Formations of Fantasy* (London: Methuen, 1979), pp. 167–99.
32. See, for example, J. Mills, *Womanwords* (Harlow, Essex: Longman, 1989). Mills's book is a dictionary of words that define women; a 'lexical category for women' that gives the etymology of the word as well as contemporary feminist commentary. The entry for *Girl/Girlie* is particularly useful for my discussion in this essay.
33. Belasco, *The Girl*, *op. cit.*, p. 197.
34. *ibid.*, p. 198.
35. *ibid.*, p. 218.
36. *ibid.*, p. 200.
37. *ibid.*, p. 188.
38. A. K. Clark, 'The Girl: A rhetoric of desire', *Cultural Studies*, vol. 1, no. 2 (1987), p. 139.
39. Very little has been written about Lotta Crabtree which makes an in-depth assessment to her contributions to the history of American theatre. Irene Comer, in her research – 'Little Nell and the Marchioness: Milestone in the development of the American musical comedy' (Ph.D dissertation, Tufts University, 1979) – mounts a convincing case for Lotta's performance work as an important early source for the American musical. Claudia D. Johnson in her recent work, *American Actress: Perspective on the nineteenth century* (Chicago: Nelson Hall, 1984), devotes a chapter to Lotta's considerable talents as a comedian. No one, to my knowledge, has examined Lotta's relationship to one of the most successful theatre directors of the early twentieth century, David Belasco.

40. C. Rourke, *Troupers of the Gold Coast or the Rise of Lotta Crabtree* (New York: Harcourt, Brace, Javanovich, 1928), p. 81.
41. Cited in Comer, *op. cit.*, p. 7.
42. D. Dempsey, *The Triumphs and Trials of Lotta Crabtree* (New York: William Morrow, 1968), p. 170.
43. Rourke, *Troupers*, *op. cit.*, p. 326.
44. C. Timberlake, *The Bishop of Broadway: The life and work of David Belasco* (New York: Liberty, 1954), p. 89.
45. Comer, '*Little Nell*', *op. cit.*, pp. 19–20.
46. Dempsey, *Triumphs and Trials*, *op. cit.*, p. 225.
47. L. L. Marker, *David Belasco: Naturalism in the American theatre* (Princeton, N.J.: Princeton University Press, 1975), p. 99.
48. Dempsey, *Triumphs and Trials*, *op. cit.*, p. 187.
49. *ibid.*, p. 125.
50. *ibid.*, p. 190.
51. C. D. Johnson, *American Actress*, *op. cit.*, p. 167.
52. Timberlake, *The Bishop of Broadway*, *op. cit.*, p. 284. As Timberlake points out, Belasco was outraged that critics suggested a parallel between his Girl and Bret Harte's Western heroine, Miggles. Miggles, from Harte's short story of the same name, was a feisty, strong-willed 'girl', who also ran the Polka Saloon. Timberlake himself – ignoring other theatrical precedents, such as Lotta – suggests that Belasco's Girl was a composite of the Harte Western heroines.
53. Comer, '*Little Nell*', *op. cit.*, p. 6.

PART II

Women Dressing as men

3

Princess Ĥamlet

JILL EDMONDS

'Innovations and experiments'

When Hazlitt wrote 'It is we who are Hamlet,'[1] it was probably 'we men' he had in mind. Nevertheless, Princess Hamlet had been born two years before Hazlitt, when Mrs Siddons played the part in Birmingham in 1776 and again in the following year in Manchester and Liverpool. In 1781 she played in Bristol and her last recorded Hamlet was in Dublin in 1802. Her friend, Mrs Inchbald, also acted Hamlet 'for her son-in-law's benefit' in 1795, an event recorded by Tate Wilkinson in *The Wandering Patentee*: 'I need not say that Denmark's Prince was not by any means destitute of grace and elegance; not that I approve such innovations and experiments.'[2]

He was more severe about the less well-known Mrs Edmead who 'has been tempted, *for her own amusement*, to perform Hamlet', a motive he found hard to condone: 'How a woman of good sense could be so determinately wrong is to me inconceivable.' He goes on to express a distaste for breeches parts in general, describing Mrs Edmead's enthusiasm for them as 'a failing which has seldom added to female reputation'. His description of her appearance, even allowing for his evident cattiness, suggests that she had a strong rather than conventionally pretty face, 'her features are by no means handsome and her mouth is not one of the least apertures'.[3]

Despite Wilkinson's protests, the 'innovations and experiments' continued. Mrs Glover was one of the most successful of the early-nineteenth-century Hamlets when she played the part at the Lyceum in 1821 to impress Edmund Kean. He congratulated her after the performance with 'Excellent, excellent', to which she replied, 'Away you flatterer! You come in mockery to scorn and scoff at our solemnity',[4] but there is no evidence that his admiration was other than genuine. Her long and full career at the Haymarket was not matched by an altogether happy family life; according to McQueen Pope

> she had been an unselfish and perhaps too dutiful daughter, she was a badly treated wife, an admirable mother to her children (whom her scoundrel of a husband tried to take from her) but no breath of scandal ever touched her.[5]

Her benefit at Drury Lane not long before her death in 1850 was attended by Queen Victoria, a tribute not only to her theatrical successes but also perhaps to her painful but blameless private life.

By the second half of the century the number of female Hamlets was growing. In America in 1851 Charlotte Cushman borrowed Edwin Booth's costume to play the part when she was thirty-five. Ten years later she made a second attempt despite the fact that she had put on weight and found Booth's costume a tight fit on this occasion. In the same year (1861) in England Alice Marriott was playing Hamlet for the first time at the age of thirty-seven at the Marylebone Theatre. When she and her husband, Robert Edgar, took over the management of Sadlers Wells in 1863, she continued to play Hamlet to considerable popular acclaim. Her admirers included a very young Arthur Pinero and a slightly older Chance Newton, theatre critic of *The Referee*, who, looking back on a long theatre-going career, maintained a warm affection for her and remembered that 'this brilliant actress's presentation of the part gradually came out as one of the very best I have ever seen',[6] a judgement which may have been influenced by the rosy glow of nostalgia but is nevertheless instructive in that it makes no distinction between male and female performers.

No longer could female Hamlets be considered innovatory or experimental: in the last decade of the century Millicent Bandmann-Palmer was well on her way to holding the record for over a thousand performances of the role in the provinces while Sarah Bernhardt's visit to England with her controversial *Hamlet* in 1899 fixed their high water mark. After the turn of the century their popularity appears to have been in decline as increasingly naturalistic styles of playing and the influence of 'the new drama' began to alter the focus of the repertoire and of approaches to Shakespeare. Significantly, many of the nineteenth-century actresses who played the role were actor–managers in their own right, able to choose what they wished to play rather than waiting to be cast by male directors.

The twentieth century has tended again to see female Hamlets as experimental. The critics of a 1938 production sound not unlike Tate Wilkinson when they reviewed the sixty-two-year-old Esme Beringer at the Arts Theatre with her younger sister as Gertrude. Harold Hobson, theatre critic of the *Observer* wrote: 'The question "Can a woman play Hamlet?" was raised again at the Arts Theatre by Miss Esme Beringer. She raised it in a practical way by her interesting performance. The answer, however, would still seem to be

"No".[7] Other reviewers responded with varying degrees of hostility; W. A. Darlington noted that 'the part is too long for a woman', while acknowledging that, 'Given the difficulties Miss Beringer did admirably.'[8]

Hamlet's sexual ambiguity

Frances de la Tour played Hamlet in a promenade production at the Half Moon Theatre in 1979 to much warmer reviews. Michael Billington in the *Guardian* wrote of her: 'She is tough, abrasive, virile and impassioned. Indeed it's a good performance compact with every female virtue except femininity.'[9] The virtues he admired in her performance raise the question of how far an actor reveals to an audience the feminine in Hamlet while an actress might demonstrate, as Brecht suggested, that 'a lot of details we usually think of as general human characteristics are typically masculine.'[10]

Sarah Bernhardt was certainly aware of the teasing sexual ambiguity of playing the role of a man considered by her contemporaries to be rather feminine. Interviewed by a correspondent from the *Daily Chronicle*, she was asked: 'Can any man quite grasp the inner nature of Hamlet?', to which she replied, 'Perhaps not. There is much that is feminine in it', and added disarmingly to her (presumably) male interviewers, 'it takes the brains of a man and the intuitive almost psychic power of a woman to give a true rendering of it.'[11]

The thrust of the interviewer's question suggests that the ability to convey the interiority of a character is a particularly feminine one and Bernhardt, perhaps ironically, supports him by polarising feminine intuition and masculine brain power.

Max Beerbohm, writing disparagingly of her Princess Hamlet, allowed, 'No doubt Hamlet in the complexity of his nature had traces of femininity . . . this I take it would be Sarah's excuse for having played the part', but concluded, 'Hamlet is none the less a man because he is not consistently manly, just as Lady Macbeth is none the less a woman for being a trifle unsexed.'[12]

Such an acknowledgement of the sexual ambiguity of the character hardly appears typical of the age. In contrast, Edmund Vining, an American Yale-educated southern Baptist, attempted to solve the problem in *The Mystery of Hamlet* (1881) by claiming that 'he' was a princess born to the Queen while Old Hamlet was away fighting the Norwegian King. The Queen, afraid that her husband might have been killed in battle, dare not acknowledge the daughter who could not succeed to the throne, so disguised the child as a boy, a disguise that Princess Hamlet had to play out to the bitter end.[13] Vining's version (which may owe something to the Danish legend of Princess Hamlet on which the 1920 film with Asta Nielsen was based) throws a new light on Hamlet's relationship with Ophelia, who is seen as a rival for Horatio's love.

Having found a satisfactory answer to the difficulty of admiring a hero who 'lacks the energy, the conscious strength, the readiness for action that adhere in the perfect manly character', the theory also has the advantage of providing Vining with an explanation of Hamlet's less attractive characteristics:

> Woman with less of strength to accomplish her desires by straightforward action, is compelled to bring them to pass by more of shrewdness and subtlety. Where strength fails, finesse succeeds. . . . His feigned madness, his trial of the mimic play, are all strategies that a woman might attempt and that are far more in keeping with a feminine than with a masculine nature.[14]

Moreover, though he does not at any point discuss the play as a performance, Vining does reveal some of the physical attractions of the part for a female player:

> A very plain-looking woman will pass for a very handsome man when suitably attired and the natural brightness and freshness of her complexion, combined with the absence of beard, will give her a boyish appearance making her look far younger than her real age.[15]

Charlotte Cushman was described by contemporaries as 'a plain woman with a protruding chin and a beaky nose, and a big raw-boned figure like a man'.[16] Vining was too young to have seen her performance but his description of the disguised princess sounds very like her.

Bernhardt, though far from plain, was probably working on the same principle when, playing Hamlet for the first time at the age of fifty-four, she announced with breath-taking confidence, 'Instead of making Hamlet a man of thirty-five, I have endeavoured to impersonate a youth of twenty summers whom his friends speak of as "young Hamlet"'.[17] That very sexual ambiguity which discomfited Vining may suggest why conservative critics could accept the solution offered by female Hamlets, while the more sophisticated Max Beerbohm could not. Hamlet's virility would not be in question if the part were played by an Alice Marriott, and the relationships between Hamlet, his Mother and Ophelia could remain romantically undefined while the melancholy beauty of the philosophical, death-seeking Prince came into focus.

The players' own perceptions may, however, have been rather different: Charlotte Cushman was a flamboyant lesbian who enjoyed playing a variety of male roles and cross-dressed off-stage as well as on. A fellow-American, Winetta Montague, married an English actor, Walter Montomery, who shot himself two days after the wedding. She is reputed to have gone on tour after his death playing Hamlet in her dead husband's costume. If the story is true, what a tangled web of motives might exist there.[18] Mrs Bandmann-Palmer had in her youth played Ophelia to the Hamlet of her husband, Daniel Bandmann, a German–American who, though 'a clever actor' and 'a rugged Hamlet', was, according to Chance Newton, a formidable man, 'of the fiercest and most ungovernable temper and at rehearsals this temper would rage so volcanically that he would knock people down, mostly taking care to select the weaker sex for his victims.'[19] Was his wife's Hamlet an act of vengeance against her violent husband? The actresses' responses to the insights they could convey as women playing men can only be guessed at but circumstantial evidence would suggest that they might have brought more complex and ambivalent feelings to the part than their audiences recognised.

Male role models for female Hamlets

The actresses who played Hamlet did not live in a theatrical vacuum and it is inconceivable that they were entirely uninfluenced by some of their contemporary male Hamlets, even leaving aside those who had first played Ophelia to the Hamlets of their husbands. An examination of three significant male Hamlets from mid- to late nineteenth century will attempt to highlight some of the connections between male and female performers.

Samuel Phelps managed Sadlers Wells Theatre for eighteen years (1844–62) during which time he presented almost all of Shakespeare's plays and appeared as Hamlet 171 times. Alice Marriott and her husband, Robert Edgar, took over the management from Phelps at a time when Miss Marriott had already played Hamlet at the Marylebone Theatre in 1861. In the year of the tercentenary, 1864, she was to play Hamlet at Sadlers Wells while Phelps was nursing considerable grievance at not being chosen to play Hamlet for the Shakespeare Tercentenary at Stratford. His Hamlet was by then considered slow and old-fashioned; nevertheless, the photograph of Alice Marriott shows her adopting a very similar style of dress: her tunic is in cut, length and decoration very like his. She also wears the Danish Order of the Elephant on a wide blue ribbon. (The badge belonging to Phelps is still in existence in the Museum of London Costume Collection.[20]) Her leading man during the tercentenary season was the Irish actor Gustavus Brooke, who played Shylock to her Portia on Shakespeare's birthday and had in 1848 had a promising London season in which he had played a number of leading Shakespeare roles, including Hamlet in a costume much like the one Phelps wore and had displayed the Order of the Elephant and a large Danish Silver star on his sable-edged cape. Dickens's description of Mr Wopsle's inept performance of Hamlet suggests that when *Great Expectations* was published in 1861 such decoration as the Order of the Elephant which Edmund Kean had worn was beginning to look absurdly old-fashioned. Mr Wopsle is dressed in conventional black, 'with the addition of a large Danish sun or star hanging round his neck by a blue ribbon that had given him the appearance of being insured in some extraordinary Fire Office'.[21]

According to Chance Newton, Phelps wore his hair in the then fashionable 'Newgate Knocker' style in which a lock of hair was twisted back from the

Figure 3.1 Alice Marriott as Hamlet

temple to the ear. Whether Miss Marriott followed this style is difficult to determine from the photograph: one can only say that Alice Marriott's appearance, allowing for her somewhat plump figure, was close to Phelps and probably seemed (at best) traditional, and (at worst) old-fashioned, by 1864.

Charles Fechter's Hamlet at the Princess's Theatre in 1861 aroused considerable excitement: he was praised for his 'naturalness' and for 'his admirable conception of character'. He was the only man who had until then played the part in a fair wig, 'a cross between golden and ginger', a Scandinavian colour, according to the actor.[22]

His interpretation, as described by Chance Newton, might suggest that some of the 'feminine' qualities came through:

> Coming as he did in the middle of a rather barn-storming period in the Hamlet succession, Fechter created a profound impression, in the first place by the wonderful meditative, almost unspoken, method in which he gave the great soliloquies. For example, in the 'To be or not to be', which I often heard in those days shouted by tragedians to the gallery, Fechter dreamily 'thought' it out before you, toying the while with his little jewelled dagger.[23]

Julia Seaman, who played Hamlet first in 1865, when she was twenty-eight, was said to have been influenced by the new style of Fechter's Hamlet. W. J. Lawrence, writing in the *Illustrated London News* in 1899 asserted that,

> Among women Miss Julia Seaman takes rank as the first colloquial Hamlet. Thirty years ago she did valuable work as a pioneer of the new school in the provinces. In her efforts to popularise the Fechterian conception of the Prince, she bore her flaxen wig to many a victory.[24]

Despite the changed hairstyle Julia Seaman's appearance still looks as though it belongs to the Phelps tradition rather than the Fechterian. Her career had certain parallels with Alice Marriott's: both had suffered seasons with the alcoholic Gustavus Brooke; both played Hamlet for their American débuts (female Hamlets seem to have been particularly popular there) and years later in 1888, both appeared in Irving's revival of *Macbeth* at the Lyceum, when Alice Marriott played the first and Julia Seaman the third witch. The second witch, Miss Desborough, had also been a female Hamlet.

Later, Clement Scott was to link Fechter's interpretation with Bernhardt's. He describes them as both exhibiting the French temperament and claims that their charm consisted of 'that dominant note of comedy, that rare vein of humour, that eccentric capriciousness which are in the very veins of Hamlet'. By contrast, he found the English Hamlets, with the exception of Irving and Forbes-Robertson, inclined to 'force the tragedy and ignore the comedy'.[25]

Towards the end of the century, the influence of the aesthetic movement was to become apparent in the appearance of both male and female Hamlets. As early as 1878 Irving's Hamlet at the Lyceum illustrates some of the changes

Figure 3.2 Julia Seaman as Ḥamlet

that were taking place. He looked very unlike Fechter: his hair, according to
Ellen Terry, was 'blue-black like the plumage of a crow' and his extremely
short tunic had the effect of lengthening the legs 'to make Henry look extraordinarily tall and thin'.[26] (He had by this time, and at her suggestion, given
up padding his calves.) Ellen Terry claims that the whole effect 'probably cost
him around £2'.[27]

By the 1890s the female Hamlets are dressed in similarly pre-Raphaelite style: Mrs Bandmann-Palmer, who was apparently squat, followed Irving in wearing a very short tunic which may have had the effect of making her look taller but she retained the dark-plumed hat which Irving had much earlier

Figure 3.3 Millicent Bandmann-Palmer as Hamlet

Figure 3.4 Sarah Bernhardt as Hamlet

abandoned at Ellen Terry's suggestion. Bernhardt was consciously creating an image of the young Raphael and all the photographic poses make much of her elegant legs. Undoubtedly, the short tunics did focus attention on the legs and may have provided attraction for some audiences but Mrs Bandmann-Palmer, renowned for the seriousness of her tragic performances, was forty-seven when she started playing Hamlet and it seems unlikely that either she or her audiences saw the role primarily as an opportunity for displaying her legs.

The popularity of *Hamlet*

F. A. Marshall gives a clear indication of the popularity of *Hamlet* in the later-nineteenth-century theatre in his introduction to Irving's edition of Shakespeare (1889) when he writes: 'Managers in town and country will tell you that you only have to put Hamlet up, even with a bad cast, and you may rely on a fairly good house.'[28] While it would be unfair to suggest that the success of so many female Hamlets in the provinces and suburbs depended solely on the popularity of the play, however badly performed, it is true that it frequently took its place in a repertoire that consisted in the main of romantic melodrama. Mrs Bandmann-Palmer, for instance, in the 1890s and early 1900s played Hamlet alongside a number of 'heavy' melodramatic roles which included Leah (in *Leah the Forsaken*), Jane Shore and Lady Isabel in *East Lynne*.

In London Clare Howard, the leading lady at the Pavilion Theatre, played a highly melodramatic version of the play to considerable acclaim and Sophie Miles ('a brilliant and versatile actress and a great favourite'[29]) played Hamlet at the Britannia, Hoxton, while she was leading lady there.

The Portable Theatre had its female Hamlets too. Ellen Terry, on holiday in Droitwich in August 1900 and invited to choose what she would see at Jennings Portable Theatre, decided on Julia Jennings, the wife of the proprietor, as Hamlet. After the performance Mrs Jennings received a signed photograph of Ellen Terry and a letter praising her 'excellent representation of the part'.[30] A century after Tate Wilkinson's strictures female Hamlets had become an accepted part of a popular theatrical culture.

Text and performance

If 'the purpose of playing' is, as Hamlet suggests 'to hold the mirror up to nature', and 'to show the very age and body of the time its forms and pressure' (Act III, scene ii) it follows that productions at different periods will choose to emphasise particular aspects of a play that is remarkably responsive to the concerns, beliefs and characteristics of an age. One of the ways in which such changes are reflected is in the cutting of an unusually long play.

The nineteenth century, with its emphasis on the individual and drawing on the work of the romantic poets, comes up with a poetic dreamer who, towards the end of the century, is transformed into a spiritual pre-Raphaelite. The rest of the play was seen as largely background to the central character and for this reason Fortinbras, Cornelius, Voltemund and Reynaldo disappeared entirely while heavy cuts in Act IV allowed Hamelt to return from his sea voyage and resume centre stage as fast as possible. Ophelia's mad scene remained but was cleansed of all sexual innuendo. Forbes-Robertson was the first to re-instate Fortinbras in 1897 but it is perhaps unsurprising that in an England confident of its position in the world, the threat of invasion posed to Denmark by Norway might not seem of paramount interest, and the example of Fortinbras, the warrior prince, had limited romantic appeal. Bernhardt, however, did include Fortinbras in her heavily cut French version by Eugene Morand and Marcel Schwob with incidental music by Gabriel Pierre. It was distinguished from English versions by being entirely in prose and divided into twelve scenes, each preceded by a spectacular tableau.

Clement Scott gives a vivid description of some of the moments in Bernhardt's *Hamlet* that he particularly admired:

> The crossing of herself before she follows the Ghost, the speaking of the speech to the players on the miniature stage, making Hamlet for the moment an actor addressing his audience; the feeling of his father's picture on the walls when the ghost has gone and materialism has come again; the effect of the poison in Hamlet's veins when his hand is scratched in the duel with Laertes; the kissing of his dead mother's hair.[31]

All these details he describes as 'never before imagined', though they probably influenced later performers. Her Hamlet was far from effete; indeed the *Birmingham Gazette*'s reviewer complains that 'she makes him too short a time the philosopher and too much the man of wrath and vengeance'.[32] Translated into physical terms, she was much praised for her fencing in Act V and was described by one critic as 'a master of the art',[33] suggesting that she was being praised for being as skilful as a male performer. Unlike Viola in *Twelfth Night* (Act III, scene iv), afraid to fight Sir Andrew because 'A little thing would make me tell them how much I lack of a man', the actresses who played Hamlet need to display their fencing skills and to do so at the climactic end of a long performance. No female role in Shakespeare could provide such opportunity for physical action, and it is noticeable that other breeches roles popular with female Hamlets also offered the chance to demonstrate the ability to fence and fight. The swashbuckling role of William in Jerrold's *Black-Eyed Susan*, for instance, was played by both Charlotte Cushman and Julia Seaman and required the actress to fight heroically and to dance a hornpipe.

Clarence Derwent makes no mention of Mrs Bandmann-Palmer's fencing in his somewhat satirical portrait of her in his autobiography, *The Derwent*

Story. By the time he played Horatio to her Hamlet in 1902 the actress was fifty-seven, weighed fourteen stone and suffered from rheumatism, so it seems likely that the duel was not one of the play's highlights. Instead, Derwent recalls one of her innovations at the end of the play:

> as Hamlet was dying he, or rather she, attempted to reach the throne which was set center of stage on a rostrum four steps up from stage level. . . . I had been promoted to the part of Horatio and it was my duty to support the dying prince in this effort. On the night in question, however, one of us must have missed a step and to our intense consternation and the audience's delighted approbation we found ourselves catapulted down the four steps landing full length at the bottom, myself under the full weight of Mrs Bandmann's two hundred pounds on top of me. From such a position it would only have added insult to injury to attempt the 'Now cracks a noble heart' speech, so the curtain descended, for the only time in history of the play to the accompaniment of unrestrained gales of laughter. [34]

This unfortunate performance was near the end of Mrs Bandmann-Palmer's career, and Derwent admits that, despite his relishing the tale, 'There was never any doubt of her knowledge and ability and many of her individual performances must have been very fine in earlier days.'[35]

W. J. Lawrence in an article in the *Illustrated London News* in June 1899 celebrating Bernhardt's arrival in England, surveyed the variety of female Hamlets he had seen and picked out Millicent Bandmann-Palmer's interpretation as a thoughtful and interesting one: 'making little or no pretence at aping masculinity, she offers her Hamlet rather as a psychological study than a vivid impersonation.'[36] His assessment implies that her Hamlet was not naturalistic in style and in that respect, at least, she might be compared to Bernhardt, who, despite frequently using the term 'impersonation', as did many other performers and critics of the period, did not necessarily mean by it naturalistic characterisation. John Stokes suggests that her approach was 'symbolist rather than Naturalistic, . . . elevated by a transparent purity of feeling between player and role that turned physical performance into eternal manifestation and left the audience transfixed by yearning.'[37] Reviews of Fechter's Hamlet in 1861 had drawn attention to the contrast between his '"impersonation" of the character and English actors' who aim but little at the strict impersonation of Shakespeare's heroes', and such criticism may well apply equally to the actresses who played Hamlet. Despite earlier recognition that Julia Seaman had been influenced by Fechter's less declamatory style, in her obituary in 1908 the *Telegraph* spoke of her Hamlet as 'elocutionary and a trifle heavy. But the actress had great faith in it.'[38] What appeared 'natural' in the 1860s probably appeared less so in retrospect.

Clare Howard's performance was a highly melodramatic one at the Britannia in Hoxton. She was described by Chance Newton as 'a pizzicato Hamlet' 'much addicted to music cues'. She spoke 'through sundry bars of pizzicato agitato and other such strains of music. At this or that situation there was heard a melodramatic chord or crash! Nevertheless he found it a striking and artificially dramatic performance', though he may have been influenced by the fact that she included, at his suggestion, 'those extremely melodramatic passages which relate to the hero's very thrillful arrangements to have the spies Rosencrantz and Guildernstern murdered on their arrival in England' (Act IV, scene vi).[39]

In the same year as Bernhardt and Howard were playing Hamlet, an American actress, Janette Steer, who had come to England in the 1880s, was taking a radically new approach to the role by chopping her hair to do so. Of her performance in Birmingham, W. J. Lawrence said she 'assumed the character' and notes that she was 'enthusiastically received'.[40] She had already been noticed by William Archer in 1897 when, playing in Henry Arthur Jones *The Liars* at the Criterion theatre, Archer praised her 'very high order of dramatic intelligence', despite 'harshness of voice'.[41]

These actresses needed considerable vocal power and projection to fill theatres like Sadlers Wells, the Pavilion in Whitechapel and the 3,000 seater Britannia at Hoxton. Clare Howard at the Pavilion and Sophie Miles at the Britannia as leading ladies at those theatres must have known the acoustics well and Alice Marriott at Sadlers Wells was described as having 'a wonderful voice in this character'.[42] While the soliloquies in the play might have been considered appropriately 'feminine' since they convey Hamlet's interior life of feeling, they also challenge the actress to explore a fuller and darker vocal range than any of the female roles could offer. A number of the actresses having played Ophelia as young women, moved on to Hamlet in middle age and might be seen as discovering a richer, bigger and more interesting role for a 'heavy' woman than could be provided by a Gertrude or Emilia.

New Women?

To what extent can the female Hamlets be seen as New Women? Their appearance in costumes modelled on contemporary male Hamlets, their 'safe' repertoire of old-fashioned melodrama, pantomime, 'standard plays' and Shakespeare and their popularity at such theatres as the Britannia and the Pavilion might suggest that they were not seen as breaking new ground. Set against this, however, are the independence and the power of women who earned their own livings. Alice Marriott, Millicent Bandmann-Palmer and Sarah Bernhardt were all actor–managers choosing their own roles. As Frances de la Tour said when interviewed by Ian Cotton for the *Sunday Telegraph*: 'In those days the thought behind the casting was simple: a good woman actress would play Hamlet because it was the best part in the repertoire.'[43]

Alice Marriott headed her company at Sadlers Wells through the 1860s, playing Macbeth as well as Hamlet in 1864. When she left for an American tour in 1869 her admirers, led by a Colonel Addison, presented her with a marble bust of herself.[44] Julia Seaman, her younger contemporary, also appears to have been a forceful, spirited woman. Her obituary speaks of the 'fire and energy which marked her histrionic career' and describes how, when her Hamlet was 'vigorously criticised by some of the newspapers – she retorted on them with considerable fervour'.[45] Nevertheless, in her last years of poverty and ill-health she showed a touching regard for respectability as she wrote to one of her daughters in 1908 putting her affairs in order: 'I hope you will think better of me when I am gone; there's no secrets, no startling revelations, no scandal; everything true and untrue has been well sifted out by me in my lifetime so it saves a lot of trouble.[46]

The adjectives most frequently used to describe Mrs Bandmann-Palmer by those who worked for her are 'massive', 'formidable' and 'redoubtable', though it would be fair to add that they were applied when she was middle-aged and elderly. As a young woman, she had toured in Germany with her husband, Daniel Bandmann, and spoke fluent German. A report in the *Era Almanack* runs: 'In 1887 I gave a performance at Berlin before 80 royal personages and was personally complimented by the Emperor Frederick.'[49]

From 1892 Mrs Bandmann-Palmer was managing her own touring company. Though Daniel Bandmann lived until 1905 he appears to have taken no part in it and the hiring and firing was carried out entirely by his wife. Whitford Kane, a young actor changing trains at Normanton Junction and looking for another engagement, met friends who took him to the Bandmann-Palmer train 'where the redoubtable Mrs Bandmann-Palmer interviewed and hired him'.[48] Later, the same actor was to recall the 'tragic power' of her Hamlet, 'though because of rheumatism she could have difficulty in rising from her knees'.[49] Bamber Gascoigne gives an amusing account of his grandmother as a young, aspiring actress being interviewed by Mrs Bandmann-Palmer, 'massive in maroon silk', and being surprised that the company appeared to be run by one person despite the two names.[50]

Some of the actors who later became Bensonians had been young members of her company: one, her daughter-in-law, Gertrude Evans, found the Benson Company 'more relaxed', while another, Clarence Derwent, had acted with 'the massive Mrs Bandmann-Palmer, enough to sober anyone'. Baliol Holloway in old age still remembered

> the strange woman who paid out tiny salaries with a grudging hand, to the accompaniment of scathing criticism. Linen in need of laundering would come under her vocal scrutiny, but what young actor on thirty shillings a week could run to a clean shirt for every performance?[51]

The picture that emerges is of a martinet keeping a stern grip on a young company and a tight rein on the finances. Off-stage 'the Lancashire tragedienne'[52] (she was born in Lancaster in 1845) usually wore tweeds and hob-nailed boots,[53] doubtless 'rational dress' for the northern climate.

While her repertoire of 'High Class Comedies, Tragedies and Standard

Plays'[54] in no way suggests that she was a 'New Woman', it is hard to reconcile the impression of a strong-minded authoritarian with Vining's view of the feminine Hamlet 'whose gentleness and dependence on others are his inherent qualities',[55] and it seems doubtful that this could have been the thrust of Mrs Bandmann-Palmer's interpretation. Though it is tempting to see the actress who played Ophelia to her husband's Hamlet moving on to take centre stage and play his part as 'the New Woman' takes over, the evidence does not support such a neat conclusion. Nevertheless, if Millicent Bandmann-Palmer was not strictly 'a New Woman', neither was she in any sense of the word the archetypal 'little woman'.

Because of her fame both on and off the stage Sarah Bernhardt's position was very different. She had never known what it was to be confined in the doll's house. As Christopher Kent suggests:

> to Victorians the profession of actress . . . offered striking opportunities for independence, fame and fortune . . . in the notion that there was an area of special dispensation from the normal categories, moral and social, that defined woman's place.[56]

Bernhardt was not at all bourgeois, nevertheless; as Stokes observes, though she 'could become rich, famous and powerful . . . she could only achieve that success by allowing herself to be bought by her public'.[57] Bernhardt may have been a force of nature rather than an early feminist but by 1911 she was speaking out in favour of women's suffrage: 'That women should possess the vote is merest justice.'[58]

A more clearly defined link between female Hamlets and the New Woman is discernable in the career of Janette Steer, who was involved in the Actresses' Franchise League from its inception: in July 1908 she gave an at home for actresses, to be addressed by Christabel Pankhurst.[59] Among those who attended were Mary Moore, Lilian Braithwaite and Violet Fairbrother. Not only was Janette Steer a committee member of the League but in 1912 received a two/three-week sentence in Holloway, probably for window-breaking.[60]

By this time, however, the heydey of the female Hamlets was over and few of the earlier actresses who played the role can confidently be identified as feminists, though they might be seen as making an appropriate reply to a play that started its stage life with a male Ophelia and Gertrude. Perhaps Shakespeare's audience responded to them in the same way as Goethe did to an all-male version of Goldoni's *Locandiera* in Rome in 1788, where he discovered 'a double charm from the fact that these people are not women but play the part of women'. Moreover, he found that the rest of the audience shared his delight in the young man who played the role of Mirandolina, the mistress of the inn:

> rejoicing that he knew so well the dangerous qualities of the loved sex, and that by a happy imitation of their behaviour he revenged us, as it were, on the fair ones for all the ills of that kind we had suffered at their hands.[61]

The man–woman of Goldoni's comedy and Goethe's chauvinistic enjoyment of the female impersonation might be translated in reverse into 'the loved sex' playing the part of Hamlet and discovering for themselves and their audiences that 'double charm' compounded of celebration, revelation, recognition and revenge, the thrilling mixture that was central to the nature of the Victorian 'Princess Hamlet'.

Notes

1. W. Hazlitt, *Characters of Shakespeare's Plays* (London: Dent, 1906).
2. T. Wilkinson, *The Wandering Patentee*, 4 vols (1795: facsimile edn, London: Scolar Press, 1973), vol. III, pp. 14–15.
3. *ibid.* Mrs Edmead played the part in 1792.
4. Quoted by R. Mandler and J. Mitchenson in *Hamlet through the Ages* (London: Rockliffe, 1955), p. 123.
5. W. McQueen Pope, *Haymarket: Theatre of perfection* (London: W. H. Allen, 1948), p. 226.
6. C. Newton, 'My four score Hamlets', in Newton, *Cues and Curtain Calls* (London: Bodley Head, 1927), p. 187.
7. H. Hobson review in the *Observer*, 23 January 1938.
8. W. A. Darlington review in the *Daily Telegraph*, 23 January 1938.
9. M. Billington review in the *Guardian*, 20 October 1979.
10. B. Brecht, *The Messingkauf Dialogues*, trans. John Willett (London: Methuen, 1965), p. 59.
11. Anon., interview with Sarah Bernhardt in the *Daily Chronicle*, 17 June 1899.
12. M. Beerbohm, 'Hamlet, Princess of Denmark', 19 June 1899, reprinted in Sir Max Beerbohm, *Around Theatres* (London: Rupert Hart-Davis, 1953), pp. 34–6.
13. E. P. Vining, *The Mystery of Hamlet* (Philadelphia: Lippincott & Co, 1881), p. 61.
14. *ibid.*
15. *ibid.*, p. 80.
16. Quoted by McQueen Pope in *Haymarket, op. cit.*, p. 286.
17. Anon., interview with Sarah Bernhardt in the *Daily Chronicle*, 17 June 1899.
18. Chance Newton tells this story in 'My four score Hamlets', *op. cit.*, p. 217, but in *Victorian Theatre* (London: A. & C. Black, 1989), pp. 119–20, Russell Jackson includes a report from *Era* (10 November 1872) of the Sale of Walter Montogmery's theatrical wardrobe: the first lot was a costume for Hamlet which consisted of 'shirt, tabard, belt, pocket, striped drapery, shoes, hat and feather and black disguise cloak'. Whether this is the costume his widow wore and later sold or whether the story is apochryphal is not clear.
19. Newton, 'My four score Hamlets', *op. cit.*, p. 225.
20. M. R. Holmes, *Stage Costumes and Accessories* (Hamlet 1850–60, no. 10), Museum of London Catalogue (London: HMSO, 1968).
21. C. Dickens, *Great Expectations* (London: Dent, 1963), ch. XXXI.
22. Anon., review in *Illustrated London News*, 4 May 1861.
23. Newton, 'My four score Hamlets', *op. cit.*, p. 191.
24. W. J. Lawrence, *Illustrated London News*, 17 June 1899.
25. C. Scott, *Some Notable Hamlets* (London 1905: repr. New York and London: Benjamin Blom, 1969), p. 18.
26. E. Terry, *The Story of My Life* (London: Hutchinson, 1907), p. 127.

27. *ibid.*, p. 129.

28. F. A. Marshall, Introduction to *The Henry Irving Shakespeare*, 1888–90: *Hamlet* (London: Blackie, 1889).

29. Newton, 'My four score Hamlets', *op. cit.*, p. 189.

30. Family papers of Mona Fortescue, a descendant of the Jennings and Seaman families.

31. Scott, *Some Notable Hamlets*, *op. cit.*, p. 18.

32. Anon., review in *Birmingham Gazette*, 24 June 1899.

33. Anon., review in *Birmingham Weekly Post*, 24 June 1899.

34. C. Derwent, *The Derwent Story* (New York: Henry Schuman, 1953), p. 21.

35. *ibid.*, p. 20.

36. Lawrence, *Illustrated London News, ibid.*

37. J. Stokes, M. R. Booth and S. Bassnett, *Bernhardt, Terry, Duse: The actress in her time* (Cambridge: Cambridge University Press, 1988), p. 30.

38. Anon., obituary of Julia Seaman, 'A noted female Hamlet', in the *Daily Telegraph*, 1909 (undated).

39. Newton, 'My four score Hamlets', *op. cit.*, pp. 215–16.

40. Lawrence, *The Illustrated London News, ibid.*

41. W. Archer, *Theatrical World*, no. 161 (London: Walter Scott Ltd., 1897).

42. Newton, 'My four score Hamlets', *op. cit.*

43. Frances de la Tour in an interview with Ian Cotton in the *Sunday Telegraph*, 15 June 1979.

44. *Era Almanack*, 1870 (19 February 1869).

45. Anon., obituary of Julia Seaman, *Daily Telegraph*, 1909.

46. Letter from Julia Seaman, now in the possession of Mona Fortescue.

47. *Era Almanack*, 1888.

48. Whitford Kane, *Are We All Met?* (London: E. Mathews & Merrot, 1931), ch. v.

49. *ibid.*

50. B. Gascoigne, *The Heyday* (London: Cape, 1973), partially repr. in *The Times Saturday Review*, 29 September 1973.

51. Quoted in N. Nicholson, *Chameleon's Dish* (London: Paul Eleck, 1973), p. 146.

52. J. C. Trewin, 'A few Hamlettes', the *Birmingham Post*, 20 August 1965.

53. *ibid.*

54. Advertisement for Bradford Theatre Royal, 24 April 1908; illustration to *The Times Saturday Review*, article referred to in note 49.

55. Vining, *The Mystery of Hamlet*, *op. cit.*, p. 61.

56. C. Kent, 'Image and reality: The actress and society', in M. Vicinus (ed.), *A Widening Sphere: Changing roles of Victorian women* (London: Methuen, 1977), p. 94.

57. Stokes, Booth and Bassnett, *Bernhardt, Terry, Duse, op. cit.*, p. 5.

58. S. Bernhardt, 'Votes for women', 13 October 1911, quoted by J. Holledge, *Innocent Flowers: Women in the Edwardian theatre* (London: Virago, 1987), p. 47.

59. M. Sanderson, *From Irving to Olivier* (London: Athlone Press, 1984), p. 110.

60. *ibid.*

61. J. W. Goethe, 'Women's parts played by men in the Roman theatre', in *Goethe's Travels in Italy*, trans. Charles Nisbeth (London: George Bell, 1883), pp. 569–70, partially repr. in A. M. Nayler (ed.), *A Source Book in Theatrical History* (New York: Dover, 1952), pp. 433–4.

4 Irrational Dress

J. S. BRATTON

In the *Era* music-hall columns on 18 May 1895 the review of the bill at the Palace in London included this paragraph:

> Emmaline Ethardo gives a graceful and pleasing melange of juggling and contortion. She first appears in male attire, and does some smart tossing about of oranges and other articles. By a quick change, the 'lounge suit' is removed; and Miss Ethardo's shapely figure stands revealed in a very pretty costume composed of tights and 'shape', both of delicate shell pink. Thus daintily clad she bends herself, and dislocates her joints, with suppleness and skill, revolving on a pedestal and doing rapid flip-flaps on a table covered with red velvet. Miss Ethardo is a pretty young lady, and her beauty is as important a factor of her success as her skill and adroitness.

The bizarre complexity of the practices of dress and display on the late-Victorian music-hall stage should never be underestimated.

In the 1980s there was a remarkable outburst of scholarly, primarily feminist, interest in cross-dressing by women. One focus of this scrutiny has been the assumption of male dress by some famous female radicals and activists in the early part of the twentieth century, and there has consequently been an attempt to read the Victorian and Edwardian phenomenon of male impersonation on the stage in the light of this contemporary radicalism. The desire to do so is perhaps part of modern theatrical and critical concern about how to intervene in the cultural reproduction of sexual difference without always being already entangled in it – a particularly difficult trick for an actress, akin to doing flipflaps with dislocated limbs on a red velvet tablecloth. In pursuit of such suppleness and skill both practitioners and commentators

have attempted to read cross-dressing as a sign that can be used to destabilise
and disrupt the subjective sense of the relation between sexuality and ideology.
There were experiments in reviving male impersonation by feminist theatre
groups in the early 1980s, and theatre historians have attempted to explore
the possibility that women on the halls were aware of the subversive potential
of their assumption of trousers. It seems to be felt that there must be a political
dimension to the phenomenon of the male impersonators, if only because it
cannot be a coincidence that the high-water mark of male impersonation on
the halls coincided with the period of suffrage agitation.[1] Such an assumption
makes good sense as a starting point for historical analysis – but only until one
tries to apply it to the likes of Emmaline Ethardo.

It is very difficult to find an analytical approach that can deal with such performances; all the arguments so far have simplified the discussion by attending
only to the interpretation of outstanding or exceptional cross-dressers in the
past, whether on or off the stage. The most recent interventions have appeared
in the field of lesbian history, where attempts are being made to find fore-
mothers within a newly self-conscious identity politics, in which, at the
moment, the issue of dress is under hot debate: *Feminist Review* carried
articles on the politics of lesbian dress style in consecutive issues in Spring
and Summer 1990, and the second issue followed up with lengthy description
and analysis of the wardrobe of Radclyffe Hall in the 1920s and 1930s.[2] The
starting point for this approach to the appropriations of male style for female
self-presentation in the past is probably Susan Gubar's long article on cross-
dressing by female modernists, published in 1981, where she demonstrates
that 'cross-dressing becomes a way of ad-dressing and re-dressing the inequalities of culturally-defined categories of masculinity and femininity'; she
can say without qualification 'by the turn of the century . . . many identified
male clothing with . . . a costume of freedom.'[3] She is concerned here with a
self-consciously homosexual community of artists; it is difficult to find the
same meanings for that freedom in less politically aware and radical groups,
and Julie Wheelwright, attempting to carry the reclamation further by examining the women who, over the centuries, have dressed as men in order to become
soldiers and sailors, finds that for them

> adoption of masculinity was successful but ultimately limited; entering the
> military meant conforming to a masculine, hierarchical world. The combatants
> did not claim their equality as newly-appropriate for women. Rather they
> divorced themselves from assocation with other women, often mocking and
> denigrating them to ensure their own status amongst their male comrades.[4]

There is, it seems, no subversion here, only the eager appropriation of an
extreme stereotype of masculinity; lesbian historians find a similar absence of
any critical stance or intent in certain recent styles.[5]

It is equally difficult to establish subversive or self-assertive intention in
the gender play of the popular stage at the turn of this century. Elaine Aston

has suggested that the leading male impersonator, Vesta Tilley, was a dissenter, promoting an image of the 'unwomanly woman' which presented a significant challenge to the 'womanly' stereotype.[6] She points to Tilley's slender, potentially androgynous figure, very unlike the majority of successful female music-hall performers, and to her combination of flawlessly realistic male attire with a soprano voice, to argue that the game she played with gender signs was an attack upon them, and consequently liberating for her audience. While this may be true, it does not deal with the fact that off stage, and in significant ways on stage too, Tilley undercut any challenge she made by a parade of essential womanliness; she was most definitely not a dissenter in her public and private life off stage, acting as 'The Lady Bountiful of the Music Halls' whose husband became a Tory MP. Perhaps her stage act could be seen as subversive in its reception, or even in its secret or subconscious intent; but to interpret it in this way we must posit audiences at the time who read against the grain, or at least differently from the contemporary commentators. Aston attempts to explore this possibility by the most directly effective method, addressing Tilley's material and her reception; but it is extremely difficult to be conclusive in retrospective analysis of performance. Sara Maitland, examining the same act, but concerned to use Tilley as an minatory example in the current dress debate, is outspokenly condemnatory:

> the act of male-impersonation (whatever its radical intention or potential) is an act of collusion, of reaction. It is also an act of self-denial, of self-destruction . . . male impersonation – within the theatrical conventions available – does not seek to confuse; finally, it does not require deception. It *pretends* to be deceptive, and is thus, so to speak, doubly deceptive.[7]

The weakness of Maitland's argument is that it is polemical rather than historical, not based on the study of the operation of theatre in general and the halls in particular; but transposed to a more sophisticated reading of performance, and the perspective of cultural materialism, the charge of collusion, is central to how we may conceptualise the issues of gender and power that are raised.

It is possible to find individual cases amongst the male impersonators where the intention to challenge and subvert gender categories seems to be as overt and conscious in the popular performers as it was in the modernist women. Laurence Senelick has unearthed several examples to substantiate his contention that male impersonation was 'directly tied to opportunities for women in the New World . . . [and] an expression of Lesbian wish-fulfillment as well.'[8] His chief instance is an obscure British serio-comic called Annie Hindle who was one of the 1860s' breed of 'King of the Boys' impersonators, who eventually settled in America and made herself some minor notoriety by marrying her (female) dresser in 1886. Here perhaps is a lesbian foremother who can be confidently claimed, and who demonstrates at least a connection between male impersonation and the popular stage as a place for the expression of deviant sexuality. The connection with American women's liberation is somewhat tenuous, however, since Hindle was British, and is not recorded as having anything to do with feminist or proto-feminist circles.

Figure 4.1 Miss Pop Carson

Figure 4.2 Carlotta Mossetti

There also exist old pin-up picture postcards of a number of women presenting themselves in the Hindle style – heavily butch, often uniformed,
adopting postures of masculine casualness or, in some cases, grotesque
extremes of physical imbalance, frozen moments of inelegant dance – which
suggest the existence of a group of British performers with some sort of lesbian
appeal. Nothing more is known of these minor figures, beyond the evidence of
the pictures that they cultivated such a following,[9] but it seems that the
famous performers generated the same response, whether deliberately or not:

Ella Shields and Hetty King, the longest-surviving well-known male impersonators in Britain, are reported by Don Ross and Daniel Farson to have been repeatedly wooed and propositioned by admiring women. But so, of course, was Marie Lloyd – and George Eliot.[10]

It would appear that deviant sexuality found some expression on the popular stage; but that is not enough to account for the appeal of male impersonation during the twenty years or so of its heyday on the halls; nor does it follow that lesbian popular performers, any more than the military cross-dressers described by Wheelwright, can be automatically recruited to an explicitly feminist history. It is difficult even to situate them within the history of the impersonation, given their obscurity, and the strong denial of such appeal by more famous performers. The pin-up photographs, which almost certainly date from the turn of the twentieth century, undercut Senelick's developmental view of male impersonation, by which 'raucous depictions of loose-living dudes' in the 1860s and 1870s were transformed into Tilley's neat performance as part of the 'willed refinement of the stage in the 1890s'.[11] More importantly, 'willed refinement' seems less than adequate as a generalisation about the 1890s music hall at large, and cross-dressing practices in particular, when we glance at Emmaline Ethardo dislocated on her pedestal in the shell-pink shape; Vesta Tilley was exceptional, and only represented the ultimate example of one strand of male impersonation.

The argument *ad feminam* is not an adequate account of the character of cross-dressed performance in general. What is needed is an analysis of the conventional practice as such, of the assumption of the outward signs of the masculine by women stage performers, by means of various permutations and transformations of male dress, partially or completely covering the signs offered by their female bodies, and interacting with them. Such an analysis needs to accommodate all the shades of political consciousness that might – or might not – be expressed by means of the enactment, reinforcement or subversion *of that convention*. It should begin with a re-vision of the long historical perspective within which the convention developed, and in relation to which the music-hall practice of the 1890s should be seen.

The history of female cross-dressing is normally begun with a discussion of 'the breeches role' as undertaken by actresses from Nell Gwynne and Moll Davis during the Restoration to Mme Vestris in the 1830s, and then followed up by an attempt to construct a rationale for the Victorian phenomenon of the female principal boy in pantomime; all approached in terms, usually, of male sexuality and desire, the male gaze. The argument is that women wore trousers (or, rather, tights and tight-fitting breeches) on stage to display themselves for the delectation of the male audience, to add the frisson of role reversals, flagellatory fantasies and other games to their sexual promise, and sometimes thereby also to defuse fears of the possibility of a real assumption of power by women, by charging it with sexuality and so returning it to its proper sphere. In this account the performers never actually impersonate men, but simply adopt a particularly sexually charged costume, in order to titillate them.[12] But by confining itself to the area of popular dance and song, extravaganza and pantomime, and at the furthest certain comedies in which cross-casting was for some particular reason expected, such an account gives a false sense of the parameters of such performance on the nineteenth-century stage. The extravaganza and pantomime performances need to be seen in a wider context of theatrical sensibilities and conventions.

On the legitimate stage, at the turn of the nineteenth century, it was the rule, rather than the exception, for boys to be played by women. Boy and young-man roles in straight plays – from deaf and dumb foundlings to the boy king of Sicily and William Tell's brave son – were allotted to young women as a matter of course; the admiration of youthful beauty, the culture of idealised androgyny (found in attitudes to the stage from Elizabethan times),[13] came to be perceived as properly directed towards the 'true sex' female, whatever the role. The androgyny of Priscilla Horton's appearance extended her range from starring in Vestris's extravaganzas to being the first performer of the role of the Fool in *King Lear* since the seventeenth century. By the 1840s feeling against the bodily display of the male had destroyed all appreciation for male ballet dancers, and created the sensuous and explicit admiration of the androgynous, as expressed by Theophile Gautier in his admiration of cross-playing ballerinas like Fanny Elssler.[14] Not merely in the dance, but in the general representation of beauty, activity and grace, girls were the representatives of youth. Boys of all sorts, roistering young blades like Midshipman Easy and the criminal hero Jack Sheppard as well as pathetic infants, were normally played by women, who in the more active roles were expected to be cheeky and dashing and pansexually attractive; in this they were analogous to pantomime boys, but they often wore costumes and played in a style as 'realistic' and mimetic as anyone else on stage, and naval roles required not only swearing and spitting, arms drill and hornpipes, but the ability to climb the scenery and fire pistols with bravado in the finale.[15]

It is possible to look beyond the appeal to male sexual response in these performances, and to discover suggestions of a challenging and potentially subversive consciousness. Several women who were particularly attractive in such roles in the 1830s, such as Mary Keeley, Fanny Fitzwilliam and Louisa Nisbett, began to find or to inspire plays which explore sexual and gender stereotyping. Nisbett in particular played Rosalind with 'exhilarating animal spirits' and Beatrice in an uncomfortably similar way, and created the role of Lady Gay Spanker in Boucicault's *London Assurance* (1841);[16] this role, of the athletic, dominant, horsey woman who drags her gentle husband round in her wake and has to be tamed, to some degree at least, after her sexual promise has been tacitly admired throughout the play, had a huge impact. Boucicault was always alive to the latest theatrical trends, and he might have drawn the inspiration for Lady Gay from an earlier performance of Nisbett's, in *Is She a Woman?* by William Collier, at the Queen's Theatre in 1835, in which a brother and sister have changed role: she hunts and shoots and he draws and dresses exquisitely. The threat of such a challenge to the stereotype of delicate, passive and asexual femininity currently being established is indicated by the fact that when this character survived all trials and did not lose her dominance at the end of the story, Nisbett felt it necessary to step out of role and deflect potential hostility by means of the play's tag-line:

> Ladies and Gentlemen, as I have so often appeared before you as one of *'the Lords of Creation'* I think it as well to inform you that I have no wish to be taken for anything but a woman, and one whose sole ambition is to please her friends *(curtseys).*[17]

There is a certain irony here, since a woman's 'friends' within the hetero-patriarchy were her family and guardians, expecting from her passive self-effacement, while those of a self-supporting actress were the audience, whom she must please in a very different way. Nisbett was secure enough about their approval of her to extend her gender games further, into a virtuoso interplay of masculinised dominant woman and actual male impersonation, in *The Rifle Brigade* by Charles Selby at the Adelphi 1838. In this she played 'an enter-prising lady, an agitator, and a young rifle' – the latter role being in full uniform drag, appearing to be a charming and good-looking young fellow who woos the wife of a jealous man before his own face, kissing and embracing her, and then gives him a very cool lecture about his unreasonable behaviour.

The ambiguities of these performances, their offering on the one hand pornography-fuelled pleasure to men in the audience, and on the other a potentially challenging vision of strong women enjoying and controlling their own sexuality, were one of the dangerous aspects of theatre over which the respectable middle classes asserted hegemonic control in the 1843 Theatres Act. In the nascent music halls, the spaces into which the lower-class or less-respectable audiences were to be syphoned off, Lady Gay Spanker, the woman who enjoys the masculine pleasures of riding, betting, drinking and, tacitly, sex, developed into the 'King of the Boys', the first music-hall style of male impersonation practised by large, jolly women. Wearing a deliberately gender-confused costume of masculine coat and tie with skirts, or full evening dress over a very curvacious figure emphasised by tight-laced stays, Annie Adams, Fanny Robina and their like sang about being 'Happy and free where 'ere I may be, fond of a frolic and noise,/ King of your game, and king of your fun, the monarch that leads you to joys',[18] offering a fantasy of female approbation and participation in masculine pleasures quite at odds with the notions of propriety dominating more respectable representations. In the new West End theatres, the convention of cross-playing was stripped of such overt provoca-tion, but remained viable for the casting of boy roles. Pathetic waifs such as Smike and Poor Jo in Dickensian adaptations were still successfully played by specialist actresses; and comic and active female boys, in the burlesque tradition, were found a role within the new style of serious drama. It has been argued[19] that in plays like Tom Taylor's *The Ticket-of-Leave Man*, at the Olympic in 1863, such casting began to have a satirical dimension. In this proto-social-problem drama, dwelling upon the temptations to which young men were exposed by attending places of entertainment like music halls, Sam Willoughby, a boy clerk rescued from dissipation by the hero, was played by a woman, Miss Raynham. Her critical representation of the young would-be swell was perhaps enhanced by audience consciousness of her true sex.

The second generation of music-hall male impersonators drew upon this continuation of 'realistic' cross-playing traditions in the legitimate theatre, creatively blended with the gender-mixed costuming of Adams and Robina. Nellie Power, a slight and pretty young woman, used the deliberately mixed messages of a corsetted figure within ultra-fashionable men's clothes to participate in the music-hall persecution of the 'swell', the overdressed gentleman. Her songs about the narcissistic clerk who 'does the Heavy in the City' and his flashy pretensions ('And he wears a penny flower in his coat, la di dah!/ And a penny paper collar round his throat, la di dah!') were so provocative to the section of the audience they portrayed that one night in 1885 she had a soda-syphon hurled at her from the stalls.[20] Jennie Hill's acts, grounded in class consciousness and often powerfully exposing patriarchal privilege, featured similar attacks upon the 'Boy about Town' and skilfully mobilised the hostility of the working-class men in the audience against the sniggering 'chappies' in the stalls; and she also presented passionately serious portrayals of waifs and strays of both sexes who were not just pathetic innocents, but able to give mordant expression to their own oppression.[21] Like Vesta Tilley in the next generation, she claimed a larger female than male following of fans; but her songs clearly suggest that the grounds of their admiration are more likely to have been recognition of oppression they shared and delighted amusement at her showing up of the privileged young men, rather than any longing for, or admiration of, the males she impersonated.

While this vein of class mockery and protest developed within the acts of individual women performers, the newly formed sketch companies who acted on the halls from the 1880s onwards availed themselves straightforwardly of the established convention of cross-playing to make good gaps in their numbers, when a stable-lad or a barman or an extra soldier were required by the text. A rich variety of implications, therefore, already informed the convention of cross-dressing when music-hall performers began, in the 1890s, to seek for ways of embodying an increasingly sophisticated and very widespread consciousness of the politics of gender, and of theatrical gender games as directly related to it. For at that period it becomes evident that the battle for ownership of gender definition was once again engaged on the stage, this time in the music halls. The antagonists were women performers, who had varying degrees of awareness and of radicalism themselves, and the audiences and commentators, newly augmented by an influx of demi-mondaine, and indeed fashionable, patrons who had just discovered the delights of visiting the halls.

The wide class spectrum and the variety of levels of consciousness and differences of attitude present made the West End music halls an exciting and potentially explosive arena for such a struggle.

The most obvious sign of political gender awareness is the steadily rising tally of songs, sketches and burlesques which are explicitly on the subject of the New Woman, and offer as the sign thereof what are always called 'bifurcated garments' and bicycles. Marie Lloyd had a song called 'Salute My Bicycle' throughout 1895, and was enthusiastically received in her divided skirt. Lloyd was easy to laugh at and with, and offered little threat to the sexual status quo in such a song. But there were others whose material seems to have provoked uneasy responses. Nellie L'Estrange, a serio who was also a male impersonator, had a turn in 1890 which began with her in a Prussian White Hussar's uniform in which she looked 'exceedingly handsome' and sang a song which 'of course, makes fun of the Service' and followed it up with a song 'in which she asserted the claims of the ladies to equality with the men. With such a charming and eloquent adocate', the *Era* reviewer goes on, 'the ladies' position ought speedily to be strengthened, and their possession of the parliamentary franchise should be brought within the range of practical politics.'[22] The journalist is in a privileged position to be heard; but his sarcasm in print could not entirely control the responses in the halls where L'Estrange made her statement.

What he and his fraternity have done, of course, is to make it almost impossible for us to discover what those responses were. The history of the halls is told almost entirely through the mouths of men. It is evident, however, that scores, perhaps hundreds, of very various female performers made use of the trappings of masculinity. Women announcing themselves on their professional cards as male impersonators in 1890 and 1895 included Nellie Selwyn, Violet Nelson, Millie Hylton, Billie Barlow, Con Moxon, Lizzie Chipchase, Lily Laurel, Florrie Villars, Maude Boyce, Emily Lindale, Bessie Bonehill, the youngest of the Black Swan Trio, Nellie L'Estrange and very many more. These represent the top slice of the profession; there must have been hundreds like them with no money to spare for such advertisements. The range of acts they offered was very wide. At one extreme were Vesta Tilley and others like her who aimed at illusionist perfection of disguise, women like Flo Windsor, who in a newspaper interview in 1891 stressed her careful study of male body language, and proudly boasted of the day when she was sent round to wait at the men's side of the stage by a confused stage manager. But they were surrounded by a world of cross-gender and parodic and confused or comical dressing and impersonating which is bewilderingly various in its signification; not only Miss Ethardo the lounge-suited juggler, but Miss Billie Butt the dancing sailor, Miss St George Hussey the female Irishman, the three sisters Oliver impersonating in quick succession New Women in rational costume, Gaiety girls and coon dancers – this last would be in drag; Constance Moxon, a well-known mezzo, including in her impersonation impressions of

Chirgwin the White-eyed Kaffir (while Chirgwin himself, a black-face falsetto singer, did a song on the same bill in female makeup), Bessie Bellwood, a voluptuous serio impersonating a cab driver and then singing about the New Woman in the character of an old one, and many more serios doing a song as a coster boy or a policeman or some other stereotypical male, in full costume, in the course of their act; and then there were acts like Gracie Whiteford, who played Romeo to John Sheridan's Juliet, and the Leons, who introduced 'the gigantic gentleman in petticoats and the petite lady in the garb of a masher of the first water. The sight of the very small male making love to the very large female excited much laughter.'[23]

Superficially, all this is treated by the reviewers as absolutely routine. But there are moments when something can be glimpsed disturbing them, behind the oracular orotundity of their well-lubricated style. One begins to wonder whether something is being deliberately played down, when the *Era* interviews first Nellie L'Estrange, an old-established male impersonator almost ready to retire on her substantial earnings, and then two weeks later Con Moxon, who has just made a major career change from musical-comedy mezzo to become a music-hall male impersonator (from the descriptions of her act, she is clearly of the full-evening-dress-and-cigar variety) and somehow in neither case, in the whole column length, is male impersonation mentioned.[24] These and similar straws in the wind suggest that there is a deliberate silence, an unmentionable area somewhere in these representations. It is notable that although the fact of her success and the details of her off-stage doings are fulsomely reported, Vesta Tilley's act is almost never described; the only review I have found dwells on the fact that she is about to marry, and imputes to her a desire to have a baby.[25] Few of the male impersonators' acts ever get more than a blandly appreciative line or two. One is led to ask whether the reticence is because of their unimportance – these are acts chiefly appreciated by women, which the men find dull – or perhaps because of their unhandlability, their potential dangerousness – exciting acts in the hall, but impossible to translate safely into words, to frame within the bland, recuperative discourse of the trade press.

As a means, therefore, of reading the complex, enigmatic and often bizarre disruption of the ordinary sign systems of gender and display which 1890s' cross-dressing represents, and accounting for its central ambiguity – its sudden huge popularity, on the one hand, and its unmentionable, apparently threatening qualities on the other – I would propose that a future analysis should attempt to read this practice, in all its enormous variety, including the pantomime boy and Emmaline Ethardo as well as Flo Windsor 'passing' in the wings and Vesta Tilley in her mockingly perfect uniform of gendered wealth and power, as part of the construct of carnival.

Carnival is, of course, by no means a simple and universally acceptable set of ideas. Bakhtin's original optimistic proposals for a reading of early modern culture in a way that celebrates the cultural strength of the common people have been hedged round with more politically and intellectually cautious reformulations by cultural materialists and anthropologists.[26] It is necessary to avoid either celebrating carnival practices as an assertion of class resistance when they were, in fact, an instrument of the hegemony in maintaining the status quo, or making an easy equation between festive practices of pre-capitalist cultures, expressive of shared value systems, and the theatrical or holiday diversions of modern societies which are inauthentic, nostalgic or an expression of shared play. It is particularly controversial to claim to detect carnivalesque practices and meanings beyond the watershed of the transition from a feudal to a capitalist society in Britain, and whenever that might be said to have taken place, it was certainly accomplished by the 1890s. But if one accepts the defining description of carnival proposed by Stallybrass and White,[27] as the transgressive manipulation of the sign systems of a culture, whereby three symbolic processes, which they call demonisation, inversion and hybridisation, are used as ways of manipulating the relationship between 'high' and 'low' social strata, in events which can be mobilised more or less politically, then music-hall male impersonation does come sharply into focus, with Emmaline Ethardo, rather than Vesta Tilley, at its symbolic centre.

Few descriptions of carnival afford women any place amongst its active participants. If they appear at all, they are most usually targets of demonisation, attacked and denigrated, or represented in a very equivocal way by masquerading men. Much has been said of past and present festivals in which male transvestites are the leaders of the ritual overturning of categories, and this is taken to represent the essential femininity of disorder, its opposition to the rational – the identification of 'woman and the demon'.[28] Such formulations tacitly dismiss women entirely from the public festive arena of streets, fairs and the music hall, and confine them to their proper sphere, the private domestic order of the bourgeois home, where alone men can feel them to be safe and unthreatening. But there were women on the streets, and in the halls; and in the 1890s they began to challenge for a place in the carnival, by dressing up as men.

The claim of the New Woman was, of course, to take part in public life; but the basis of the claim, in the sober daylight world, was that they were as rational as men – hence trousers are 'rational dress' – and that they wished to offer no challenge to their symbolic placement in the domestic sphere by doing so, and would not shrug off the dutiful wife and mother, but simply represent the best of domestic bourgeois values drawn from the home. The music hall, with its ritualised disorder, drinking, display, physical freedom and sexuality, could only mock those claims, and expose the paradoxes of all rational ordering. Emmaline Ethardo's act was, in a strictly Bakhtinian sense, grotesque, an offence offered to the values of reason and high art. In a symbolic gender-inversion she first appeared in male clothes, and displayed a male characteristic, physical skill and activity, by her juggling. Then, dropping her mask, revealing her shape, she presented not the reality of the female body, but a parody of its representation in classical, high art: mounting a pedestal, apparently nude as a statue, she proceeded to a grotesque distortion, a dislocating, splitting, of her form. The commentator who has preserved this for us confirms its irony in his concluding assertion that it is important (that is, important to him, in understanding the pleasure he derives from her) that Miss Ethardo is beautiful. Her act had all the defining characteristics of Bakhtin's 'grotesque body': heterogeneity, impurity and masking in her male impersonation; eccentricity, distension, disproportion and the focus upon gaps and dislocations in her contortions; and in both parts the superaddition of the parody of 'high' forms – the classical statue, and the man.

The challenge this sort of thing presented to the daylight political world is clear enough in the 1890s' campaigns (symbolically headed by a woman, Mrs Ormiston Chant) to make the halls respectable or snuff them out. It is a significant sign of a growing power and danger in the licensed foolery of the carnival when it is suddenly reprobated and more aggressively policed, and said by the authorities to be getting out of hand. Incidents of disorder accompanying music-hall and pantomime performance began to provoke disproportionately outraged responses, particularly from those whose business it was to profit from the harmless operation of the entertainment industry. At Christmas 1889 Jenny Hill was the principal boy in *Aladdin* at the Theatre Royal in Birmingham, wearing a scarlet carnival version of the fashionable suit of the 'masher' and satirising the 'eccentric strut, the ineffable simper, the vacuous expression' of the young man about town.[29] On the last night of the show, at the end of February 1890, the panto suddenly disintegrated into a row between the principal boy and the principal girl, a Miss Shirley, both of them attempting to recruit the other players and the audience to their sides. On 8 March the *Era* devoted its leader to a furious attack upon them, upon female performers in other provincial shows who had also allowed aggressive personal feelings to find expression in public, and especially on their audiences, for permitting the ordinary theatrical rules to be outraged, liberty to degenerate into licence and the barrier that confines such unladylike behaviour within the unreality of the theatrical world to be dangerously breached.

Contemplating the cross-dressed woman in the 1890s' music halls, and the curiously defensive reactions to her, one is attempting to read the subtext of the commentaries, and to understand audiences and performers only half-conscious of what is happening, and wholly unwilling to verbalise even what they do perceive. I think it is reasonable and helpful, when one considers the full range of distorted, mocking, exaggerated images of masculinity projected by these women from the music-hall stage, to read male impersonation as carnivalesque, and to interpret it as transgressive, provocative, an act of clowning that is a subversive manipulation of the masks of stereotype. It may be called feminist; but it is quite profoundly at odds, in its dark suggestiveness and anarchy, with the rationality of the New Woman.

Notes

1. The performances included Eve Merriam's *The Club*, and Timberlake Wertenbaker's *New Anatomies*, performed by the London Women's Theatre Group in 1981. David Cheshire was the first to remark the temporal coincidence between male impersonation and suffrage agitation, in 'Male impersonators', *The Saturday Book*, 29 (1969), pp. 245–52.

2. I. Blackman and K. Perry, 'Skirting the issue: Lesbian fashion for the 1990s', *Feminist Review*, 34 (Spring 1990), pp. 67–78; K. Rolley, 'Cutting a dash: The dress of Radclyffe Hall and Una Troubridge', *Feminist Review*, 35 (Summer 1990), pp. 54–66, and Elizabeth Wilson, 'Deviant dress', *Feminist Review*, 35 (Summer 1990), pp. 67–74.

3. S. Gubar, 'Blessings in disguise: Cross-dressing as re-dressing for female Modernists', *Massachusetts Review*, Autumn 1981, pp. 477–508, pp. 479, 478.

4. Julie Wheelwright, *Amazons and Military Maids: Women who dressed as men in the pursuit of life, liberty and happiness* (London: Pandora, 1989), p. 78.

5. For example, Blackman and Perry, 'Skirting the issue', *op. cit.*, and S. Ardill and S. O'Sullivan, 'Butch/femme obsessions', *Feminist Review* 34 (Spring 1990), pp. 79–85.

6. E. Aston, 'Male impersonation and the music hall: The case of Vesta Tilley,' *New Theatre Quarterly*, 15 (August 1988), pp. 247–57.

7. S. Maitland, *Vesta Tilley* (London: Virago, 1986), pp. 9–10.

8. L. Senelick, 'The evolution of the male impersonator on the nineteenth-century popular stage', *Essays in Theatre*, vol. 1, no. 1 (1982), pp. 30–44, p. 33.

9. Or were pursued by it: in the *Era* for 15 June 1895, p. 17, there is a strangely inexplicit report of a court case in which an unnamed but 'fashionably attired young lady, who stated she performed on the stage as a male impersonator' was granted an injunction to stop a photographer, to whom she had paid 8 shillings on account for four dozen photographs of herself 'in various characters', from hawking copies of them around the city. His customers were, or at least included, women: a 'canvasser' had offered to sell the complainant a picture of herself.

10. D. Farson, *Marie Lloyd and Music Hall* (London: Tom Stacey, 1972), p. 140. Farson reports King as rejecting lesbianism very explicitly – 'I loathe it. I find it horrible.' Marie Lloyd was adored by Naomi Jacob, who wrote her biography; George Eliot's best-known female admirer was Edith Simcox; see P. Johnson, 'Edith Simcox and heterosexism in biography: A lesbian–feminist exploration', in The Lesbian History Group, *Not a Passing Phase* (London: The Women's Press, 1989), pp. 55–76.

11. Senelick, 'Evolution of the male impersonator', *op. cit.*, p. 38.

12. Aston and Senelick offer accounts along these lines; see also D. Mayer, 'The sexuality of pantomime', *Theatre Quarterly*, vol. 4, no. 3 (1974), pp. 55–64; J. Steadman, 'From dame to woman: W. S. Gilbert and theatrical transvestism', in M. Vicinius (ed.) *Suffer and Be Still* (Bloomington and London: Indiana University Press, 1972), pp. 20–37; and K. Fletcher, 'Planche, Vestris and the transvestite role: Sexuality and gender in Victorian popular theatre', *Nineteenth Century Theatre*, vol. 15, no. 1 (Summer 1987), pp. 7–33.

13. See P. Racklin, 'Androgyny, mimesis, and the marriage of the boy heroine on the English Renaissance stage', *PMLA*, vol. 102 (January 1987), pp. 29–41.

14. See, for example, I. Guest, *Fanny Elssler* (London: Adam & Charles Black, 1970), p. 88, where he quotes from Gaultier's description of Elssler in *Le Figaro*, 9 October 1843. Sexual excitement was not openly voiced in British theatrical criticism, but see T. C. Davis, 'The actress in Victorian pornography', *Theatre Journal*, vol. 41 (October 1989), pp. 294–315, on the pervasive subtext of the enjoyment of women on stage by most men in London audiences, and its erotic focus upon the legs and buttocks.

15. Miss Martin accomplished this feat when she played Midshipman Easy in an adaptation of Marryat's novel by W. H. Oxberry and J. Cann, at the Surrey in March 1837.

16. See W. Marston, *Our Recent Actors* (London: Sampson Low, Marston, Searle and Rivington, 1890), pp. 291–2. 'Lady Gay Spanker' is, of course, a thoroughly provocative name for a character: 'gay' in Victorian slang indicates prostitution, and the flagellatory patronymic is suggestive of delights which in a breeches role would be hinted at more overtly. The moralising critic Clement Scott recorded, apparently in all innocence, that when Nisbett fixed her eyes on the audience and strode back and forth across the stage cracking her whip, 'the effect was electrical' (*The Drama of Yesterday and Today*, 2 vols (London: Macmillan, 1899), vol. 2, p. 36).

17. William Collier, *Is She a Woman?* (London: Duncombe, n.d.), p. 30.

18. *King of the Boys*, written by C. St Leonards and James Manhill, composed by Joseph Cleve (London: Francis, Day and Hunter, 1893).

19. H. Day, V. Gardner, M. Holt and D. Mayer, *An A-Level Study Book for The Ticket-of-Leave Man* (Manchester: Department of Drama, University of Manchester, 1986).

20. *Daily News*, 28 December 1885, cited in P. Bailey, 'Champagne Charlie: Performance and ideology in the music-hall swell song', in J. S. Bratton (ed.), *Music Hall: Performance and style* (Stony Stratford: Open University Press, 1986), pp. 49–69, p. 65.

21. For further discussion of Hill's songs, see A. Bennett, 'Music in the halls' in Bratton (ed.), *Music Hall, op. cit.*, pp. 1–22, p. 18, and my 'Jenny Hill: Sex and sexism in Victorian music hall' in the same volume, pp. 92–110.

22. *Era*, 2 August 1890, p. 15 in a review of the reopening night at the Canterbury.

23. *Era*, 21 June 1890, p. 15, in a review of the Alhambra. All the acts cited are similarly reviewed in the *Era* during 1890 or 1895.

24. 'A chat with Nellie L'Estrange', *Era*, 13 April 1895, p. 16, and 'A chat with Miss Constance Moxton', *Era*, 27 April 1895, p. 16.

25. *Era*, 16 August 1890, p. 14.

26. M. Bakhtin, *Rabelais and his World*, tr. H. Iswolsky (Cambridge, Mass.: MIT Press, 1968); M. Gluckman, *Order and Rebellion in Tribal Africa* (London: Cohen, 1963) and *Custom and Conflict in Africa* (Oxford: Blackwell, 1965); G. Balandier, *Political Anthropology* (London: Allen Lane, 1970); T. Eagleton, *The Function of Criticism* (London: Verso, 1984).

27. P. Stallybrass and A. White, *The Politics and Poetics of Transgression* (London: Methuen, 1986), pp. 56–8 and *passim*.

28. See, for example, Barbara Babcock, *The Reversable World: Symbolic Inversion in Art and Society* (Ithaca: Cornell University Press, 1978).

29. *Birmingham Daily Times*, 27 December 1889.

PART III

Women Singing

The Voice of Freedom: Images of the prima donna

SUSAN RUTHERFORD

> Oh, I am happy! The great masters write
> For women's voices, and great Music wants me!
> I need not crush myself within a mould
> Of theory called Nature: I have room
> To breathe and grow unstunted.[1]

So proclaims the prima donna protagonist of George Eliot's dramatic poem *Armgart* (1871), flushed with the triumph of her operatic debut, savouring the ecstasy of the moment when the cage-door of Victorian domesticity was at last flung wide and a seemingly limitless horizon of possibilities lay before her. Armgart is, of course, a fictional representation of the prima donna, not a historical figure. Yet Eliot, like George Sand in *Consuelo*, Willa Cather in *The Song of the Lark* and Gertrude Atherton in *Tower of Ivory*, presents a particular nineteenth-century and wholly female perception of the prima donna: that of the prima donna as a positive symbol of liberation and artistic fulfilment, whose voice is quintessentially the voice of freedom. It is this notion of the prima donna as free woman, apparent not only in women's fiction but also in women's journals, memoirs and other writing, which precedes and supersedes the *fin-de-siècle* phenomenon of the New Woman, and which in part accounts for the absence of a precise depiction of the New Woman on the operatic stage. My intention is to examine the manifestation and the significance of this definition of the prima donna in the context of other nineteenth-century readings of the female voice, and to assess its applicability or otherwise to real singers of this era.

Against the prevailing model of the 'feminine ideal', the prima donna was certainly a striking, even iconoclastic figure: not only in terms of her public life, her professional career and her financial independence, but often equally in the very mode of her performance, as may be glimpsed from a review of Giulia Grisi in Marliani's opera *Ildegonda* at Her Majesty's Theatre in 1837:

> The whole of Grisi's performance . . . was marked by extraordinary boldness, energy, and power. Her ability in sustaining herself against that immense body of voices and instruments in the finale already mentioned, was quite tremendous. What she wants is tenderness of expression: her very mode of taking her notes is in keeping with her general character of performance – it is abrupt and defying: 'You may take it if you like; if not you may let it alone.'[2]

Yet female access to this self-possessed and potent image of womanhood, as either fictional or actual heroine, had first to negotiate a difficult path encumbered with the obstacles of male suspicion and distrust. For the purposes of this study, these obstacles are perhaps most clearly illustrated by Offenbach's *Les Contes d'Hoffmann* (1881),[3] which usefully combines all the major nineteenth-century patriarchal interpretations of the meaning, possession and use of the female voice in the single figure of Stella, an Italian prima donna. That the opera presents purely a male perspective of the prima donna is emphasised by the fact that Stella herself appears only briefly and mutely in the final scene: instead, she is portrayed to the audience solely through the eyes of her male lover, the poet Hoffmann. Hoffmann, drinking in a tavern with his male friends, relates his 'folles amours' with three different women: Olympia, the doll; Antonia, the singer and artist; and Giulietta, the courtesan. Yet these apparently separate female characters ultimately prove to be but multiple facets of Hoffmann's mistress, Stella. Stella, the prima donna, is 'trois femmes dans la même femme/ Trois âmes dans la seule âme!/ Artiste, jeune fille et courtisane':[4] she encompasses Antonia's voice and artistry, Olympia's youthful promise, and Giulietta's abundant eroticism.

Hoffmann's tripartite analysis of Stella essentially springs from the traditional male readings of the female voice. Giulietta, whose voice 'comme un concert divin'[5] persuades Hoffmann to surrender his reflection to the devil and to kill a male rival, is derived from the ancient mythological figure of the syren. Part-woman and part-bird, the syren belonged to a sisterhood: a coven of prima donnas who, from the corpse-strewn meadows of their island home, lured sailors to their death by means of the 'high clear tones' and 'honeysweet music'[6] of their voices. This powerful myth, associating women's singing with the death-hungry outpourings of a darkly erotic and hostile female sexuality, lingered throughout later cultures; its influence was further re-inforced by the traditional antipathy of the Christian church towards the female singer (whose 'beautiful but deluding sweetness' of voice Bishop Hippolytus damned as being 'full of seduction to sin');[7] and, as Bram Dijkstra has indicated, it was still highly present in the art and literature of the nineteenth century.[8] That the prima donna of this era, commonly described as 'syren',[9] was inevitably construed in the sensual terms of this predatory creature is demonstrated, for example, by Mayhew's use of the nomenclature 'prima donna' as a synonym for 'prostitute',[10] and by the publication of pornographic 'memoirs', erroneously purporting to be based on the sexual adventures of singers such as Elizabeth Billington, Lucia Vestris and Wilhemina Schröder-Devrient.[11]

Nevertheless, as Hofffmann's tale of the life-sized puppet Olympia illustrates, the syrens were not absolutely invincible. If the early Christian church, by proscribing women's voices from men's hearing, had essentially aped the advice of Circe to stop the ears of Odysseus' crew with melted wax,[12] the nineteenth century mimicked that other Greek hero, Jason, who conquered the syrens by the means of Orpheus and his lyre:[13] the syrens, outsung and outcharmed by this male competitor, reportedly committed suicide in despair. *Ottocento* society employed the same device, and pitted the much-vaunted 'moral'[14] qualities of man-made music against the syrens' intrinsically female and supernatural vocalising by establishing the teaching of singing, the harmonious reordering of voice, as a standard item in the education (and therefore containment) of women. The battle against the syren, against female will and eroticism, was thus directly fought in women's throats and minds. Singing, with its potent mixture of melodious music and wholesome words, became especially prized for female study as 'almost the only branch of education, aside from divine truth, whose direct tendency is to *cultivate the feelings*':[15] that is, as a means of inculcating the desired lessons of genteel femininity. In contrast to the syren/prima donna, the drawing-room singer's voice was therefore carefully restricted in terms of tonal quality, manner and use of singing, as is apparent from Ruskin's advice to young women in *Sesame and Lilies*:

> In music especially you will soon find what personal benefit there is in being serviceable: it is probable that, however limited your powers, you have voice and ear enough to sustain a note of moderate compass in a concerted piece; that then, is the first thing to make sure you can do. Get your voice disciplined and clear, and think only of accuracy; never of effect or expression: if you have any soul worth expressing, it will show itself in your singing; but most likely there are very few feelings in you at present, needing particular expression; and the one thing you have to do is to make a clear-voiced little instrument of yourself, which other people can entirely depend on for the note wanted.[16]

There is no suggestion here that woman herself might savour pleasure from her singing, or that she might use her singing for her own purposes; only that she must cleanse her voice of its troublesome egotistical desires, and subject its purified tone to the demands of others. Olympia, the doll who trills her coloratura aria in display of feminine accomplishment for the edification of her 'father's' guests (and thereby further entrances Hoffmann), is just such an evocation of the bourgeois daughter as music-maker: she is a syren caged, whose active and knowing eroticism has been changed into the passive, ignorant sensuality of the songbird.

The third element in Hoffmann's division of the prima donna, the 'artiste' Antonia, encapsulates that other popular Victorian notion that artistry was too great a burden for woman's frail physique,[17] for Antonia's beautiful voice, inherited from her dead mother, kills her by overstraining her dangerously weak constitution. Yet the perils of artistry to Antonia are not merely physical but also spiritual, for she is portrayed as in constant conflict with herself; pulled alternately by her syren and songbird selves between fame and domesticity, between unwomanliness and femininity, she must choose or indeed lose either her soul/life or her career. This image of the prima donna is manifest in a variety of male fiction of the era: the singing heroines of writers such as E. T. A. Hoffmann, George Meredith, George Moore and George Du Maurier, are invariably robbed of their voices by maternity or religious zeal or mortality.[18] No womanly woman, these writers imply, can remain as a prima donna and truly live happily ever after.

Offenbach's prima donna Stella, the synthesis of songbird, artist and syren, clearly fails the test of 'womanliness', for when she finally appears in person she is condemned by the drunk and disillusioned poet: 'Vous êtes Olympia? Brisée. . . Antonia? Morte! Giulietta? Damnée.'[19] Her subsequent exit on the arm of Hoffmann's triumphant rival, Lindorf (the devil-figure who has plagued all Hoffmann's attempts to woo Olympia/Antonia/Giulietta) emphasises that she is sponsored by satanic elements, whilst Hoffmann remains to be comforted by *his* Muse, an angelic female figure who promises to appease his sufferings by enabling him to transform his grief into art. The opera's ultimate images of Stella and Hoffmann thus explicitly uphold the association of female art with the disruptive forces of evil, and male art with the forces of goodness and morality.

Such marginalisation of women's creativity did not go wholly unchallenged. Nineteenth century female writers, themselves women with 'voice' and ambition, similarly employed the prima donna as fictional heroine, but claimed her instrument as a positive expression of female independence, individuality and artistry. Their imaginary singers are quasi-feminists, inversions and subversions of the conventional configuration of the female artist as doubly 'other', and they invariably share certain key characteristics: a proud self-confidence, a dedication to their art, an intelligent creativity and an unconventionality of manner, ideas and behaviour. The recurrence of this 'fantasy of the performing heroine' (as Ellen Moers terms it) in women's literature has been noted in other studies,[20] but their approaches have been understandably confined to literary as opposed to theatrical matters. My emphasis is rather the reverse, for whilst the problematic relationship between fiction and reality obviously precludes the examination of these invented prima donnas as axiomatic of the actuality of the woman singer's experience, they are nevertheless a form of evidence of a specifically female perception or reading of the prima donna both as stage artist and as woman. As such, they offer a limited and oblique solution to the theatre historian's perennial problem: that is, the difficulty of accurate assessment of the spectator's response to theatrical image.

The works of three of these women writers, George Sand, George Eliot and Willa Cather (all of whom regularly attended and enjoyed operatic performances), are unified by the appearance in various guises of a particular and actual *cantatrice*: Pauline Viardot (1821–1910). The plain younger sister of an equally famous singer, Maria Malibran, Viardot was a Spanish prima donna of prodigious talent: a superb vocalist, a gifted musician and composer and a compelling actress. Her closest female friend was George Sand, who regarded her as

> the foremost, the only, the great, the true singer . . . you are the priestess of the ideal in music and your mission is to spread it, to make it understood, and to reveal to the incalcitrant and the ignorant the True and the Beautiful.[21]

Sand's passionate admiration was given fictional shape in her two-volume romantic novel, *Consuelo* (1842), which celebrates Viardot's character and profession in its idealised depiction of an eighteenth-century opera singer. Here, Sand directly challenges the notion of the prima donna as erotic syren, and instead presents the female singer's profession 'as sacred . . . the loftiest which a woman can embrace'. She uses a man, Consuelo's lover, Albert, to argue that originally the arts and religion were one: that 'Music and poetry were the highest expressions of faith, and a woman endowed with genius and beauty was at once a sibyl and a priestess.' Yet 'absurd and culpable distinctions' destroyed women's liturgical participation in religious ceremony:

> Religion proscribed beauty from its festivals, and woman from its solemnities. Instead of ennobling and directing love, it banished and condemned it. Beauty, woman, love, cannot lose their empire. Men have raised for themselves other temples which they call theaters, and where no other god presides.

Admittedly, these new temples have become 'dens of corruption', but Albert believes that Consuelo 'would be as pure in the theater as in the cloister', and that nature has specifically formed her to 'shed over the world' her 'power and genius'. In this reassessing of the source and motive of women's creativity, Consuelo recognises 'sentiments which she herself had frequently experienced in all their force':

> Devout, and an actress, she every day heard the canoness and the chaplain unceasingly condemn the brethren of the stage. In seeing herself restored to her proper sphere by a serious and reflecting man, she felt her heart throb and her bosom swell with exultation, as if she had been carried up into a more elevated and more congenial life.[22]

Consuelo, dedicated to her art and faith, is 'consolation' personified;[23] her innate goodness and 'tender and sensitive heart' disseminate compassion, hope and renewal to all those around her. Sand (as author and in the guise of Albert) thus lifts up the prima donna from the mire of male denigration, and accords her a moral status of unimpeachable virtue. However, because of her artist's nature, Consuelo the woman is also provided with freedom; she has a 'love of liberty, and a proud and lofty independence';[24] she relishes danger and 'deeds of courage and address';[25] she willingly assumes male attire, is physically strong and agile, and invariably frank and outspoken in her opinions. Sand showers gifts on her heroine like a fairy god-mother; she invents a husband who supports and cherishes her profession; grants her motherhood of five children; organises a satisfying career (which ends only when Consuelo's voice finally fades); and involves her in political intrigue and adventure. Importantly, she also finds Consuelo an operatic role (Predieri's *Zenobia*) in which she could be 'herself', and 'manifest, in their full force, all her purity, strength, and tenderness, without, by an artificial effort, identifying herself with an uncongenial character'.[26] In marrying Consuelo's 'otherness', signified by her assumed gipsy identity and artist's calling, with her virtuous and generous character, Sand confirms and illustrates Consuelo's own statement: 'I would make art loved and understood, without making the artist . . . feared or hated.'[27]

Sand, in idealising Viardot as Consuelo, immerses herself and the reader in an enjoyable (if over-wordy) wish-fulfilled fantasy of the prima donna's life, motives and attributes. George Eliot's depiction of the prima donna in her dramatic poem *Armgart* (1871) is more problematic than Sand's, and Viardot's influence is necessarily more oblique. Throughout the poem the shadow of Viardot/Consuelo appears variously as Armgart's alter ego, foremother and rival,[28] symbolising female artistic prowess, whilst Eliot, in the shape of her own rebellious and strong-willed heroine, explicitly defines the significance of the prima donna as free woman. Armgart's voice directly liberates her from the conventional constraints of her sex: it supplies her life with 'meaning';[29] it is the instrument which gives her soul 'freedom'[30] and which releases the 'rage' that would otherwise have made her a 'Maenad' setting fire to forests in her wrath:

> 'Poor wretch!' she says, of any murderess –
> The world was cruel, and she could not sing:
> I carry my revenges in my throat;
> I love in singing, and am loved again.'[31]

Moreover, her singing has wider implications: it is a refutation of the argument that 'Nature has willed' woman's role as one of 'pure subservience', for it is nature herself who has given her both voice, 'such as she only gives a woman child', and also ambition, 'That sense transcendent which can taste the joy . . . of being adored/ For such achievement.'[32] Because 'the great

masters write/ For women's voices', Armgart is not only afforded access to
the otherwise male world of professional music-making but her specifically
female talents cannot be usurped by male expertise:

> Men did not say, when I had sung last night,
> '"Twas good, nay, wonderful, considering
> She is a woman' – and then turn to add,
> 'Tenor or baritone had sung her songs
> Better, of course: she's but a woman spoiled.'[33]

Rather, the reverse is true, for Armgart's performing of Gluck's *Orpheus*
suggests an appropriation not only of a role originally written for a male
castrati (Viardot was the first female Orpheus), but also of the very nature of
Orpheus himself and his supposedly 'moral' music. The suggestion that she
should relinquish this active music-making on the public stage to 'Sing in the
chimney corner to inspire/ My husband reading news'[34] is met with scorn;
claiming she can 'live unmated, but not live/ Without the bliss of singing to
the world',[35] she refuses marriage to the wealthy and aristocratic Graf and
disdains to shackle herself to one who believes ambition has 'unwomaned'[36]
her:

> I will not take for husband one who deems
> The thing my soul acknowledges as good –
> The thing I hold worth striving, suffering for,
> To be a thing dispensed with easily,
> Or else the idol of a mind infirm.[37]

Yet if Eliot heightens the feminist connotations of the prima donna, she
also counters Sand's exuberant romanticism by delineating the transient nature
of the singer's art, and the subsequent pain entailed by a loss of creativity.
In an earlier essay Eliot had written sympathetically of the temporality of the
performer's career,[38] and here she elucidates the double tragedy of the prima
donna who loses not only her creativity but her emancipated status. Armgart's
voice is 'murdered' through illness, leaving her 'meaningless', a 'power turned
to pain',[39] the mere 'torso of a soul',[40] forced to contemplate a future she
bitterly names as 'The Woman's Lot: a Tale of Everyday'.[41] This, then, is
the 'burthen' of the artist's rank, the 'peril' of failure Armgart had proudly
accepted: 'I choose to walk higher with sublimer dread/ Rather than crawl in
safety'.[42] Although she will always now be a 'broken thing',[43] her decision to
disseminate her gifts to other women in a new career as a teacher, and to
acknowledge, in the final image of the poem, that her rival Paulina 'sings
Fidelio,/ And they will welcome her tonight'[44] nevertheless implies a continuation of women's artistry.

Eliot returned to the complex figure of the prima donna in her last novel,
Daniel Deronda (1876), and developed a number of themes originally raised
in *Armgart*. Armgart's evocation of the 'murderess' who 'could not sing' is

here realised in the person of Gwendolen Harleth, the drawing-room singer
who vainly seeks the operatic stage in order to avoid marriage and because
she wishes to 'achieve substantiality for herself and know gratified ambition
without bondage';[45] forced instead to marry, she does not precisely murder
her odious husband but makes no attempt to save him from his death by
drowning. Armgart's destiny as a teacher is further elaborated in the figure of
Mirah Lapidoth, whose 'exquisite'[46] voice was not 'strong enough'[47] for the
stage, who found theatrical life 'repugnant' and rebelled against it,[48] and who
therefore teaches singing and performs at modest concerts. Mirah has no
desire to make 'great claims' for herself;[49] and the smallness and fragility of
her voice, 'like a thread of gold dust',[50] is echoed in her acceptance of the
feminine role in its entirety: in her purity of character, her dutiful devotion to
family and her eventual marriage to Deronda.

In contrast, the singing of Alcharisi (the retired prima donna who is the
character most closely aligned to Armgart) provided a 'chance of escaping
from bondage', of eluding the oppressive domesticity her Jewish father
imposed upon her. Alcharisi wanted to 'live a large life, with freedom to do
what everyone else did, and to be carried along in a great current, not obliged
to care.' She castigates her son, Daniel Deronda, when he assumes an understanding of her:

> You are not a woman. You may try – but you can never imagine what it is to have
> a man's force of genius in you, and yet to suffer the slavery of being a girl. To
> have a pattern cut out – 'this is the Jewish woman; this is what you must be; this
> is what you are wanted for; a woman's heart must be of such a size and no larger;
> else it must be pressed small, like Chinese feet; her happiness is to be made as
> cakes are, by a fixed receipt.' That was what my father wanted.[51]

However, Alcharisi lacks the 'talent to love';[52] wholly absorbed in her career,
she gives away the care of her baby son because she 'did not want a child'[53]
and because she wished further to defy her dead father by denying him a
Jewish grandson. Yet she defends herself from the unspoken accusation that
she must therefore be somehow perverted:

> Every woman is supposed to have the same set of motives, or else to be a
> monster. I am not a monster, but I have not felt exactly what other women feel
> – or say they feel, for fear of being thought unlike others.[54]

Eliot portrays Alcharisi not as unnatural, but supernatural: as a supreme
female 'other', a woman reminiscent of a 'sorceress'[55] or a 'dreamed visitant
from some realm of departed mortals';[56] 'Her worn beauty had a strangeness
in it as if she were not quite a human mother, but a Melusina, who had ties
with some world which is independent of ours.'[57] Alcharisi, an artist, is thus
a being that spans two realms, and thereby transcends the nineteenth-century
limitations of female sexuality. Deronda was the child of her father's dictates:

the product of a forced marriage and a patriarchal concept of woman's place. Implicitly, Alcharisi's real child is her art; a wholly female art she alone gave birth to and nourished, and which brought her a precious nine years of liberation and achievement before, as in a 'fit of forgetfulness', she began to 'sing out of tune'.[58] Despite her subsequent marriage to a Russian prince and the five children that relationship produced (and therefore her possession of the traditional rewards of a 'womanly' woman), life without that art remains eternally impoverished for Alcharisi, it is 'little more than a sense of what was'.[59] Though she is now ill and dying, the over-riding image is of a woman who found absolute freedom and fulfilment in her career; a woman who 'was never willingly subject to any man'.[60]

Towards the end of *The Song of the Lark* (1915), Willa Cather writes that 'Artistic growth is, more than anything else, a refining of the sense of truthfulness. The stupid believe that to be truthful is easy; only the artist, the great artist, knows how difficult it is.'[61] This is the heart of Cather's portrayal of the prima donna, for her heroine Thea Kronborg is just such a 'great artist' engaged in the long, hard struggle to fulfil ambition and achieve artistic maturity. An amalgamation of the actual singer Olive Fremstad and Cather herself, Thea is born and raised from plain, 'rough people'[62] in a small town in Nebraska: her earliest inspiration is Wunsch, her alcoholic German music teacher who, via a score of Gluck's *Orpheus*, and his memories of the Spanish prima donna who sang the title-role, enthuses Thea with the idea of an operatic career. The Spanish singer is, of course, Viardot, although she is never named as such;[63] and it is again this potent appropriation of the male music-god Orpheus by the female voice of the prima donna, which, encapsulated in the recurring first lines of Gluck's famous lament,[64] accompanies, inspires and comforts Thea in the years ahead.

Cather draws a deliberately unglamourous picture of the prima donna's profession. Thea is a 'strange, crude girl'[65] to whom nothing comes easily; her learning is painful and tedious, and even as a mature singer she grimly comments: 'I have to work hard to do my worst, let alone my best.'[66] Her career contains 'many disappointments' and 'bitter, bitter contempts';[67] yet she is eventually rewarded, not simply by monetary success or worldly approbation (though she achieves both), but by 'full possession of things she had been refining and perfecting for so long';[68] by the rare sense of creative fulfilment and freedom which is the direct result of her hard work, her determination and her 'fierce, stubborn self-assertion'.[69] Throughout this account of the making of an artist, Thea's gender is virtually incidental; there is no suggestion that her female sex excludes her from following such a path, nor any overt alignment of the prima donna with woman's emancipation: simply the figure of a strong-minded, independent woman energetically forging a life for herself. However, on stage there are indications of a clearly feminist perspective in Thea's interpretations of Wagner's heroines: for example, she dramatically transforms the limpid Elsa in *Lohengrin* (who collapses into death on the departure of her lover) into an abbess, a woman 'made to live with ideas and enthusiasms, not a husband', a woman who, rather than dying, is 'just beginning'.[70] Effectively combining elements both of Sand's optimism and Eliot's realism, Cather therefore constructs a warmly human prima donna: a woman who dreams and achieves, whose abrupt and resolute character inspires love and respect in those around her, and who embodies the prosaic, earthy qualities of dedication and honesty that Cather believed were so essential to the creation of genuine art.

The female writers thus countered the male myths about woman's voice, illuminated the nature of the prima donna's profession and its rewards and penalties and argued for woman's right to creativity. It is perhaps important to stress that the real prima donnas largely welcomed these sympathetic fictional accounts. Pauline Viardot was highly flattered by her portrait in *Consuelo*, and, according to her biographer, was actively influenced by it:

> Certainly in her letters she was often to express herself in a way which is reminscent of the book, and certain actions in her subsequent life seem to be consciously or unconsciously modelled on those of Consuelo.[71]

Eliot's *Daniel Deronda* also met with approval: in her *Memoirs of an American Prima Donna* (1913), Clara Louise Kellogg cited the pragmatic advice given to Gwendolen Harleth as essential reading for those young women singers 'who think of trying to make a career',[72] and moreover echoes Alcharisi in her description of her own sense of loss on her retirement from the stage:

> It was not easy to stop. When each autumn came around, it was very difficult not to go back to the public. I had an empty feeling. There is no sensation in the world like singing to an audience and knowing that you have it with you. I would not change my experience for that of any crowned head.[73]

And although Olive Fremstad was less convinced by the personal accuracy of her counterpart in *The Song of the Lark*, reportedly saying to Cather with characteristic frankness, 'My poor Willa . . . it wasn't really much like that. But after all, what can you know about me? Nothing!',[74] she also felt the novel was 'the only such book . . . where "there was something doing" in the artist'.[75]

It is impossible to estimate precisely the degree of influence, if indeed any, these and other such novels exerted on the wider female readership. There is the occasional tantalising clue that they may have aided the legitimisation of the singer's profession: in her 1877 address on 'Woman as a Musician' to an American feminist organisation, the Association for the Advancement of Women, Fanny Raymond Ritter (an 'English poetess and musician'), describes Consuelo as 'the ideal character of a pure and noble artist woman, too deeply imbued by lofty enthusiasm for her fine vocation to barter its true principles for transitory success, social flattery, or pecuniary advantage', and employs Sand's fictional image to support her own representation of the actual prima donna as a proud example of woman's musical achievements and possibilities. Ritter, too, lays claim to the Orpheus myth: her vision of the female singer is not the dispossessed songbird whose warbling signifies her passivity, but rather a beneficent activist:

> [The singer] also exercises a positive moral force upon her hearers. The voice is an instrument which the singer carries with her; and as goodness, beauty and happiness are almost the sole objects of unperverted artistic expression, and as even grief and terror are themselves ennobled when illustrated by art, the singer, merely by the action of communicating elevated emotion to her hearers by means of her voice, becomes, for the time, a moral agent.[76]

As the syrens' death by suicide turned out to be mere rumour (at least two were alive when Ulysses sailed past their island a year later),[77] so the strategy of containing women's will by a specific ordering of the female voice thus proved unsustainable. Whether as a result of her personal appraisal of the prima donna, or of her response to the fictional representations cited above, or of her experience of her own music-making, the drawing-room singer either subverted the moral intent of music tuition, by claiming her right as 'agent' rather than 'object', or, like Marie Bashkirtseff, she interpreted her singing in terms of potency and freedom. Bashkirtseff, who harboured ambitions to become a singer until the onset of consumption destroyed her voice, enthused in her journal in 1874 that when singing 'one is more than a woman, one feels immortal',[78] and regarded the female voice as a formidable weapon of female sexuality: 'Singing is to woman what eloquence is to a man, a power without limits.'[79] Other women sought the prima donna's career as a means of escape; the novelist Gertrude Atherton recalls sharing her 'dreams of a future when I should be free to live my own life' in the late 1880s with the then would-be prima donna Sibyl Sanderson, the daughter of a wealthy Californian judge:

> we used to take long despairing walks over the steep hills of the city, wondering if we should ever get out of it. She wanted to be an opera singer, and her father wouldn't hear of it. A few years later she was the rage of Paris and Massenet had written *Esclarmonde* for her début. At that time, however, life seemed a dreary waste.[80]

Whilst in the earlier part of the nineteenth century the majority of singers originated from families of working musicians, by the end of the century the operatic stage therefore had become a career to be chosen by women from all social classes and backgrounds. Women flocked to the music colleges (the composer C. V. Stanford grumbled that the British institutions had been over-run by women[81]), or sought tuition abroad: influenced by hugely popular books such as the pianist Amy Fay's *Music-Study in Germany* (1880), or articles like the one printed in 1890 in *The Musical World*, describing a female singer's lessons in Paris with Pauline Viardot who, even then, could still inspire the apprentice prima donna with a longing to be 'a true artist'.[82]

Ostensibly, this influx of eager young women may be seen as exemplars of New Womanhood: they were seeking a career and financial independence; they were educated in musical terms; and many (such as Kathleen Howard, who severed her engagement when her fiancé told her 'that no married woman should follow a profession'[83]) deliberately chose their vocation above marriage. Some also became actively involved in the women's suffrage movement, the most prominent of these being the American prima donna Lilian Nordica, who sang at several suffrage meetings in the United States and made speeches in support of the Pankhursts' policy of militant action,[84] and the British mezzo-soprano, Marie Brema, who was a vice-president of the Actresses' Franchise League. Yet the *zeitgeist* of the early twentieth-century operatic stage is perhaps more truly typified by the Scottish–American prima donna, Mary Garden (1874–1967): an innovative and controversial performer who, from her début at the Paris Opéra-Comique in 1900 until her retirement in 1934, enjoyed a long and extraordinarily successful career in Europe and America. Although there was much of the 'new' about Garden's personal image of female sexuality, it accorded little with the pictures of New Women contained in *Punch* cartoons. Indeed, her originality was such that one critic, James Huneker, invented an entirely different category for her:

> A condor, an eagle, a peacock, a nightingale, a panther, a society dame, a gallery of moving-pictures, a siren, an indomitable fighter, a human woman with a heart as big as a house, a lover of sport, an electric personality, and a canny Scotch lassie who can force wails of anguish because of her close bargaining over a contract; in a word, a Superwoman.[85]

The standard Victorian descriptions of the female singer as 'nightingale' and 'siren' are still present in this listing of Garden's attributes, but here they are not only combined together but also countered by a whole host of other qualities, denoting Garden's apparent escape from the more reductive definitions of the past. That she was interpreted in such terms undoubtedly owed much to the era's changing delineations of womanhood, but it was also a reflection of Garden's own capacity to project a more complex and multi-faceted image than previous prima donnas.

Garden was fiercely independent, stating that her 'motto' had always been 'liberty'.[86] Although there is no evidence that she read the works of Sand or Eliot, unpublished letters certainly reveal that during her early period of study in Paris in 1890s she enjoyed the first of the 'performing heroine' novels, Mme de Stael's *Corinne, ou l'Italie* (1807), which she thought was 'grand';[87] and in later years, she was to review her approach to her career in terminology that possibly confirms the realism of Eliot and Cather's fictional characterisations of prima donnas:

> I believed in myself, and I never permitted anything or anybody to destroy that belief. My eye never wavered from the goal, and my whole life went into the operas I sang. I wanted liberty and I went my own way. Some called it a lonely way, but that wasn't true. I had myself and my music, and I was and am a very happy person. I owe nothing to anyone but Mary Garden, and for that I paid the price of hard work. My help always came from myself, never from outside.[88]

Yet if, as Rupert Christiansen suggests, Garden appears to possess a 'flawlessly armoured personality',[89] the letters to her Chicago sponsors, written between 1896 and 1899, indicate a conscious acquisition of such protection as a defence against the murky manoeuvrings of the operatic impresarios, the 'disgusting men' who she implies were prepared to offer her a début in exchange for sexual favours, and also against the scandal that dogged her life; one frantic epistle declares that

> the world is *so cruel* for a woman all alone! If they can put her down they do it – and one has to have a character of iron to stand up against it all and come out in the end as honest and pure as when I went into it – I'll do it I know I will and then when I am at last *there* perhaps I can have my peace.[90]

Perhaps it is not so surprising that, having achieved success, she then guarded her freedom jealously: for her, 'music always came first'; and although she 'valued' her male lovers for their 'companionship', the 'only real "romance"' of her life was opera.[91] Like Eliot's Alcharisi, Garden 'never *really* loved anybody. I had a fondness for men, yes, but very little passion, and *no need*.' Besides, men were poor substitutes for the endless fascination of her working life: 'My career never gave me any pain. It never gave me anything but joy, and what man could give that?'[92] Far from feeling deprived of affection, she gloried in her solitude: 'When I sit and think that I can be alone in this world, that I can go into my bedroom and sleep alone, it gives me a shiver of freedom. That is my ecstasy, that knowledge of freedom.'[93]

Undisturbed by conventionalities off stage, on stage Garden similarly eschewed traditional practices. She prided herself on her reputation as a 'singing actress',[94] and established a highly distinctive and modern performance style of her own, which Huneker claimed was influenced by her study of the *café-concert* singer Yvette Guilbert and also Eleanora Duse.[95] Her hallmark was her ability to colour her voice imaginatively according to the needs of each individual role, and a minuteness of dramatic detail that apparently stemmed from a trance-like emergence in the character. Her effects were undoubtedly both novel and memorable; the mezzo-soprano Kathleen Howard (1880–1956) contrasted her experience of the stuffy, old-fashioned modes of operatic acting promulgated by the French studios, where every gesture was conceived from some ancient pattern of expression, with the 'inspiration' of Garden's 'new order' of sung performance:[96] 'Her power of suggestion in those days was capable of conveying any shade of thought or delicate mood to the spectator.'[97]

Yet if the women writers presented their imaginary prima donnas enacting lofty, heroic roles on stage, Garden's theatrical speciality was the modern erotic heroine of the 'New Opera'[98] of the *fin de siècle*. She sang virtually the entire repertoire of these often overtly sensual and rebellious women: Louise (Charpentier), Melisande (Debussy), Thais, Manon, Sapho, Cleopatra (Massanet), Aphrodite (Erlanger), Monna Vanna (Fevrier), Tosca (Puccini) and also their progenitor, Bizet's Carmen. Of them all, the character which had a 'deeper effect' on her more than 'any other'[99] was the title-role of Richard Strauss's setting of Oscar Wilde's *Salome* (1905), which she first performed on 28 January 1909 at the Manhattan Opera House, New York. Salome, who attracts male lust but who finds her own sexual satisfaction in her necrophiliac feasting on Jokanaan's dead lips, has obvious connotations with the figure of the syren. But this is a syren given a new dimension: Jane Marcus argues that Salome is 'Oscar Wilde's New Woman', and that the play should 'be read as a parable of the woman artist's struggle to break free of being the stereotype of sex object'.[100] It is tempting to interpret Garden's enactment of the role in similar terms but, like Aino Ackte (who, when singing the role in London in 1911, provocatively declared that 'there is more than a spice of Salome in every modern woman'[101]), Garden seems to have revelled in precisely the most sexually stereotyped part of the opera, the Dance of the Seven Veils: wearing only the 'thinnest, thinnest muslin', her rendition was (in her words) 'glorious and nude and suggestive'.[102] Her performances made her notorious; amongst many other similar reactions, the *New York Herald Tribune* commented that she 'had realized a conception of incarnate bestiality which has so much power that it is a dreadful thing to contemplate', whilst in 1910 the Chicago Law and Order League denounced her as 'a great degenerator of public morals'.[103]

Garden's delight in such roles, her pride in erotic physical exhibition and her seeming obsession with the numerous 'beautiful' deaths she enacted on stage,[104] contrast oddly with her own controlled and independent life, and the awareness of feminist issues she displayed in statements such as:

> It is fine women do no longer love as they once did. It will be even finer if they can win absolute freedom. Formerly we were under the man's heel. Now just his little toe is on us. Yet how conscious we are of that little toe.[105]

This dichotomy between Garden's on-stage and off-stage images effectively poses the same problem for feminist critics that Madonna, who also juxtaposes arguably negative performance images of women with public comments of a pro-feminist nature, does today.[106] For both women, the power seems to lie in the playing with forbidden fire, with the extremes of sexual submission or domination, whilst they themselves remain apparently untouched by the flames. And like Madonna, who has a wide female following, Garden interestingly claimed that her public too consisted mainly of women, who 'were so eager to know about the new things', and who 'dragged' their husbands to see her performances: 'It was the women of America, not the men and certainly not the critics, who made me. . . . It was they who understood my art and the secret of modern French opera.'[107] Provoking the excesses of both fanatical hatred (one man tried to kill her because 'she talks too much'[108]) and fanatical admiration (a girl committed suicide after being refused entry to her dressing-room), attaining an exceptional degree of authority (as the first prima donna to assume control of a major opera house when she became general manager of Chicago Opera from 1921 to 1922), Garden sought and achieved freedoms which were essentially personal rather than political, based around ideas of artistry and aesthetics, and rooted in a strong sense of individual autonomy. In so doing, she is perhaps far more recognisably the prima donna as 'free woman' rather than as 'New Woman'.

The notion of the prima donna as free woman is therefore apparent both in the perception of certain female spectators, as is indicated by the women writers, and also in the self-descriptions and the actions of some of the prima donnas themselves, as is demonstrated by Mary Garden. Both writers and singers contributed differently to the defining, articulation and dissemination of this image to the wider public, yet it should not be assumed that its effects were wholly or necessarily emancipatory: Clara Louise Kellogg wrote soberly of the 'lighthouse of success' that falsely lured many young women to 'break their wings' against its implacably enclosed beam.[109] Even so, whilst the prima donna's voice of freedom undeniably directly liberated only a few immensely talented and dedicated women, it also signalled to many others the possibility of a life outside the traditional roles of wife and mother; it proclaimed women's right to vocation and creativity, to 'voice' in the widest sense of utterance.

Notes

1. G. Eliot, 'Armgart', in *The Legend of Jubal and Other Poems, Old and New* (1871; London: Blackwood, 1879), p. 98.
2. *The Musical World*, 28 July 1837, p. 110.
3. J. Offenbach, *Les Contes d'Hoffmann* (1881), libretto by Jules Barbier based on his own and Michel Carre's play, *Les Contes fantastiques d'Hoffmann* (1851). As the work was incomplete at Offenbach's death, and has undergone numerous revisions since its first performance in 1881, I have chosen to use the libretto printed to accompany the recording of Deutsche Grammophon, 1989, which combines elements of both the traditional version performed since 1905 and Fritz Oeser's scholarly reconstruction of 1977.
4. *ibid.*, p. 124.
5. *ibid.*, p. 246.
6. Homer, *The Odyssey*, trans. Walter Shewring (Oxford: Oxford University Press, 1980), pp. 144–7.
7. Bishop Hippolytus, third century AD, cited by S. Drinker, *Music and Women* (New

York: Coward-McCann, 1948), p. 179. Drinker discusses at length the exclusion of women's voices from the early Christian churches from the fourth century onwards. The gradual reform of the Protestant churches in allowing women to sing in church choirs during the nineteenth century is noted by N. Temperley, *The Music of the English Parish Church* (Cambridge: Cambridge University Press, 1979), vol. 1, p. 281; however, the ban against women choristers in the Catholic church in this era continued, and was reinforced by the *Motu Proprio* of Pope Pius x in 1903.

8. B. Dijkstra, *Idols of Perversity: Fantasies of feminine evil in fin-de-siècle culture* (Oxford: Oxford University Press, 1988), pp. 258–71.

9. For example, see Rev. H. R. Haweis, *Music and Morals* (London: W. H. Allen, 1874), p. 61.

10. H. Mayhew, *London Labour and the London Poor* (1861; repr. New York: Dover, 1968), vol. iv, p. 217.

11. For Elizabeth Billington, see R. Christiansen, *Prima Donna* (London: Penguin, 1986), p. 46; for Wilhemina Schröder-Devrient see *ibid.*, p. 142. For Lucia Vestris see *Confessions of Madame Vestris* (London and New York: The Erotica Biblion Society, 1899).

12. Homer, *The Odyssey*, p. 144.

13. Pausanias and Homer, cited by R. Graves, *The Greek Myths* (London: Penguin, 1955), vol. 2, p. 245.

14. For example:

> Music acts upon the moral feeling. Simple and beautiful melodies refine it; pure and majestic harmonies connected with them, correct, ennoble [sic], and confirm it; the significant and characteristic movement, order, and feeling of relation throughout, work powerfully on the mind, and the connexion of the parts, when properly displayed by a sufficient performer, awakens high and heavenly thoughts and elevates devotion.

Anonymous contributor to *The Musical World*, 12 April 1838. See also Haweis, *Music and Morals*.

15. L. Mason, 'General observations on vocal music', *The Musical World*, 16 June 1837. See also J. Mainzer, *Singing for the Million* (London: 1841; repr. Kilkenny, Ireland: Boethius Press, 1984).

16. J. Ruskin, *Sesame and Lilies* (London: George Allen, 1893), p. xviii.

17. For example: 'We hold music to be altogether too *laborious* a profession for women' (editorial in *The Musical World*, 11 April 1839, p. 222); see also Haweis, *Music and Morals*, p. 65.

18. See E. T. A. Hoffmann, 'Councillor Krespel' (1818) in *Tales of Hoffmann*, trans. R. J. Hollingdale (London: Penguin, 1982); G. Meredith, *Emilia in England* (1864; as *Sandra Belloni*, Westminster: Archibald Constable, 1902) and *Vittoria* (1866; London: Constable, 1924); G. Moore, *Evelyn Innes* (London: T. Fisher Unwin, 1898) and *Sister Theresa* (London: T. Fisher Unwin, 1901); and G. Du Maurier, *Trilby* (1894; London: Dent, 1931).

19. Offenbach, *Les contes d'Hoffmann*, p. 268.

20. See E. Moers, 'Performing heroinism: The myth of Corinne', in her *Literary Women* (London: The Women's Press, 1978), pp. 173–210. Also R. Morhmann, 'Women's work as portrayed in women's literature' in R.-E. B. Joeres and M. J. Haynes (eds), *German Women in the Eighteenth and Nineteenth Centuries* (Bloomington: Indiana Press, 1986), pp. 70–3.

21. Letter from Sand to Viardot, dated June 1842; cited by Fitzlyon, *The Price of Genius: A life of Pauline Viardot* (Lodnon: John Calder, 1964), p. 121.

22. G. Sand, *Consuelo: A romance of Venice* (1842), trans. unknown (New York: A. L. Burt, n.d.; repr. New York: Da Capo Press, 1979), pp. 335–7. See also the sequel, *The Countess of Rudolstadt*, trans. Fayette Robinson (London: A & F Denny, n.d.).

23. *ibid.*, p. 200.
24. *ibid.*, p. 599.
25. *ibid.*, p. 504.
26. *ibid.*, p. 709.
27. *ibid.*, p. 616.
28. G. Eliot, *Armgart*. Like Viardot, Armgart is a 'plain brown girl', who makes her début as Gluck's *Orpheus*, the role which marked the 'culminating point' of Viardot's career. Viardot's fictional representation as Consuelo is also evoked: Armgart's teacher, the composer Leo, is surely named after Leonardo Leo, an eighteenth-century composer whose music Consuelo uses to teach singing to the young Joseph Haydn. The truncation of Armgart's career and her final decision to teach is further reminiscent of Viardot's own situation at the time Eliot wrote the poem. Finally, Viardot is possibly reflected as the 'Paulina', who sings Beethoven's *Fidelio* (another of Viardot's most successful roles) on the night when Armgart had hoped to return to the stage.
29. *ibid.*, p. 105.
30. *ibid.*, p. 126.
31. *ibid.*, p. 75.
32. *ibid.*, pp. 95–6.
33. *ibid.*, p. 96.
34. *ibid.*, p. 97.
35. *ibid.*, p. 106.
36. *ibid.*, p. 76.
37. *ibid.*, p. 102–3.
38. See 'Liszt, Wagner, and Weimar', in T. Pinney (ed.) *Essays of George Eliot* (London: Routledge & Kegan Paul, 1963), pp. 98–9.
39. 'Armgart', p. 113.
40. *ibid.*, p. 119.
41. *ibid.*, p. 124.
42. *ibid.*, pp. 93–4.
43. *ibid.*, p. 138.
44. *ibid.*, p. 140.
45. Eliot, *Daniel Deronda* (1876; repr. London: Penguin Classics, 1986), p. 295.
46. *ibid.*, p. 729.
47. *ibid.*, p. 256.
48. *ibid.*, pp. 253–4.
49. *ibid.*, p. 728.
50. *ibid.*, p. 256.
51. *ibid.*, pp. 693–4.
52. *ibid.*, p. 730.
53. *ibid.*, p. 689.
54. *ibid.*, p. 691.
55. *ibid.*, p. 723.
56. *ibid.*, p. 730.
57. *ibid.*, pp. 687–8.
58. *ibid.*, p. 702.
59. *ibid.*, p. 727.
60. *ibid.*, p. 730.
61. W. Cather, *The Song of the Lark* (1915; London: Virago, 1982), p. 571.
62. *ibid.*, p. 266.
63. *ibid.*, p. 91. Viardot is clearly recognisable in Wunsch's description of the Spanish singer as '"ugly; big mouth, big teeth, no figure. . . . A pole, a post! But for the voice – *ach!* She have something in there, behind the eyes", tapping his temples.'

64. Commonly known in Italian as 'Che faro senza Euridice'; Cather here uses the German translation, 'Ach, ich habe sie verloren'.
65. *ibid.*, p. 237.
66. *ibid.*, p. 544.
67. *ibid.*, p. 550.
68. *ibid.*, p. 571.
69. *ibid.*, p. 274.
70. *ibid.*, p. 510.
71. Fitzlyon, *The Price of Genius*, *op. cit.*, p. 118.
72. C. L. Kellogg, *Memoirs of an American Prima Donna* (New York and London: G. P. Putnam, 1913), p. 314.
73. *ibid.*, p. 365.
74. M. W. Cushing, *The Rainbow Bridge* (New York: G. P. Putnam, 1954), p. 244.
75. Moers, *Literary Women*, *op. cit.*, p. 191.
76. F. R. Ritter, *Woman as a Musician: An art-historical study* (London: William Reeves, n.d.), pp. 8–12.
77. Graves, *The Greek Myths*, *op. cit.*, p. 245.
78. M. Bashkirtseff, *Journal*. trans. Mathilde Blind (1891; repr. London: Virago, 1985), p. 28.
79. *ibid.*, p. 416.
80. G. Atherton, *Adventures of a Novelist* (London: Cape, 1932), p. 118.
81. C. V. Stanford, *Studies and Memories* (London: Archibald Constable, 1908), p. 5. See also C. Ehrlich, *The Music Profession in Britain Since the Eighteenth Century* (Oxford: Clarendon Press, 1985), p. 110.
82. Anon. 'Singing lessons in Paris', *The Musical World*, 4 January 1890, p. 10.
83. K. Howard, *Confessions of an Opera Singer* (London: Kegan Paul, 1920), p. 261.
84. I. Glackens, *Yankee Diva: Lilian Nordica and the golden days of opera* (New York: Coleridge Press, 1963), p. 241.
85. J. Huncker, *Bedouins* (1920; London: T. Werner Laurie, n.d.), p. 108.
86. M. Garden and L. Biancolli, *Mary Garden's Story* (London: Michael Joseph, 1952), p. 137.
87. Undated letter of Mary Garden to her sponsor (Florence Mayer of Chicago), probably written in the autumn of 1897. I am indebted to Mario Goetschel and Dr David Mayer for granting me permission to publish this and the letter quoted below, note 90.
88. Garden and Biancolli, *Mary Garden's Story*, *op. cit.*, p. 271.
89. Christiansen, *Prima Donna*, *op. cit.*, p. 281.
90. Undated letter of Mary Garden to David L. Mayer of Chicago, probably written in the summer of 1899.
91. Garden and Biancolli, *Mary Garden's Story*, *op. cit.*, p. 272.
92. *ibid.*, p. 146.
93. *ibid.*, p. 137.
94. *ibid.*, p. 105; also pp. 145 and 268.
95. Huneker, *Bedouins*, *op. cit.*, p. 10.
96. Howard, *Confessions of an Opera Singer*, *op. cit.*, pp. 53–4.
97. *ibid.*, p. 43.
98. Huneker, *Bedouins*, *op. cit.*, p. 10.
99. Garden and Biancolli, *Mary Garden's Story*, *op. cit.*, p. 234.
100. J. Marcus, *Art and Anger* (Columbus: Ohio State University Press, 1988), pp. 10–12.
101. Cited by R. Christiansen, *The Grand Obsession* (London: Collins, 1988), pp. 362–4.
102. Garden and Biancolli, *Mary Garden's Story*, *op. cit.*, p. 119.
103. Cited by R. D. Fletcher, '"Our own" Mary Garden', *Chicago History*, vol. ii, no. i (Spring 1972), p. 42.

104. Garden and Biancolli, *Mary Garden's Story*, *op. cit.*, see p. 66, also p. 156.
105. Cited by Christiansen, *Prima Donna*, *op. cit.*, p. 280.
106. See, for example, C. Paglia, *Guardian*, 27 December 1990, p. 40; also R. Coward in the *Observer*, 5 May 1991, p. 52.
107. Garden and Biancolli, *Mary Garden's Story*, *op. cit.*, p. 263.
108. *ibid.*, p. 171.
109. Kellogg, *Memoirs of an American Prima Donna*, *op. cit.*, p. 323.

Yvette Guilbert: *La Femme Moderne* on the British stage

GERALDINE HARRIS

On Wednesday 9 May 1894 Yvette Guilbert, *la diseuse fin de siècle* and reigning 'diva' of the Parisian *café concert*, gave her first British performance at the Empire Music Hall in London. Her act caused some consternation amongst both critics and public. *The Times* described her reception as 'cordial but by no means enthusiastic' and concluded that her act was 'little calculated to appeal to a public unacquainted with the argot of the boulevards'.[1] Max Beerbohm's assessment was less polite: 'of course the audience applauds her, the educated part of it, lest it be thought not to understand her, the uneducated part of it because she receives a fabulous sum for her every performance.'[2] Even Harold Simpson, one of her most staunch admirers, desperately trying to make the best of it, had to admit that the audience was 'a little at a loss how to take her act',[3] and a favourable review from George Bernard Shaw was undermined by the admission that 'despite her superb diction I did not understand half her lines myself'.[4]

This reaction could hardly have been surprising to Guilbert. Most of the *chansons* she performed were written in a Parisian slang that would not necessarily be comprehensible to a native of the French provinces. Yet this problem does not seem to have occurred to anyone before she was booked at the Empire for a 'fabulous sum'. Exchange of artists from both the popular and legitimate stages across the Channel was not uncommon during this period. In the early 1880s British audiences had some difficulty understanding the text of Racine's *Phèdre* played by Bernhardt, but the force of her performance outweighed this problem. In her own field, Guilbert was not a lesser artist than Bernhardt, a fact acknowledged by other performers of quality, such as Eleanora Duse.[5]

115

The unintelligibility of Guilbert's performance was, in fact, not purely a question of language in the simplest sense but clearly related to questions of culture, class and expectations of a British audience with regard to a female music-hall performer. *Phèdre* as a 'classic' would, of course, be hard to follow, but surely the French equivalent of 'A little of what you fancy' should be easy?

Simpson attempted to explain it in terms of her repertoire as a reflection of 'national character':

> English songs as a rule, though they may dip into pathos, avoid direct tragedy. It is partly the outcome of our national character. The French as a nation are more hysterical and morbidly emotional than we are; prone to sudden transilience from comedy to tragedy and vice versa. . . . In our comedy songs too, we miss that light touch which makes the French *chansonette* so dainty a thing. One or two of the songs of this class which Yvette Guilbert sings have, when considered in the cold light of an English translation, a distinctly 'naughty' tendency. But the French have such a way of expressing these things that they become in their interpretation irresistibly droll and innocent of all offence.[6]

Ironically, Guilbert had already been described by one French critic as a 'very English artist',[7] and seldom seems to have shown signs of hysteria or morbid emotionalism in performance. In fact, the opposite was nearer the truth. Further, whilst most French commentators would have agreed on major differences between the *chanson* and the British popular song due to 'national character', Guilbert was clearly recognised as something very new, if not unique, in Paris.

The *café concert* was not the exact equivalent of the British music hall but many of the performers would have been fairly unproblematic to a British audience. Both Thérésa[8] and Mme Demay, to cite two 'typical' examples, used repertoires and performance styles very similar to Marie Lloyd.

Guilbert, however, presented a conundrum. Her songs were often not so much 'naughty', that is based on *double entendre*, as frankly dealing with sexual matters. Yet her performance was, as Beerbohm complained, 'full of nuances and half tones',[9] too subtle for the average Empire audience. Shaw felt it necessary to defend Guilbert in terms of the artist's right to deal with all aspects of life, even the most unsavoury, but at the same time thought she could

> furnish an object lesson to Miss Marie Lloyd and Miss Katie Lawrence and other eminent English prima donnas in order that they might be encouraged to believe that there is room in Music Hall singing for the art of classic self possession and delicacy, without any loss of gaiety'.[10]

Equally confusing to the British public, perhaps, was the fact that, whilst many of her songs were sung in the first person as a male speaking subject, she made no attempt at creating the external illusion of a masculine persona.

Critics were at a loss to find a performer who might be Guilbert's British equivalent. Eventually, it was Albert Chevalier, the male 'coster' singer, who was thought to be comparable; on several ocasions they shared the bill in England and in 1896 toured America together. Guilbert herself is noticeably silent over this association and generally the comparison seems strained. In attempting to establish common ground between the two, Harold Simpson was forced to contradict himself and qualify his statements. To summarise his argument, while they had much in common they actually presented a striking contrast. Max Beerbohm was more articulate when discussing a joint appearance at the Duke of York's Theatre in 1906:

> It seems appropriate that these two should be together. The name of each conjures up visions of the early nineties. Both were innovators in method and subject matter, Mme. Guilbert depicting in hard sharp outline the tragedies and comedies of the least pleasant persons in Paris, Mr Chevalier weaving a network of romance around costermongers. Altogether there is a distinct kinship between the two artists. And thus the differences between them have a certain significance as illustrating the differences between the French and English art.[11]

I would suggest that this 'kinship' was rather removed. Guilbert's act did embody certain specific elements within French culture of the 1890s, hence the sobriquet *la diseuse fin de siècle*. However, the manner in which she absorbed and transformed these elements sets her apart from Chevalier. His stage persona suggested a direct identification with the characters of the songs, while Guilbert had a highly complex relationship with the characters and contents of her repertoire: to the extent that Beerbohm commented, 'How she does it is (at the moment of watching) a mystery. And but for that mystery she couldn't do it'.[12]

What Guilbert brought to the Empire stage, to the confusion of the British audience, was *la Femme Moderne*. That is, firstly to use the term in a specific sense, she performed within a style of modernism directly inherited from Baudelaire. The way she manipulated this inheritance gives us a second, more colloquial, definition of her as a 'modern' female performer engaged with the problematic issue of the representation of 'woman' on stage. Finally, I would like to use this term in regard to Guilbert as a private individual to indicate that these operations were not completely unconscious and accidental.

The notion of Guilbert as *la Femme Moderne* is not entirely removed from the idea of the 'New Woman' but (to borrow from Simpson) while they have elements in common, they actually form a striking contrast for a number of reasons. The concept of the 'New Woman' seems to have been firmly situated within a middle-class idea of female emancipation. Although Guilbert's family was originally of solid bourgeois extraction, the failure of the family business and the desertion of her father meant that she had to go out to work at an early age. As for the majority of performers, a career within the *café concert* was for her an alternative to the sweat shop. The audiences in these venues were, like the characters in most of the songs, drawn predominantly from the working class or *petit bourgeoisie*. Latchkeys and cigarettes, the transgressive symbols associated with the popular construction of the 'New Woman', had no currency here and I have found no evidence of a treatment of a type even similar to the 'New Woman' within the *café-concert* songs.

A version of *la Femme Nouvelle* did certainly exist on the French legitimate stage. A general upsurge in French feminist activity in the 1890s included the foundation of a short-lived *Théâtre Feministe*, dedicated to the encouragement of women playwrights and composers. This initiative provoked discussion of the role and representation of women in theatre generally. In 1901 a special feature in *La Revue d'art dramatique* included articles on *la Femme Nouvelle* in plays written by both men and women. The plays cited seemed mainly to have dealt with the institution of marriage and the double moral standard in regard to adultery and sexual freedom. There is evidence of feminist activity as early as 1790, and in fact the words *la Femme Nouvelle* were used in the title of a feminist newspaper in 1832.[13] The development of an organised movement, however, was fractured and fragmented due to the general turbulence of nineteenth-century French politics. Women's issues emerged strongly during the frequent periods of unrest but were forcibly suppressed upon the re-establishment of order.

Feminism was also chiefly linked with several socialist groups but the divisions amongst these, together with the dominating influence of the Catholic majority, hindered the formulation of cohesive, coherent policies on key issues. It has also been suggested by Chafetz and Dworkin that France had a smaller proportion of literate, urban-middle-class women essential to the development of the women's movements in Britain and the United States.[14] The strongest elements in French feminism tended to be liberal and reformist, concerned with familial problems rather than suffrage, which is reflected in the fact that women in France did not get the vote until 1945.

Guilbert, then, perhaps typically of her class and nationality, seldom expressed any direct feminist political consciousness. In 1914 she was recorded as condemning the violence employed by English suffragettes. In 1916, however, she was a speaker at the American Congressional Union for Women's Suffrage, where she made a passionate spech declaring that women would never be free whilst being prepared to support 'Man . . . the eternal fighter, the eternal killer and destroyer'.[15] She now urged American women to be 'brutal' in their struggle for independence. The implicit separatism of this speech is contradicted by the fact that she herself was, by all accounts, very happily married to a German biochemist (Max Schiller) at the time. It is likely that the sources of this speech were more to do with the horrors of the First World War than a feminist consciousness.

Due to various socio-cultural factors, then, the links between Guilbert as *la Femme Moderne* and the 'New Woman' were most likely to exist in the spheres of family life and sexuality. Guilbert's relationship with Schiller appears to have been a model of 'role swapping', with him giving up both his country and career in order to support her, without assuming control. Apparently, he effaced himself to the extent of signing himself as 'Maxyvette' after her death.

In her biography of Guilbert, Bettina Knapp claims that there were 'echoes of feminism' in the 'innumerable depictions of wronged women'.[16] This remark actually fails to take into account the sources of her repertoire but it is true to say that many of the *chansons* she performed did recognise the existence of an active female sexuality. A notable example is Jean Lorrain's *Fleur de Berge*. Here the female narrator describes her relationship with her lover in explicitly erotic terms.

> J'étais foll' de lui et d'sa peau
> Y'm caréssait fallait voir comme
> C'était un gars, c'était un homme.

('I was crazy about him and his skin/ He used to caress me like anything/ He was a lad, he was a man'.)

In *The Song of my Life* Guilbert states with some puzzlement that the French publisher insisted on changing the first line quoted here, to 'Y'm'bassait la bouche, fou de ma peu' ('He kissed my mouth, mad about my skin'). Clearly, changing this line alters the emphasis in an important fashion, making the female character sexually passive rather than active. Guilbert describes the song as a whole as being about 'the delights of the senses' and half-way through we discover that the narrator has died of consumption and so presumably speaks from some unidentified after life. The song ends with a complaint: 'Heaven always does the dirty on you – you've got to die just when you are happy.' This conforms with nineteenth-century popular tradition, so clearly encoded within melodrama, that evidence of active female sexuality was usually punishable by death. However, the truly remarkable thing about this song was its interpretation by Guilbert. She sang it in the voice of a 'pure virgin', thereby working against the moral superstructure and allowing the audience to be 'deeply moved' rather than judgemental. On the other hand, this character, like most of the women in Guilbert's repertoire, was a prostitute and her 'gars' was her pimp. This form of love, then, was far from free.[17]

Equally, 'echoes of feminism' may be found in another of her *chansons*: Maurice Donnay's *Eros Vanné*, which apparently acknowledges the possibility of the female as desiring subject and also admits the fact of sexual love between women. Again the framework eventually mitigates against positive portrayals. This is a 'Jaded Eros'.

> Très vieux malgré mes vingt années
> Usé, blasé
> Car je suis né

Sur un lit de roses fanées.
Et je suis un Eros Vanné.

('Very old, despite my twenty years. Worn out, satiated/ Because I was born/ On a bed of faded roses. And I am a jaded Eros')

This is the Eros of Baudelaire's damned, born of a liaison between a 'red haired bookmaker and a tart in the backroom of a shop'. The 'amours Saphiques', as they are called here, are by turns pitied, celebrated and condemned. Guilbert cut out the verse referring to lesbian love when performing in the *café concert* due to complaints that the term *saphiques* was incomprehensible to the majority of the audience.[18]

This is not to deny the possibility of a retrospective feminist reading of Guilbert's act. However, this is not simply a question of representations of wronged women but involves a complex interplay of form, content and interpretation in performance. Apart from one or two of her own compositions, Guilbert's *chansons* were written by male *chansonniers* coming out of the literary avant-garde centred around the 'artistic cabarets', and in particular the Chat Noir. These *chansonniers* self-consciously took on the mantle of Baudelaire and within this type of modernism there is a certain ambiguous and paradoxical relationship between the writer and the written. Absorbing these paradoxes may have allowed Guilbert to work in 'the gaps' in between nineteenth-century notions of masculinity and femininity through the employment of something very like *Verfremsdungeffekt*. This subverted, or rather transcended, contemporary ideas concerning the female performer. The contrast she employed within *Fleur de Berge* indicates something of her technique on a simple level but to grasp fully its implications it is necessary to go back to Baudelaire.

Discussing her work in *The Song of my Life*, Guilbert stated: 'When I say "my" art I know that I have a right to claim it as mine, as it has been born of my own will-power. I am aware of how it came into being. I am its mother.'[19] It is interesting that Guilbert describes her art in terms of motherhood but this comment is even more significant when compared to a statement by Baudelaire on the problems of the modern artist. 'In the salon of 1845, will-power has to be well developed and always very fruitful to be able to give the stamp of uniqueness even to the second rate.'[20] Throughout the various volumes of her autobiography Guilbert frequently stresses the creation of her stage persona in terms of an exercise of will. In the 1880s the *café concert* was also generally considered to be 'second rate'. When she first decided to embark on a career in the concerts, Guilbert herself was appalled by the stupidity of the songs and the vulgarity of the performances. Her reaction was that she must 'strike an absolutely new note . . . something more artistic'.[21]

The critical consensus was that the *chanson* had been debased by exploitation within the form. Historically, the *chanson* had been the vehicle for the dissemination of either political opinions or the 'old gaulois spirit'. Political *chansonniers* such as Beranger, Dupont and Pottier had been acknowledged as both poets and social commentators. The old gaulois spirit referred not to 'naughtiness' but the frank acceptance of the earthier side of human nature as demonstrated by Rabelais. The *café concert* had transformed this minor branch of poetry into a silly, repetitive excuse for smutty jokes. By the late 1880s a reaction had already set in. Mme Saint-Ange, owner and manager of the Eden *café concert*, had had some success with a series of evenings based around the *chansons classiques*, reviving songs from earlier in the century. Guilbert wanted to transform the second-rate, utilising something more in sympathy with her own era.

Even before discovering her repertoire, she was already creating a stage presence in keeping with Baudelairian modernism. She rejected the elaborate dress, cosmetics, hairstyles and jewellery that were the norm for female performers within the *café concert* and created a style based on bizarre simplicity. This was a plain dress, no jewels, simply styled hennaed hair, no cosmetics other than bright red lips and, most importantly, long black evening gloves. Guilbert originally claimed that the choice of black rather than the more usual white was purely a question of economy but later agreed that they also emphasised the thinness of her arms and drew attention to her very restrained use of gesture.

Black gloves also functioned as signifiers on numerous levels for her audience. The notable predominance of black, particularly in male clothing in the nineteenth century, had been analysed from Baudelaire to Louis Veuillot. Baudelaire wrote: 'Is this not the attire that is needed by our epoch, suffering and dressed up to its thin narrow shoulders in the symbol of constant mourning.'[22] Guilbert was almost the personification of this quotation, quite literally dressed up to her famously thin narrow shoulders in black. In an evocation of *fin-de-siècle* Paris, Maurice Donnay commented:

> And in 1890 there were in ideas and morals, an ease and freedom which we found very new. We breathed the air not of liberty but of liberties and that air at first seemed very light. At the Moulin Rouge the *quadrille naturaliste* was danced, a symbol of *La Vie Parisienne*. Soon the expression *Fin de Siècle* flew from mouth to mouth. We went out of Boulangerism into Pantheism. We spoke of the black horse of the brave General, the black corset of Mme. Marnier, the black gloves of Yvette Guilbert, women wore black stockings, we sang the refrains of the Chat Noir and saw *La Vie en Rose*.'[23]

The black gloves and the Black Cat were, of course, related. Black indicated the bohemian, an alternative, slightly seedy elegance, perverse, provocative sexuality, the satanic, death, decadence, the outsider – the modernist. Outside the Chat Noir, the sign showed a black cat trampling on a goose (the bourgeoisie) with the inscription underneath 'Passer-by. Be modern.'

As the Donnay quotation indicates, many of the writers and artists gathered around the Chat Noir were undergoing a period of youthful rebellion before taking their places within 'the establishment'. They created and inhabited a myth of bohemian Montmartre, where the chief concern was to *épater la bourgeoisie*'. Some of the *chansons* emerging from the Chat Noir and performed by Guilbert were written to fulfil this function, such as MacNab's *Macabre Dance of the Foetuses* or Jouy's *How to Incinerate a Corpse*. Other *chansons* dabbled in social satire, particularly around the theme of bourgeois sexual hypocrisy, as in Donnay's *Le Petit Cochon* (about a *ménage à trois*), or 'Xanrof's *Le Fiacre* (where an adulterous couple accidentally run over the woman's husband with their coach). Such *chansons*, written under ironic modernist influence, tended to be classified as *Zutiste*[24] or *La Chanson ironique*, but the songs that became collectively known as *La Chanson moderne*, typified by the works of Aristide Bruant and Jules Jouy, were more clearly marked by the spirit of Baudelaire to the point of plagiarism. Jouy's *La Chant des ouvriers*, for example, can be clearly seen as a less effective reworking of *Le Crépuscule du matin*. Chiefly, however, *chansonniers* like Bruant and Jouy took up Baudelaire's subject matter and something of his persona as a poet.

Earlier in the century Baudelaire had complained of contemporary writers who confined themselves to official or historical topics on the principle that 'There are subjects from private life which are heroic in quite another way. The spectacle of elegant life and the thousands of irregular existences led in the basements of the big city by criminals and kept women'. [25] The Chat Noir writers seized upon the 'heroic' aspects of these 'irregular existences' and, like Baudelaire, constantly returned to the themes of the criminal, the prostitute, the drug addict and the *chiffoniers* (rag-pickers), the outcasts or, rather, the 'damned'. These *chansons* expressed the modernist's vision of the big city as a jungle or prairie, a mysterious place full of danger inhabited by 'apaches' and 'mohicans'.

In London in 1894, Guilbert presented a repertoire that included several 'ironic' or *Zutiste chansons* such as *Les Vièrges*, a song based around a series of sly jokes about virginity. It was with *la Chanson moderne* proper, however, that she had the most impact and created the most confusion. *Les Vièrges* clearly signals its use of irony, whilst Bruant's *À la Villette* or Jouy's *La Soularde*, like most of such *chansons*, operate through an ironic contrast of form and content which is far more subtle. Stylistically, they read and sound like bitter nursery rhymes. They usually have a three-line structure with a two- or three-word refrain and a musical accompaniment that is similarly simple and repetitive. In contrast to this deliberate naivety, the content is very adult. In the first verse of *À la Villette* the 'hero' is introduced:

> Il avait pas encor vingt ans
> Il connait pas ses parents
> On l'appelait Toto Larpiette
> À la Villette.

('He was not yet twenty/ He didn't know who his parents were/ They called him Toto Larpiette/ In la Villette.')

As in *Fleur de Berge*, it is not until verse 6 that we realise that the narrator here is Larpiette's girlfriend/prostitute. She gives the bare details of his life:

De son métier i'faissait rien
Dans l'jour i'baladait son chien
La nuit i'comptait ma galette
À la Villette.

('He didn't have a job/ In the daytime he walked his dog/ At night he counted my takings/ In la Villette.')

Again like *Fleur de Berge* this is a love story with a tragic ending:

I'm aimait que j'l'amais
Nous nous aurions quittés jamais
Si la police étais pas faite
À la Villette.

('He loved me as much as I loved him/ We would never have parted/ If the police hadn't done it/ In la Villette.')

Exactly why the police arrested him is never made clear, except that generally the fate of men from La Villette seems to be to end up in La Roquette prison on the guillotine:

La dernier fois que je l'ai vu
Il avait l'torse moitié nu
Et le cou pris dans la Lunette
À la Roquette.

('The last time I saw him/ He was bare chested/ With his neck in the guillotine/ In la Roquette.')[26]

La Soûlarde ('The Drunkard') is very similar in style and structure, except that the identity of the narrator is never revealed. Again in the first verse the main character of the drunkard is introduced in similar terms to Larpiette:

On n'lui aucun parent
À Clichy, pour cent francs par an
À couch par terre, dans une mansarde
La soûlarde.

('Nobody knows her parents/ In Clichy, for a hundred francs a year/ She sleeps on the floor of a garret/ The drunkard.')

The song describes various daily incidents in the drunkard's life, including the taunts and casual violence she suffers at the hands of the local children. It ends with the message:

Pourtant ouvrier ou gamin,
Laisse passer son chemin,
Qui sait le noir souci que garde,
La soûlarde?

Peut-être que pleurant un fils,
Songeant au bonheur de jadis,
Le soir, ell'trouv' sa fin tarde,
La soûlarde.

('Therefore, worker or child/ Let her pass,/ Who knows what dark secret she hides,/ The drunkard?/ Perhaps she weeps for a son/ (or) dreams of happier days,/ One evening she will find her end at last,/ The drunkard.')[27]

While *À La Villette* is not without a certain black humour, *La Soûlarde* is a much more realistic song; but in both the characters are given an heroic status through the inevitability of fate. As Stanley V. Makower wrote at the time, 'It is just this poetry of vision which robs these songs of all their horror, for it is in the beautifying of the terrible that lies the supremacy of her art.'[28]

Guilbert's British audience were then, confronted with songs that allowed the criminal, the prostitute and the drunkard an 'heroic' status that was complicated but not entirely undermined by an underlying irony in formal terms. This irony stemmed partly from a self-conscious sense of decadence but also from the ambiguous Baudelairian relationship between subject matter and poet. As Walter Benjamin put it:

The poetry of apachedom appears in an uncertain light. Do the dregs of society supply the heroes of the big city? Or is the hero the poet who fashions his work from such material? The theory of modernism admits both.[29]

The theory of modernism does not only admit both, it admits the possibility of both at the same time. In Baudelairian terms the poet and the apaches are brothers, *semblables*,[30] both suffering from the sense of futility engendered by life in the big city. The poet also identifies with the criminal hero because they are both part of the fabric of the city and yet set apart, marginalised. Like the *Flaneur* who was both part of the crowd and yet isolated amongst it, the poet enters into the world of the outcasts and yet as an artist remains at the same time an observer.

When Aristide Bruant set up Le Mirliton,[31] his own cabaret, performing his own songs, part of his enormous success owed much to this ambiguous relationship. For his predominantly bourgeois audience he embodied Toto Larpiette and yet was clearly, in fact, a *chansonnier* and a businessman.

Guilbert appears to have absorbed this relationship into her act. She represented the characters while remaining aloof or, it could be said, performed the *gestus* whilst remaining, personally, an observer. Simpson described this technique as 'being uncontaminated' by what she performed, whilst Stanley V. Makower put it more clearly:

You positively see the drunken woman, with dishevelled hair and bloodshot eyes, reeling down the street, pursued by a jeering crowd – but in the meantime Yvette Guilbert, in modern evening dress, is standing comparatively still on stage with that backdrop representing a Mauresque palace which has become the traditional drop scene at the Empire Theatre.

The effect that Yvette Guilbert produces is far removed from that of external realism. If we were to see a person imitate accurately a drunken woman, so accurately, in fact that, were it not for the stage we should be unable to guess that she was acting, we should feel much the same physical disgust that is aroused in us when we see a drunken woman reeling down the street. We should be no more edified than by the ingenuity of the man who exhibited a picture with a real face peering through the canvas. But when Yvette Guilbert is telling you about the drunken woman, though you shudder, it is not with disgust – for the thing is transfigured by her into something different. You see the scene but you see it in a new light, with something of the light that goes to make the genius of the performer and which she has such a rare power of communicating. When she steps outside of the characters of the scene, crying out against the profanity of ridicule and raising a plea for the woman to pass unmolested, she conveys in her voice a suggestion of that universal harmony which binds the world together.[32]

Aided by the modernist influence of the songs, or rather in the spirit of the songs, Guilbert showed the characters and situations whilst remaining at a distance from them as a performer. This sense of separation with the option of 'stepping outside' is partly inherent in the structure of the songs through the ironic juxtaposition of form and content. This is heightened by the frequent use of an unidentified narrative voice or by the revelation of the narrator's identity being deferred for several verses. This forces the listener to reconsider and reassess information already provided.

In other songs, written in the first person, Guilbert achieved distance through other means, for example the 'pure' voice of *Fleur de Berge*. In *Ma Tête*, portraying a male murderer, she employed a token piece of costume, a black 'hooligan's' cap. In the last verse the protagonist predicts his death on the guillotine and, on the final rendition of the refrain 'Ma Tête', Guilbert dropped the cap (which was weighted) to the floor with a dull thud. The effect was dramatic, suggesting the sound of the guillotine but at the same time the removal of the cap stripped away any illusion of Guilbert playing a character. Once again the audience was left with the female performer in evening dress.[33]

All these devices and techniques were also aided by her unusual physical presence. Her stage appearance and the black gloves marked her as an 'outsider', herself a bohemian. Further, critics continually remarked upon her restrained use of gesture, her stillness on stage. Guilbert apparently did not illustrate or act out her songs. In his comparison with Chevalier, Beerbohm complains that Chevalier makes a 'dozen gestures' a 'dozen grimaces' where one would do, and that 'He suits the action to the word so instantly that every word almost has an action all to itself.'[34]

This sort of vivacity, of playing up a song, was fairly normal music-hall practice in both Britain and France, due partly to performance conditions. Beerbohm then goes on to describe Guilbert:

> I do not think that her face, voice and hands are more naturally eloquent than
> Mr Chevalier's. But she knows just how much use to make of them. Notice in
> the famous 'Ma Grandmère', how perfectly she differentiates the words of the
> girl from those of the old woman, yet with hardly a perceptible pause, with
> hardly a perceptible change of key. Something happens in her eyes and we
> know that it is the girl speaking, and then again, in another instant we see the
> old woman. One can imagine the pauses with which Mr Chevalier would mark
> these transitions and the violent contortions he would go through before he got
> under weigh.[35]

Guilbert's performance was intellectual. Although she did at times create
an illusion of the characters she performed, she did so without recourse to
'external realism'. She 'showed' or 'told' the characters rather than attempting
to impersonate, and could (and frequently did) revert at any second to her own
persona as a performer.

In such ways the lives of 'the dregs of society' were described and demonstrated in a manner that, while not entirely unromantic, was neither sentimental nor moralising. The audience was never allowed to lose sight of Guilbert
as a performer and so although the content of the songs was often potentially
shocking, the performance was not. Makower wrote scornfully of those who
attempted to define her as a 'wicked sparkling soubrette'[36] on the grounds that
they had heard that she sang 'the most indecent songs with the most absurd
innocence'. Her style was not that of 'absurd innocence', suggesting the use
of false naivety, but a highly sophisticated interpretation and use of a particular modernist ethos. As such, her practice may be related to some of
the most important debates within twentieth-century theatre. Just as with
feminism, there were, of course, various strands and different developments
within modernism but all modernist theatre practitioners shared certain concerns. Both Artaud and Brecht, to take two apparently opposed examples,
however diverse their intentions, were engaged in the search for new forms,
new theatrical vocabularies that corresponded to the needs of the modern
period. Both were also fundamentally concerned with the issue of 'imitation'
or 'impersonation' versus the notion of 'performance' in the realm of acting
theory. Clearly, it would be possible to discuss Guilbert's work in relation to
either theorist. Her connection with the Chat Noir and the fact that later in life
she became interested in both psychoanalysis and eastern mysticism would
seem to link her to Artaud. In fact, she represented an earlier strand of
modernism more engaged with a vague sort of social realism, and never
became involved with either the Dada or Surrealist movements. It is therefore
more interesting and relevant to discuss her particular style of modernism
with reference to Brecht.

The influence of cabaret forms on Brechtian theory is well documented and
it is possible to trace a direct line descending from Guilbert, through Wedekind to Brecht himself. Despite the obvious political complications, Guilbert
apparently felt a special affinity with German culture that was strengthened

by her marriage to Schiller. Recounting some of her tours outside France, she described Germany as the most 'cultivated' and 'responsive' country, going on to declare:

> For twenty two seasons before the first World War I showed them the mind of France and of the Montmartre of my early days. It was I who inspired the German 'cabarets' which were started in hundreds after my first visit in 1897.[37]

It is difficult entirely to substantiate this claim, as the founding of the German cabaret tradition is normally attributed to other, earlier sources. However, as with the modernist cabarets in the Netherlands, Spain, Poland, Russia, Sweden and Zurich, these sources all eventually lead back to the Chat Noir. Many of those directly responsible for establishing this form in Germany, including Wedekind, had already visited Paris and absorbed the spirit of the *cabarets artistiques* before Guilbert's German début. The satirical journal *Simplicissimus* (which began life in 1896) was modelled on the *zutiste*, *Gil Blas* and frequently published translations of Bruant's *chansons*. Marc Henry, the founder of the celebrated Eleven Executioners cabaret in Munich, was himself French. In Paris, he had been a regular at the Lapin Agile[38] and was familiar enough with proceedings at the Chat Noir to reproduce them when the Executioners opened in 1901. Henry was certainly resident in Germany by 1897. Since, however, the first German cabarets did not appear until the turn of the century it seems reasonable for Guilbert to perceive her appearances as an important stimulus, if not actually the sole inspiration for this movement. In any case, the influence of the Chat Noir and of Bruant in particular are incontestable and for the German public, Guilbert would have embodied the more accessible and popular face of both the cabaret and the *chansonnier*.

The similarities between Bruant and Wedekind in terms of stage persona are striking. Brecht's famous obituary of Wedekind in performance is a remarkable echo of accounts of Bruant at his own cabaret, the Mirliton. They both sang in monotonous, metallic, harsh tones, to the barest, simplest accompaniment. They both presented threatening and 'plebeian' physical appearances. Actually, Wedekind's songs, taken alone, indicate a broader range of influences, some of them owing to specifically Germanic popular forms although many of them are distinctly Chat Noiresque in subject matter and tone. Even so, the parallels are too notable to be coincidental, and even more significantly there is again an analogue between the Guilbert/Bruant association and Wedekind's connection to Marya Delvard.

Delvard was a *diseuse* of French origin who became one of the star attractions at the Eleven Executioners. She plainly modelled herself on Guilbert to the point of impersonation. Posters for the Executioners show all the familiar Guilbert trademarks but in an exaggerated mode. Like Guilbert, Delvard was noted for the simplicity of her costume. In the early years this was a tightly fitting black dress, but later she also wore the same sort of low-cut green gown

featured on the posters advertising Guilbert in the 1890s. Like Guilbert her
plainly styled red hair contrasted with the pallor of a face relieved only by a
gash of red lipstick. Like Guilbert she was sparing in her use of gesture and
like Guilbert she was thought to represent a decadent, deathly modernity.[39]

Delvard often performed *chansons* by Bruant but her repertoire came chiefly
from German writers. Some of her greatest successes were with her interpretations of Wedekind, and her performance of his *chanson*, *Ilse*, helped to
establish her reputation and made the song famous. (*Ilse*, incidentally, is very
similar to *Fleur de Berge*.) Wedekind and Delvard together may be considered as having established a performance style for cabaret singers in
Germany that then informed, and still informs, the delivery of songs by Brecht
and Weill. This style did not develop from some generalised 'torch' singing
tradition but was unmistakably drawn from Bruant and Guilbert, who were
both considered innovators within their own milieu. Equally, many Brecht/
Weill songs recall Bruant, and certain numbers such as *Surabay Johnny*
would not have excited comment as part of Guilbert's repertoire.

In fact, in 1937 Guilbert played Mrs Peachum in a production of *L'Opéra
de Quat'sous* at the Théâtre de L'Éoile in Paris, and further research and
analysis might provide evidence of an even closer connection with Brecht
himself. The links are sufficiently clear, however, to suggest that Guilbert
may be considered a 'modern' performer in that, directly or indirectly, her
techniques foreshadow some Brechtian practice and theory. Therefore her
performance style raises issues that are still of concern to feminist theatre
theorists, particularly in relation to *Verfremsdungeffekt* and the potential of
the use of gestic acting in addressing the problems of gender in performance.
In the course of her act she was able to present male characters without any of
the sexual ambiguities of 'travesti' or cross-dressing. Further, she achieved
the portrayal of a range of female characters (mainly prostitutes), not as
'wronged women' or indeed as 'objects' but in such a way as to encourage
audiences to accept their simple humanity and suspend moral judgement.

In terms of her private life, Guilbert also seems to have overcome some of
the problems caused for the female artist by being defined mainly through
their sexuality. In *Struggles and Victories*, Harold Simpson includes a chapter
on 'Yvette Guilbert the woman', and yet this turns out to be a description of
her as a performer with no sense of her as a private individual. Few critics
ever discussed her in terms of her gender, and Makower remarked that it
was impossible to guess what she might be like off stage, from watching her
perform.[40] This is not to indicate a lack of distinctive personality, nor was the
absence of a conventional sexual presence necessarily negative, for it accorded
Guilbert freedom as an artist denied to other more sexually defined female
performers. Stars like Bernhardt, Terry and Duse frequently found their
personal lives invaded and their careers inhibited by the limited and clearly
defined manner in which each was perceived to represent different aspects of
'femininity'. Guilbert's off-stage existence was far from uneventful and she

did not avoid publicity, yet the press seldom showed an interest in the more intimate and prurient elements of her personal life.

Guilbert's own writings indicate a serious concern for the problems of the female performer. In an article entitled 'The actress of tomorrow' for *The London Evening Standard* she describes how this actress would be extensively educated, well travelled and multilingual, and concludes:

> The actress of tomorrow and this will be one of her greatest victories, will be no mere doll woman to pander to desire. She will not have to struggle any longer against dull prejudice and against social offence. Serious books will have taught her morality and the simplicity of her attitudes will defend her against all attacks upon her private sentiments. In her the woman will disappear, yielding her throne which this time will be respected to the High Priestess of Expressionism, Priestess of Noble Thought and her efforts will not be without effect upon her wisdom, for much reading of philosophy will have freed her from exaggerated ambitions and private vanities. She will pay more attention to the condition of her soul than to her face.[41]

Despite the elevated prose, this is an attempt to redefine the position and negotiate the issues for the female performer in a profession where they were expected to 'pander to desire'. In the 1920s she also wrote an incisive and perceptive analysis of what she describes as the 'unhealthy taste' for the child woman on the American stage. In the 1930s she engaged in a lively correspondence with her friend Sigmund Freud when he suggested that her act was based on the acting out of her own 'repressed desires'. Her quite angry reply seems to accept a psychological interpretation to the extent that her letter uses several terms and concepts that could have been taken directly from Stanislavsky's *An Actor Prepares*. This aside, Guilbert asserted that her work was actually intuitive and anti-logical and her portrayal of characters was based on her ability to empathise rather than her own personal problems. At such times she seems strikingly contemporary in her attitude to performance, combining Brecht, Stanislavsky and a personal, female sensibility.

Guilbert achieved many of the goals that she set for the 'actress of tomorrow' herself and was obviously an individual who would have been remarkable in any period. Shaw described his first sight of her at the London press reception in 1894 in these terms: 'When the young lady appeared, it needed only one glance to see that here was no mere Music Hall star but one of the half dozen ablest persons in the room.'[42] He goes on to call her a 'female masterspirit', and although the linguistic paradox inherent in this term probably indicates more about Shaw than Guilbert, it does suggest how Guilbert, in public and private, resisted and challenged the nineteenth-century norms of femininity and established her kinship with the New Woman.

At one point, describing the failures and rejections of her early career in *The Song of my Life*, Guilbert stated that she carried on because 'I knew I was more intelligent than they and I could become anything I chose.'[43] This statement was not pure arrogance. Despite her lack of formal education after the age of twelve, by 1894 Guilbert was already a serious student of the medieval *chanson*, beginning to collect and collate over 60,000 *chansons* dating from the twelfth century. These songs formed the basis of her second repertoire at the turn of the century, and in 1908 she gave a series of lectures, illustrated with songs, on 'Women in the song from the medieval period to the present day'. In 1916 she was invited to lecture on the medieval *chanson* at Bryn Mawr College in America and performed in the same capacity at the University of Vienna in 1924. In 1921 her achievements in this field were officially recognised through her election to the Société des Anciens Textes.

In the course of her career she wrote two novels, *La Vedette* in 1901 and *Les Demi Vielles* in 1903, although authorship of *La Vedette* has been disputed. She also wrote several volumes of autobiography and many newspaper articles. In 1910 she founded an *École de Chanson* for girls of working-class parents in Paris and in 1921 the Yvette Guilbert School of Theatre in New York. She continued to perform in the music hall, on the legitimate stage and for film and radio right up until her death in 1944.

More pertinent to this discussion, Guilbert's interest in the *chanson* extended into mainstream poetry and from the turn of the century she gave several recitations and lectures on the work of Villon, Rambaud, Verlaine and of course Baudelaire. A lecture given on Baudelaire in Britain in 1936 was poorly received but evoked a warmer response when she repeated it at the Salle Chopin in Paris in the following year. A critic from *L'Ère Nouvelle* commented:

> One went to the Salle Chopin a little out of curiosity. How would a music hall singer speak of a writer whom some people compare to a father of the church? Now Madame Yvette is as learned as she is penetrating. She made in her lecture three points:

> The idea that many of the poems of Baudelaire suggest a stage set so that one could say that this artist was a dramatic poet; the declaration that Baudelairian hysteria is not an indication of sexuality but hypersensitivity; and a corrosive and moving evocation of the life of Baudelaire.[44]

This lecture was apparently also later given at the Sorbonne. Whether Guilbert was as familiar with his work in the earlier stages of her career is a matter for speculation but considering the artistic and literary circles in which she moved, it is reasonable to assume that she was and that this lecture was the product of a long association. The sense of dramatic potential within Baudelaire's poetry and the unusual interpretation of his relation to sexuality seem self-evident influences on her performance in the 1890s. Whether her embodiment of the spirit of this style of modernism was conscious or unconscious, Guilbert was clearly one of the first modernist performers and a radical innovator in ways that are still relevant.

Much of the formal experimentation that has taken place within the arts during this century emerged from out of the artistic cabaret tradition that was originally initiated by the Chat Noir. Britain's slowness in developing its own modernist or avant-garde movements is a reflection, if not a result, of the singular lack of interest that has always been evinced in this form. In 1912 an Austrian, Frida Strindberg, opened the Cabaret Theatre Club (or, as it became known, the Cave of the Golden Calf) in London. Her chief aim was to stage the works of her former husband, the Swedish dramatist. Despite the collaboration of Jacob Epstein, Augustus John and Wyndham Lewis, the club soon became mainly a venue for drinking and dancing. It was particularly popular with officers from the Brigade of Guards. Marinetti performed there in 1913, but overall this attempt to found a modernist cabaret in Britain rapidly disintegrated and failed to make a significant impression. Compare this to the impact and importance of the Four Cats in Barcelona in 1897, the Eleven Executioners in Munich in 1901, the Green Balloon in Cracow in 1905, the Bat in Vienna in 1906, the Bat in Moscow in 1908, the Stray Dog in St Petersburg in 1911 or Cabaret Voltaire in Zurich in 1916.

When Guilbert, the popular representative of the early manifestations of this movement, first appeared in Britain the native theatre was still only just coming to terms with realism and naturalism. The concept of the New Woman was just becoming current and meeting resistance. No wonder, then, that British music-hall audiences found *la Femme Moderne* incomprehensible.

Notes

1. *The Times*, Thursday 10 May 1894.
2. M. Beerbohm, *Around Theatres*, 2 vols (London: William Heinnman, 1924), vol. I, p. 59.
3. H. Simpson, *Struggles and Victories*, with a Preface by Yvette Guilbert (London: Mills and Boon, 1910), p. 237.
4. G. B. Shaw cited *ibid.*, p. 241.
5. Guilbert and Duse were close friends from 1892 until Duse's death in 1922. They frequently discussed the possibility of working together but their plans never came to fruition.
6. Simpson, *Struggles and Victories*, op. cit., p. 263.
7. Jean Lorrain cited by P. Leslie, *A Hard Act to Follow* (London: Paddington Press, 1978), p. 99.
8. Thérésa (Emma Valadon) was the most celebrated performer in the history of the *café concert* before Guilbert.
9. Beerbohm, *Around Theatres*, op. cit., vol. I, p. 59.
10. G. B. Shaw cited by Simpson, *Struggles and Victories*, op. cit., p. 243.
11. Beerbohm, *Around Theatres*, op. cit., vol. II, p. 243.
12. *ibid.*, p. 246.
13. *La Tribune des Femmes*, founded August 1832 by a group of Saint Simonian women and so a 'socialist–feminist' publication.
14. J. S. Chafetz and A. G. Dworkin, *Female Revolt* (Totowa, NJ: Rowman and Allenheld, 1986), p. 127.

15. Cited by Bettina Knapp, *That was Yvette: The biography of the great diseuse* (London: Fredreich Muller, 1966), p. 224.

16. *ibid.*

17. Y. Guilbert, *The Song of my Life*, trans. Beatrice de Holthoir (London: George G. Harrap, 1929), p. 224.

18. *ibid.*

19. *ibid.*, p. 179.

20. C. Baudelaire, *Œuvres*, ed. Yves Gerard Le Dantec (Paris: Pléiade, 1931–2), vol. II, p. 26.

21. Guilbert, *The Song of my Life, op. cit.*, p. 45.

22. Baudelaire, *Œuvres, op. cit.*, vol. II, p. 134.

23. M. Donnay, *Autour du Chat Noir* (Paris: Arthène Fayard, 1924), pp. 43–4.

24. *Zutiste* or *Zutisme* roughly translates as 'care for nothing' or rather 'don't give a damn'.

25. Baudelaire, *Œuvres, op. cit.*, vol. II, p. 234.

26. Cited by Simpson, *Struggles and Victories, op. cit.*, pp. 324–5.

27. *ibid.*, pp. 317–19.

28. Cited *ibid.*, p. 220.

29. W. Benjamin, *Charles Baudelaire* (London: New Left Books, 1973), p. 80.

30. See Baudelaire, Prologue, *Fleurs du Mal*, any edition.

31. Bruant opened le Mirliton in 1885, purely as a commercial venture entertaining a broader audience than the Chat Noir. He liked to present himself and was accepted as *le chansonnier du peuple*. In fact, he had this legend inscribed above each of his three residences, including his country house. To be fair, he did spend some time in the early years working for the railway. F. Borgex, in *Le Fin d'un siècle* (Paris: Dentu, 1956), p. 154, summed up the opinion of many of Bruant's contemporaries when he stated, 'All things considered he had the soul of a bourgeois skunk.' Guilbert, however, described him as one who 'loved the down and outs as St Francis loved the lepers, in all pity' (*Song of my Life, op. cit.*, p. 123).

32. Cited by Simpson, *Struggles and Victories, op. cit.*, pp. 320–1.

33. *ibid.*, p. 322.

34. Beerbohm, *Around Theatres, op. cit.*, vol. II, p. 249.

35. *ibid.*

36. Cited by Simpson, *Struggles and Victories, op. cit.*, p. 248.

37. Guilbert, *The Song of my Life, op. cit.*, pp. 236–7.

38. M. Henry (Achille Georges d'Ailly-Vaucheret). The Lapin Agile was a lesser *cabaret artistique*.

39. Brecht on Wedekind:

> There he stood brutal, ugly and dangerous, with close cropped red hair, his hands in his pockets and one felt that the devil himself couldn't shift him. . . . A few weeks ago at the Bonbonniere he sang his own songs to a guitar accompaniment in a brittle voice, slightly monotonous and quite untrained. No singer ever gave me such a shock, such a thrill. It was the man's intense energy which allowed him to defy sniggering ridicule and proclaim his brazen hymn to humanity. (cited and translated by J. Willet, *Brecht on Theatre* (New York: Hill and Wang, 1964), pp. 3–4)

Arthur Symons on Bruant: 'He sang his own songs to his own music in a loud monotonous voice without emphasis, always walking to and fro' (A. Symons, *Colour Studies in Paris* (New York: E.P. Dutton, 1918), p. 63).

A. Zeveas on Bruant:

> a strong voice in which he deliberately exaggerated the plebeian accents. . . . A large man, pale, wearing a velvet jacket. There was no lack of talent, he sang true, having a brazen voice with a power and penetration that was extraordinary . . . the success of his songs where the filth and suffering of the lowest, all the abominable afflictions of this social

hell, shouts and spits its evil, in vile words of blood and fire. (A. Zeveas, *Aristide Bruant* (Paris: Editions de la Nouvelle Critique, 1943), p. 42)

Hans Carossa on Marya Delvard:

She did not perform as dead still as she appears in illustrations, nevertheless, an unexpected encounter with her in solitude might have really frightened someone. She was frightfully pale, one thought involuntarily of sin, vampiric cruelty and death. (cited by H. B. Segal, *Turn Of The Century Cabaret* (New York: Columbia University Press, 1987), p. 151)

Henri Lavedon on Guilbert: 'she is a poster . . . a macabre and insolent poster that makes one shudder' (H. Lavedon, *Yvette Guilbert: Sa carrière ses chansons* (Paris: Press collection, Bibliotéque de L'Arsenal, n.d.).

Jean Lorrain on Guilbert: 'her long thin body, the absence of gesture which contrasts to the almost diabolic distortions and grimaces of her bloodless face' (cited by Leslie, *A Hard Act to Follow, op. cit.*, p. 139).

40. Cited by Simpson, *Struggles and Victories, op. cit.*, p. 230.
41. *ibid.*, p. 173.
42. *ibid.*, p. 242.
43. Guilbert, *The Song of my Life, op. cit.*, p. 51.
44. Cited by Knapp, *That Was Yvette, op. cit.*, p. 291.

PART IV

Venturesome Women

Female Daredevils

HELEN DAY

Traditional theatre history is too often conducted on principles of segregation and exclusivity. Historians sometimes discriminate excessively and inappropriately – creating and imposing artificial hierarchies, drawing needless distinctions between texts or performances in the 'high' or 'literary' culture and those in popular entertainment. Women's theatre history, on the other hand – perhaps only because the study of women's history is still too young to have fallen into the trap of inappropriate discrimination – is inclusive rather than exclusive and without imposed hierarchies. The high and the popular co-exist and have equal status. The suffragist dramatist, the actress, the female daredevil and the female spectators in their respective audiences are all facets of the same world and are reflections of the same pressures. There is no insistence that these women be ranked and no gain in determining which of these activities is the more skilled or prestigious or significant.

However, there are unavoidable differences. The female daredevil, by her very existence, by her clamour for attention and by her (or by her promoters') insistence on her singularity, would appear to draw attention to her distinctiveness from other women. But so too does this dashing and audacious female distinguish herself from men. She does what few can or dare do. If she is not an element of high seriousness in the theatre, she is largely, although not exclusively, a product and a process of the century that produced the more up-market version of the woman who states her claim for attention and equality in the suffragette drama or the plays of the Kingsway and Court and Manchester Gaiety Theatres. The female daredevil is not without antecedents, but at the nineteenth century's beginning she is far from numerous, and it may not be too much of an exaggeration to insist that these women came

137

out of nothing and yet, by the century's end, had become a clearly identifiable group.

The existence of the female daredevil invites a cluster of questions: what, in the first place, is a daredevil or *casse-cou*, a neck-breaker? Where and when and for whom did she perform? What values and biases and enthusiasms did her audiences bring to performances, and to what extent were these pre-existent attitudes re-inforced or contradicted by the performance? What were her earnings, and how did they compare to a male daredevil's? How and what did she perform? How was she trained in her craft? What was the nature of her life away from her professional existence? I hope to address these questions, but not all answers are within reach.

My intention is to restrict my consideration of the female daredevil to two continuous and perhaps not wholly separate areas of showbusiness:[1] women in circus and women in early aviation, specifically ballooning and para-chuting. The first area, circus, is unambiguously entertainment; the second, flight, sometimes masquerades as science, sometimes actually is science, but nevertheless is by circumstances obliged or chooses to operate as a highly public form of popular entertainment. Both areas of showbusiness are com-mon to Britain, but both are substantially non-verbal – intelligible without recourse to language – and therefore international, and the female dare-devils themselves may be British or continental (usually French or Italian) or American. My study is further compromised by a necessary acknowledge-ment: there is little that female daredevils do or have done that has not first been done by males. So what? Indeed, the very fact that females do these acts of skill and bravery and do them at the time they do is a matter of significance, because I am looking back to a period of intensive repression that questions most female activity outside the home and frowns on or views suspiciously individuality, assertiveness and the acquisition and exercise of professional skills.

Details of these women's lives are sparse. We tend to know of them through their publicity, the bills and pictorial posters that advertise their most notable feats and in the follow-up news events that depict these fleeting triumphs. We also hear of them if they disturb prevailing notions of taste, decorum and propriety (usually in dress), and we have final word if, in the course of follow-ing their professions, they injure or kill themselves. Between are blanks: these women would seem to disappear between performances. Lower in social standing than actresses, they are, by and large, the untouchables of show-business and consequently, in the eyes of the press and public, socially insignificant. Can these women have been role models for anyone?

Any analytical approach to this subject is vexed by a series of questions which in the main relate to the sources available for study. Despite the over-whelming choice of female candidates which may be volunteered from the pages of Thetard[2] or Toole-Stott[3] or the infinite miscellany of bills, puffs and posters giving notice of female daredevilry, the information itself is not self-evident or self-explanatory. Perhaps because the subject is too lurid or trivial or tacky for conventional academics, there is little in the way of systematic study and analysis of daredevils of either sex. More significantly, there is scant material describing entire acts, and we are more likely to find as the subjects of writers' and artists' attentions heart-stopping key moments, perilous traverses, leaps or falls or flights.

Whilst the reporting of daredevils invites hyperbole, the very nature of that enthusiasm is suspect. Each source demands its own deconstruction. Is it reportage or publicity? Who is the would-be recipient of this communication? Is the act of daredevilry – as publicity will often have us believe – a singular and unique event, with consequent untried dangers, or is it routine, rehearsed and, if not altogether safe, at least tested and the more dangerous flaws detected and mended? This particular question arises because one of the more reliable forms of information is the accident report. Performers, male and female alike, can make auspicious appearances, then disappear for months or even years, until a terminal moment of fame in a fatal or crippling accident. However, for that moment we have a locus and a date. Is the information meant to be public? Does it come from a private letter or is it hidden in a diary? Are other accounts of the same performer available? What do discrepant versions tell us of the informants and informees as well as of the subjects?

Illustrated material, although nearly always welcome, poses further difficulties. Drawings, posters, lithographic sheet-music covers make us see what we are meant to see, but not to question. Acts appear dangerous, distances are exaggerated, safety features are elided or unrecognised and unrecorded. In many instances the female performer is subjected to the male gaze, but is sexual allure intended to dominate or to be co-equal with danger? Does danger spice sex or sex enhance danger? Or is the question circular? What is the relationship between illustrations and the accompanying text? This question intrudes because illustrations may have their own life and have been generated in distinct circumstances. Circus historians have a high regard for Hughes le Roux's *Acrobats and Mountebanks* (1890) illustrated with line drawings by Jules Garnier, but the line drawings are an afterthought, first added for the English edition, and give rise to the possibility that their inclusion lends a voyeuristic aura to le Roux's descriptions, especially as many of the illustrations of female acrobats stress the skimpiness of their dress and draw the viewer's eye to the performer's figure. Photographs might appear 'factual' but create their own problems. Few Victorian theatrical photographs were made in venues other than the photographer's studio. An 1881 photograph of Zazel is an exception because the glass transept of the Royal Aquarium afforded enough natural light to permit a picture of Zazel with her propelling cannon.

A further problematic area is the use which may be made of descriptions furnished by the Victorian diarist Arthur Munby. Munby kept a private diary between 1859 and 1889 in which he recorded numerous encounters with working women,[4] and there is little doubt that he was sexually aroused by the sight and proximity of women engaged in strenuous physical activity. There is the further possibility – probability may be as appropriate – that the acts of recalling, recording and rereading furnished further sexual pleasure. Nevertheless, Munby's diary entries for his occasional visits to the music halls

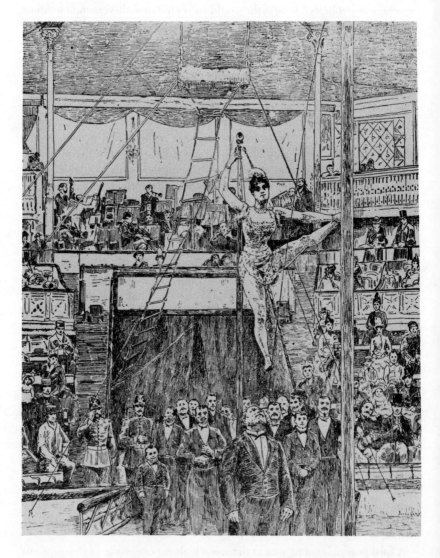

Figure 7.1 Le Roux and Garnier line-drawing: *The Slack Wire*

Figure 7.2 Le Roux and Garnier line-drawing: *Trapeze Artist*

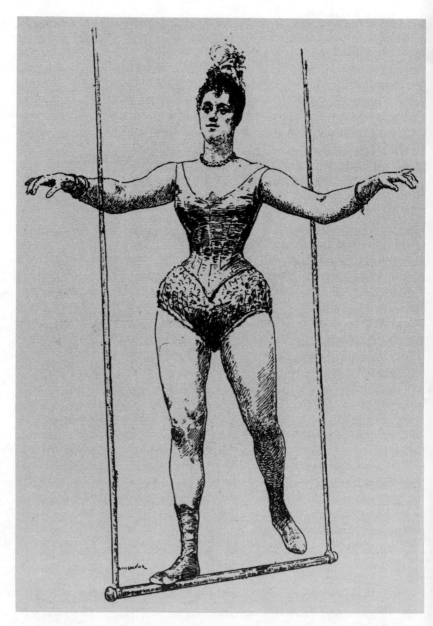

Figure 7.3 Le Roux and Garnier line-drawing: *Trapeze Artist*

Figure 7.4 Zazel

where he saw female acrobats constitute some of the richer detailed descriptions anywhere of entire performances and make Munby exceptionally valuable to any circus historian. The reader must therefore take on board the dual nature of Munby's narratives: accurately detailed accounts but, equally, material for masturbatory fantasy. With problems such as these, is it any wonder that the genuine female daredevil is difficult to locate and recognise? What we can recognise of these women's lives is the high degree of professional self-discipline and practised skill that each brought to her work. True, there were exceptions. In the 1880s there was no training for the parachutists, male or female, just as there had been no training for balloonists, but those who survived the first flights and drops got better at their jobs and, like circus aerialists and lion-tamers, managed their careers with some acumen and made adequate livings.

What may also be of significance for us here is the manner in which female daredevilry is depicted and interpreted, for in these respects – in press reporting, in pictorial representation and in public reception – there is a world of difference between male and female derring-do. One, the male daredevil, whose name is usually known and publicised in full, is bold, assertive, sometimes foolhardy and ill-judged, sometimes pushing back the frontiers of knowledge and adventure, sometimes – in the language and echoing the concept and practice of colonialism – demonstrating dominion over inferior beings, pacifying the savage through strength of character and bravery, not low cunning. The female, by contrast, is either an adjunct to a male companion (and is then, for propriety's sake, known as Mrs X or Madame Y), Mr X or Monsieur Y having given her temporary leave to neglect her domestic obligations to assist, accompany and comfort him, or – Heaven forbid – a woman who, by her close-fitting garments, invites inspection of her body (and who will then be known by a stage-name or by the provocative name of her act). There is often a sexual gaze implied in her pictorial representation. If she is shown in proximity to the savage and dangerous, she exerts not control, not dominion, but sexual allure and near-complicity which seduce and charm and make contact more risky than one based on the illusion of power and fear employed by the male. Outside the picture there is, the male or female customer may infer, a deserted kitchen, an empty nursery or an expectant double bed.

These sexual undertones infuse many accounts and were present in many female daredevils' performances even if in the main unacknowledged. Arthur Munby describes such a heady combination of disinterested professionalism and sexual allure in his uncensored diary entry for 11 June 1870. Munby had left the University Club for a visit to the nearby Oxford Music Hall. There he witnessed the performance of an acrobat performing under the stage-name of Mlle de Glorion. Arthur Munby's tone is worthy of note: it is a mixture of the heavy-breathing voyeur qualified by a mixture of gallantry and disgust. At some moments he is admiring a performer's great skill; at other moments he is describing an erotic sexual act. He wants to aid this girl, but then recalls that, like a professional prostitute, she is paid for the risks she takes. Munby records in his diary,

She came forward to the footlights hand in hand with two male acrobats; she was drest much like them; and she made a bow, not a curtsey, to the spectators as they did. A very pretty English girl she seemed, of 18 or 20 years; trim and slight and shapely, standing about 5 feet 4. The only clothing she had on was a blue satin doublet fitting close to her body and having very scanty trunk hose below it. Her arms were all bare; her legs, cased in fleshlings, were as good as bare, up to the hip: the only sign of woman about her was that she had a rose in her bosom, and another in her short curly hair. She began the performance by putting the nape of her neck in a noose at the end of a rope that hung over a pulley aloft; then, hanging so with her head thrown back, she cleverly hoisted herself up, by hauling at the other half of the same rope, to the triple swing or trapèze, some twenty feet above the stage. There she sat, side by side with her two male companions; and went through the usual gymnastics; hanging head downwards, hanging by one leg or one knee; sliding down headforemost over the body of one of the men, and then catching her feet under his armpits, and coming up again by grasping his body between her knees and his leg with her hands, whilst she brought her head and shoulders up by a strong muscular effort; and lastly, balancing herself on the small of her back upon the trapèze, till at a given signal the two men, who were hanging head downward on either side of her, each seized one of her ankles, and pulling her so by main force from her perch, flung her bodily forward and downward, and so held her upside down in the air, her limbs all sprawling apart. The shock to her brain and to all the joints and sinews of her body must have been tremendous: yet this is what she, and many other young women, do daily for a living: and she was rewarded with great applause by the crowded hall, as the men dropped their hold and left her to grasp and slide down a loose rope alone. But this was not all: for the 'chairman' got up & said 'Ladies and Gentlemen, Mdlle de Glorion will now take her daring leap for life, along the whole length of the hall'. And the fair acrobat went down from the stage among the audience, alone, and walked, half nude as she was, through the crowd, to the other end of the long hall, and there went up a staircase into the gallery. She passed close to me; taking no heed of anyone; her fair young face all crimson with heat and wet with perspiration; and climbed the rope ladder that led up from the gallery to a small platform, just big enough to stand on, which was suspended high up under the ceiling. There she stood, in sight of all the people: intent on preparing for her nightly peril, and taking no thought (nor did they, I think, just then) of the fact that she was almost utterly unclothed. Two strong parallel ropes were stretched from hooks in the roof, fifty feet off, to the platform where she was: on the stage, far beyond that, one of her mates was hanging inverted from the trapèze, awaiting her; but he was wholly hidden from her by two great discs of paper stretched on hoops, which were hung near him, one behind the other, above the footlights. And she had to swing herself, high over the heads of the crowd, across the great space of eighty feet or so, and leap through the two discs and alight in his inverted arms, which she could not even see. A fair girl of eighteen, preparing in the sight of all men for such a feat as that; perched up there, naked and unprotected, with no one to help her; anxiously testing the ropes, chalking the soles of her feet, wiping the sweat off her hands and her bonny face, and trying to smile withal. One must suppose that if she had not been an acrobat, every man present would have rushed to rescue or assist her: as it was, she had hired herself to do the thing, and they sat still to see her do it. She did it, of course; she leaped into the air, and in leaping left the ropes that swung her, and dashed through the two hoops, and was seen hanging in the arms of her mate, grasping his body, her face against his breast. A moment more, and she lowered herself by the loose rope to the stage, and was bowing and smiling amidst thunders of applause. And so I came away.

But Munby continues, moralising on the event:

Ought we forbid her to do these things? Certainly not, if she wishes to do them and if men may do them unforbidden; the woe is with those by whom such offences come. And, although it is not well to see a nude man to fling a nude girl about as she is flung, or to see her grip his body in mid air between her seemingly bare thighs, I think that an unreflecting audience takes no note of these things & looks on him and her only as two performers. Still, the familiar interlacing of male and female bodies in the sight of the public is gross and corrupting, though its purpose be mere athletics. Tonight, when the girl was sitting on the trapèze with her comrades, resting a moment after having climbed up there again from the grip of their hands or feet, she observed that one of their shoes had left a stain of dust on her pink thigh. And she called his attention to it, and wetted her handkerchief and wiped the place; just as nonchalant as if she had been in her own dressing room, and not there, aloft and under the gaze of several hundred people.[5]

Since we have come to female daredevils by way of Mlle de Glorion, let me begin with the circus performer. I use the term circus because under one heading it compresses acts that were variously and indiscriminately seen at carnivals, fairs, music halls, pleasure parks and peoples' palaces, venues as unalike and as unlikely as the windy banks of the Thames or the Canadian and New York shores of Niagara Falls linked by tight-wires, the booths outside the walls of Paris or on the moors of Bradford, the wooden circus buildings of Sheffield and Bristol or the hippodromes of Glasgow, Manchester and Madrid.

A further point before citing some examples. My choices are arbitrary. In Toole-Stott's four-volume *Circus and Allied Arts* there is evidence of hundreds, perhaps thousands, of female acts which involve physical danger. These testify, on the one hand, to the continuity of circus life in which all members of circus families are expected to pitch in as soon as they become toddlers, and for some wire-walking and trapeze work would have been less risky than childbirth. On the other hand, these numbers for female acts, increasing through the second half of the nineteenth century and substantially more in the first quarter of the twentieth, confirm that women are being less reticent or more exploitative: they are forcing changes to a conservative profession and making places for themselves.

But even then their successes and the resulting acclaim may be shorter-lived. Many have read of 'Charles Blondin' (Jean-François Gravelet), 'the hero of Niagara', who on a tight-rope crossed the cliffs between the American and Canadian sides of the Falls in 1859 and again, this time before the Prince of Wales, in 1860; but who has heard of Madame Geneviève (Selina Young), 'the female Blondin', who in 1861 crossed the Thames on a high-wire from Battersea on the Surrey side to Cremorne Gardens on the north bank? It was interpreted as an act so outrageous to public decency that, on her first attempt, the guy-wires that stabilised her cross-Thames cable were slashed by angry men, and she endured a fall and damage to her reputation. As late as 1978 some male historians were insisting that the feat could be done only by a male and that Madame Geneviève was a boy in disguise,[6] yet when, on 4 July 1863, she fell from a high-wire at Aston Park, no one insisted that Selina Young was a fake. According to one report, she was killed by the fall,[7] another account tells that she was so severely injured that one leg healed inches shorter than the other and that she could never work again.[8] Or who can describe the act and bravery of Maria Speltarini (a name that has a certain false ring about it – was she plain Mary Spelter?) who emulated Blondin's crossing of Niagara? Blondin walked across in one direction and returned trundling a wheelbarrow and gained international fame. Maria Speltarini traversed Niagara with her feet encased in wicker baskets, and such skill was dismissed by a British (male) showman as being 'fit only for the French fête booth from whence it came'.[9] True, neither Blondin's nor Young's nor Speltarini's skills were unique. Their acts had been the stuff of fair booths for generations, for centuries. What we find are hard-working professionals with practised skills taking risks, thereby gaining the public attention to increase their chances of further bookings and the likelihood of higher fees. Women are working. And sometimes they are getting injured or killed.

The nature of that attention is another matter. The clothing of acrobats is necessarily functional as well as eye-catching. Elsewhere Arthur Munby, a connoisseur of female circus performers, describes the costume of the quite respectable Lizzie Foster, a pub-keeper's daughter, who performed as an aerialist under the name of 'Zuleilah' as 'drest like a male acrobat, in tights, with spangled trunk hose and a sleeveless vest; her dark hair drest like a woman's, & with a rose coquettishly placed over one ear.'[10] It is clear from his previous description that Munby, and, one may suspect, others like him, were prepared to interpret conventional gymnasts' attire on females as 'nude' or 'naked' or 'almost utterly unclothed' and therefore dangerously provocative. Certainly, the female circus performers sketched in the late 1880s by Jules Garnier, one of the foremost artists of the circus ring and carnival mid-way, are drawn to lead the viewer's eye to the thighs, groin and buttocks. Such drawings pass without comment in *Acrobats and Mountebanks*, but a poster of Adelaide Wieland, known to the London public as Zaeo, similarly drawn and vividly coloured, raised a furore because of the alleged indecency of the performer's costume. At the insistence of the Central Vigilance Society for the Repression of Immorality, the poster was withdrawn,[11] and Zaeo's stage and music-hall act was thereafter attended as much for its supposed voyeuristic appeal as for Ms Wieland's professional skill.

Such problems of public perception of daredevil skill and supposed sexual allure are focused in the public career of Zazel, otherwise Rossi (or Rosa) Mathilde Richter. Zazel's act was one of the more exciting and dangerous of the century. More than a conventional aerialist and more than a rope-dancer, although she performed these feats with recognised skill, Zazel's was the first of the 'human-cannonball' acts. In a modern circus the human-cannonball act is managed by creating what appears to be a large-bore field gun mounted on a lorry and by having the asbestos-clad and helmeted human projectile 'shot' across an arena to a net. But the cannon is not genuine. It is a tube with either a heavy spring or a compressed-air chamber in its base, with a platform above the chamber on which the performer–projectile will rest her or his feet. As a dummy charge is fired at the 'cannon's' mouth, the spring or a compressed-air piston is released, and the human occupant is propelled on a ballistic trajectory upwards and outwards. For the performer the feat is akin to being propelled on a star-trap upward through the stage floor – but at a greater velocity and at a terrible shock to the feet, legs, knees, indeed to the whole frame. The sudden acceleration, with the resulting loss of blood from the brain, may cause momentary unconsciousness. Unlike the acrobat who lands on his feet on the stage (I can, incidentally, find no indication that women were ever fired upward on a star-trap but, instead, rose majestically and poetically on slow-traps), the human cannonball has to fly across the length of an auditorium or tent or pleasure-palace transept and land somersaulting into a distant net or grasp in flight a suspended trapeze.

Zazel's cannon was obviously such a fake, concealing within a large elastic spring rather like a child's catapult, for, as it was usually suspended from supports above the spectators' heads, it was by necessity far too lightweight to be genuine. The 'cannon's' shortness and particularly wide bore created further problems for Zazel. Her head was close to the obligatory pyrotechnic explosion at the cannon's mouth, and she therefore risked scorching; the wide bore made it harder to keep her body properly aligned for flight; the short length also reduced the sureness of the gun's aim. Refinements that were to eliminate these faults lay in the distant future. But her act was spectacular, and, not surprisingly, Arthur Munby saw her at least twice at the Royal Aquarium in early 1877, the year she first appeared in London:

Friday, 20 April. To the Aquarium at 5 & again saw 'Zazel' and again astonished (as every one was) at the courage and coolness and skill of this girl of 18: who, drest as an acrobat, walked the tightrope without a pole, lay down on it & rose again on one leg, & the like: Then swung herself about on the trapeze like a monkey, and sat on it like a strong man, with big arms folded, and sitting thus, flung her body round and round it, holding it by the hollow of her knees: Then leaped 60 feet down, head foremost: Then let herself down, feet first, into a cannon, and was literally fired thence into the air, falling on a net: and 15

minutes afterwards, was seen in neat woman's clothing, walking quietly home
with her sister, as modest and demure as any schoolgirl.[12]

Zazel was not the eighteen-year-old that Munby thought. Six days before
Munby's visit she had turned just fifteen.

That such an act as Zazel's could avoid detractors is too much to expect and
later in the same year the Zazel-mania came in for mild heckling and sexual
innuendo. Such an example is in the song 'Zazel' written by George Hunt for
George Leybourne's music-hall turn. The song allows Leybourne to impersonate a countryman who comes to London and, after seeing and describing
Zazel's act, is visited by bed-destroying erotic dreams and tumescent megalo-
mania (the weight of his 'cannon' collapses the bedframe), and he fervently
wishes that he could become a soldier so as to have Zazel-like projectiles fired
at him. The illustrated cover accompanying the song also marginalises Zazel
in depicting her one-quarter the size of Leybourne.

Zazel's act brought her to the notice of the largest of circus managements,
and by 1879 she was performing with Barnum's troupe in New York. For
eighteen months we find her playing arenas and vaudeville houses on the
Eastern Seaboard, then another eighteen months of silence, and then, in early
1883, Zazel reappears.[13] Somewhere in America her cannon had thrown her
wide of the safety net, and she had sustained serious injury. No more can-
nons. Zazel ends her few remaining performing years on the slack wire.

I stated earlier that gender defines the structures of some daredevil acts.
Wild-beast or 'cat' acts are one such area. No one has disputed Isaac van
Amburgh's skill and pre-eminent showmanship in training and displaying
captive animals. Queen Victoria herself saw him repeatedly during the 1830s
and 1840s, and at her insistence Edwin Landseer twice painted van Amburgh
in action. Landseer's paintings and their titles tell us much about presentation and public perception of the act: one painting is called *Dominion* and
expresses the lion-tamer's domination of the cowed beasts. Man is the superior
animal, the fit lord of the earth. The second, called *The Peaceable Kingdom*,
shows van Amburgh protecting a lamb as a part of a stage act that referred to
a prophetic passage from Isaiah foretelling that at the coming of a Messiah
'the lion shall lie down with the lamb'.[14] Man is the anticipating and fulfilling
instrument of God's intent.

Women in 'cat acts' had no such dominion. They controlled either by
becoming a scolding mother separating and pacifying quarrelsome children/
beasts or, more commonly, through establishing the illusion that the female
dompteuse had established a sexual relationship with the dangerous male
beasts. So common has this approach become that the usual billing for such
an act is the term first applied to Claire Heliot, 'la fiancée des lions' or 'the
lion's bride'. Technically, such an act is identified by the circus term *en
pelotage* to distinguish it from those staged *en férocité*. The latter act, where
the tamer tries to convince the audience that the beasts are ferocious, is less

dangerous because the illusion of ferocity depends upon keeping some distance from the animals, but an act performed *en pelotage* – the very term suggests sexual proximity[15] – allows little separation.

There was one alternative approach, simultaneously played *en férocité* and *en pelotage* when male and female lion-tamers worked together: the female became a stooge and actually subjected herself to great risk by putting herself among the cats. Appearing in a nightdress with her hair down, identifiable symbols of loss of control and possible impropriety, the female subject allowed

Figure 7.5 Ḫypnosis (*en férocité* and *en pelotage*)

herself to seem 'mesmerised', just as the cats were apparently 'mesmerised', by powerful male thought. Here in the cage the woman is an inferior beast, tamed, domesticated, vulnerable. There is a strong element of sexual titillation in the act, or at the least the act feeds male power fantasies.

The scientific revolution of the late eigheenth century and the accompanying industrial revolution must be held accountable for an unorthodox sort of daredevil. Many inventions, the products of the new science, found their way into primitive existence and thereupon languished for lack of funds to develop and exploit them. Those inventions which succeeded often came before the public because the scientist–inventor learned the techniques of showmanship and, in publicising and popularising, became an accomplished performer able to create interest, draw and hold crowds, even when the new device became refractory or when hostile conditions, such as bad weather, impeded public display. The principles of aerostation and the hot-air and gas balloons were such discoveries and inventions. Their inventors, Montgolfier, Lunardi, Sadler, Cocking, etc., became accomplished showmen and funded further research and experimentation with public ascents and a remarkable, if sometimes ludicrous, variety of aerial displays. I call these people, inventors who, by financial necessity, were obliged to become show-people, 'entertainer–scientists'.

But these entertainer–scientists had no monopoly on success, for a new group of people, true show-people, recognised the crowd-pulling appeal of dangerous ascents and aerial tricks and soon acquired balloons for themselves. Unlike the scientists, whose ascents were infrequent, the show-people needed durable balloons, cheap and safe fuel, reliable launching techniques, portable equipment and on-board safety features that would withstand frequent use and hard wear. These showmen were obliged to invent the equipment and safety methods that scientists had not considered and in so doing considerably advanced the new technology. I call these show-people, who may have ripped off the original scientists but who often improved the original product, 'scientist–entertainers'.

Women played a part in the latter half of the equation as scientist–entertainers, making ascents from early days, sometimes in the company of their husbands, sometimes flying alone or with other women. But these women, Mme Blanchard and Mrs Graham and Mrs Green – until their deaths we know them only by their formal married names – are, at first, a colourless lot, eschewing publicity apart from the publicity generated by and from their frequent flights. They took risks, but their risk-taking was often portrayed to be less than their husbands'. It is not at all unusual to find announcements in their handbills informing the public that in the event of stormy weather a male aeronaut will replace the female pilot. Nevertheless, Mme Blanchard was one of ballooning's earliest fatalities, and the circumstances of her death in July 1819 are typical of the risks run by the scientist–entertainers. Sometimes the aeronauts carried whole military bands aloft; sometimes they rose with domestic livestock or wild animals aboard; frequently they ascended carrying assorted fireworks and discharged these fireworks from their balloons' passenger-baskets. On this occasion Marie Martha Sophie Blanchard was casting lighted fireworks from her balloon when one ignited gas escaping

Figure 7.6 **Leona Dare by Emile Tourtin**

from a valve. She appears to have suffocated in the rapid combustion of gas.[16]

Leona Dare, an appropriate stage-name for Adelaide (or Adeline) Stuart, was anything but colourless. She flaunted her American origins, but then to be American in the 1870s and 1880s was to be modern, brash, outrageous and independent. Her first recorded performance, in 1871, was in a trapeze act at Hooley's Opera House in Brooklyn, and for a further four years she played the variety houses of East Coast and Mid-west America. We see something of her act when, in 1877, a poster for the Folies Bergère showed Leona hanging from a trapeze whilst supporting her suspended partner, possibly her brother, the one-legged acrobat Stuart Dare, by her teeth. In the autumn of 1878 she is in London. *Punch*'s correspondent saw her perform at the Oxford Music Hall, where she was billed as 'The Queen of the Antilles', and commented on the discomfort of the venue and the presence of women in the audience:

> It was crowded. The Stalls are more uncomfortable than at any other place of amusement I can just now call to mind. The stall-audience was much the same as all such audiences are, and – what invariably astonishes me at these places – the proportion of thoroughly respectable-looking women, with the comfortable air of well-to-do lodging-house keepers of the Bloomsbury Division, was really remarkable. . . . The very swell fast element does not seem to enter into the composition of an Oxford Music-Hall, to any appreciable extent . . . I insist upon the respectability of the audience, as showing what such an audience will enjoy in the way of – Heaven save the mark! – amusement.

This correspondent then goes on to describe in greater detail the act that Leona had performed in Paris:

> the feature of the evening was announced, namely, 'LEONA DARE, QUEEN OF THE ANTILLES'. I do not know what 'The Antilles' are doing in the absence of their Queen, or what Her Majesty, having been deposed from that high position – (she could, I fancy, be deposed from any high position, and bet three to one on her coming down safely – like a cat) – is now reduced to earning an honest livelihood by showing what an ex-sovereign can do when not fettered by the strict ceremonial and rigidly formal etiquette of a Court. The 'Queen of the Antilles' has evidently discarded her regal robes, unless the acrobatic costume in which she appears is the Court-dress of the Antilles. She enters, first of all, in a sort of thin wrapper, strikes an attitude – perhaps as 'Queen of the Antilles receiving the Antillesian nobility' – and then dashes aside the flimsy robe, as though it were a bathing dress, and she were going to take a plunge.
>
> How do the nobility and courtiers of the Antilles act on such a trying occasion? Do they put their hands up to their faces and turn away? Or do they at once hand her the trapèze, or the rope or the bar, or whatever it may be? I fancy so, as Her Majesty is accompanied by a small wiry man, attired similarly to herself, who seems to know what Her Majesty likes, and what she wants. And what is this poor man's reward? Why, after he has served her faithfully for over a quarter of an hour, throwing her ropes, tightening cords, seeing that everything is right,

and finally devoting himself, recklessly, to her service, by loyally flinging himself from a giddy height, and joining her on a trapèze bar, where they sit together, – she dignified as a Queen of the Antilles should be, he proud as a subject might well be at being raised to such an eminence by his own merits and by the command of his Royal mistress, and willing to obey her lightest word – he is suddenly deposed – poor favourite, and with a ring in his waistband that is linked to a ring which Her Majesty, now in a down-flying attitude, holds in her mouth, between her teeth – and thus this poor unhappy Prime Minister (or whatever he is) is suspended from office by the Queen of the Antilles.

Then she slaps him, slaps him hard and frequently, and he being thus suspended, is sent round spinning like a whipping-top, until so fast and furious are his gyrations, that I could not tell what he had become – a man or a crab, a human being or a shapeless dummy.

At last that merciless, capricious Queen of the Antilles releases her victim, and once more allows him to resume his seat on the bar, where he appears dazed, bewildered, while she looks cruelly and maliciously riante. (By the way, this was good acting on the part of both performers and looked uncommonly real.)

What was this man – her courtier, her slave, her servant? From his connection with the bar, perhaps a Q.C. – a Queen's Counsel – of the Antilles. Not a judge, surely? But suppose he were found to be the Lord Chamberlain at the Court of the Antilles, on a tour through Europe with the Queen? On a tour, and taking several 'turns' nightly.

Punch's correspondent ends with a rhetorical question and response: 'And what attraction has this entertainment for the respectable stall-audience I have already mentioned? Why, I honestly believe, simply, its peril, nothing else.'[17]

Leona Dare re-appeared in London in the spring of 1879, but this time she was not performing indoors. Instead, she was hanging by her teeth from the basket of a balloon launched from Alexandra Palace. Her act attracted such large crowds and so much adverse attention that the MP for Flintshire asked the home secretary to intervene, and another MP introduced a bill to suppress a range of dangerous performances that also included Zazel's. Some articles of the resulting Dangerous Performances legislation are still in effect. It was undeniably dangerous to hang thus from a balloon, but Leona Dare, a calculating professional, depended on the reliability of the balloon and its crew to get her aloft and to bring her safely down. To this degree she is typical of the scientist–entertainers who incorporated the latest technology into their acts and to some degree bettered it.

In 1886 Leona tried the same balloon and trapeze act in Paris, and on this occasion public opposition was too intense. Performance was forbidden. A poster, illustrating her feat and printed for the event, was never used. That year Leona was reported to be earning a remarkable 4,000 francs per month at the Cirque Franconi in an act that concluded when, supported by a bar clenched in her teeth, she slid down an oblique rope stretched from the high ceiling to the sawdust ring. Attempting this trick at the Hippodrome de l'Alma, the bar twisted, and she broke her jaw. Here her chronology becomes obscure. Sometime within this period Leona or Adelaide married an Austrian banker, then divorced him because, she claimed, she missed circus life. She attempted a return to the aerial acts, but was refused work. She then worked in *poses plastiques* and eventually retired to southern Austria, married this time to a railwayman.[18]

My final daredevil is Dolly Shepherd. Dolly, too, is difficult to keep track of, but again we start with a male performer. There had been several attempts at parachuting, but with more fatalities than successes until, in 1888, the American 'Captain' or 'Professor' Thomas Baldwin undertook a series of leaps, always for bank holiday and weekend crowds, at the Alexandra Palace and, subsequently, at other British and North American venues. The Alexandra Palace management in 1904 undertook to attract crowds by engaging a team of aeronauts, two men and two women. The men were to operate the balloons and to parachute, the women were to parachute. It must be emphasised that neither Baldwin's nor any other parachute for some decades had safety body-harnesses. Nor were these aeronauts carried in balloon baskets. The parachutist usually ascended whilst sitting on or clinging to a trapeze bar dangling beneath her parachute which was, in turn, fastened to the balloon's outer netting. Most of these acts used 'smoke balloons' that were filled with hot air from coal and wood fires on the ground. They rose swiftly, and all 'chutists had to release their parachutes and cling fast to their trapezes before the balloon collapsed and fell separately.

When Dolly was hired she was seventeen. She was given a half-hour's ground training and promised £2 10s for each jump. She kept at it until 1912, jumping frequently in London and at fairs and fêtes around the United Kingdom. We have bills of her at Grantham, Bath and London, making descents whilst sharing her trapeze with a male colleague. We also have an account and illustration of an accident, when she rescued a fellow female daredevil whose parachute had become fouled in the balloon's netting.[19] Dolly, we should note, was depicted wearing clothing similar to the other performers I have described. Even aloft she was assumed to exude sex appeal.

It would be futile to contend that any of these women, acrobats, aerialists, cannonballs, parachutists, were wholly independent in their professional lives. Their work was inescapably connected with showbusiness, which increasingly in the nineteenth century became just that: business. Profits were made, not just for themselves, but for other people, more than likely for the predominantly male show-people who owned and managed the venues at which they appeared. It is impossible to know and futile to speculate whether they saw themselves as assisting the cause of women by making places for them in the arena of public entertainment, in the circus or on the fringes of aviation. It is likely that no such thoughts crossed their minds or that, as professionals, they even compared themselves to their male counterparts.

What we can recognise – all that we can recognise – is their individual professionalism and their skill and their calculated and recurring bravery. They were singular performers and singular women.

Notes

1. I am pleased to acknowledge the assistance of David Mayer, especially in researching and describing the structures and technologies of circus performance.
2. H. le Roux and J. Garnier, *Acrobats and Mountebanks* (trans. by A. P. Morgan from *Le Jeu du cirque et la vie forain*), (Paris, 1889; London: Chapman & Hall, 1890).
3. R. Toole-Stott, *Circus and Allied Arts, a World Bibliography*, 4 vols. (Derby: Harpur, 1958–71).
4. D. Hudson, *Munby, Man of Two Worlds: The life and times of Arthur J. Munby, 1828–1910* (London: Sphere Books, 1974).
5. *ibid.*, pp. 285–7.
6. R. Mander and J. Mitchenson, *Victorian and Edwardian Entertainment from Old Photographs* (London: Batsford, 1978), p. 32.
7. *The Times*, 5 July 1863.
8. 'Trim' (ed.), *The Original, Complete, and Only Authentic Story of 'Old Wilds'* (Bradford, London: G. Vickers, 1888), p. 240; reprinted from the *Halifax Courier*, p. 224. This account, which leaves no doubt about Selina Young's female gender, identifies the locale of the accident as Highbury Barn and the place of treatment as St Bartholomew's Hospital, London. In this version Selina Young married and settled on the Surrey side of the Thames, where she and her husband kept a tavern.
9. This remark is attributed to the circus impressario John Hengeler. T. McDonald Rendle, *Swings and Roundabouts: A yokel in London* (London: Chapman and Hall, 1919), p. 207.
10. Hudson, *Munby, op. cit.*, p. 254.
11. R. Busby, *British Music Hall: An illustrated who's who from 1850 to the present day* (London: Paul Elek, 1976), p. 190. Also see T. C. Davis, 'Sex in public places: The Zaeo aquarium scandal and the Victorian moral majority', *Theatre History Studies*, x (1990), pp. 1–13.
12. Hudson, *Munby, op. cit.*, p. 389.
13. Zazel's American tour is noted in G. C. D. Odell, *Annals of the New York Stage*, 15 vols (New York: Columbia University Press, 1927–49), vols. XI, XII.
14.   And there shall come forth a rod out of the stem of Jesse
          . . .
        The Wolf also shall dwell with the lamb
        The leopard shall lie down with the kid
        And the calf and the young lion and the fatling together
        And a little child shall lead them
        And the cow and the bear shall feed
        Their young ones shall lie down together
        And the lion shall eat straw like the ox . . .
                                    (Isaiah 11, 6)
15. A. Hippisley-Coxe, *A Seat at the Circus* (London: Macmillan, 1980), pp. 130–40. The verb *peloter* means, literally, to wind a ball of wool, but the term is also applied to trifling actions, i.e., to play negligently or, in modern slang, 'to fool around'. Another meaning, echoed in the female approach to such cat acts, is to caress erotically. *Le pelotage* is an erotic caress.

16. J. Jobe (ed.), *The Romance of Ballooning: The story of the early aeronauts* (London: Patrick Stephens, 1971), pp. 84–6.
17. *Punch*, 26 October 1878.
18. H. Thétard, *La Merveilleuse Histoire du cirque*, 2 vols (Paris: Prisma, 1947), vol. ii, p. 158.
19. Undated cutting (*c.* 1910?) from *The Illustrated Police Budget*.

8

The Adventuress: *Lady Audley's Secret* as novel, play and film

ZOË ALDRICH

In writing on the relationship of the New Woman to the Victorian novel, Gail Cunningham asserts:

> It was suddenly discovered that women, who had for so long been assiduously protected from reading about sex in novels and periodicals, or from hearing about it in polite conversation, had a great deal to say on the subject themselves. . . . Venereal diseases, contraception, divorce and adultery were made the common talking points of the New Womanhood.[1]

This view arguably perpetuates the notion of the New Woman wrenching the Victorians out of a dark age of covered table legs. While the 1890s undoubtedly saw more open debate on such issues, the work of Mary Braddon and other sensation novelists demonstrates that female sexuality, desire, seduction, adultery, bigamy and crime were subjects equally popular with a female bourgeois readership thirty years earlier. Indeed, in *A Woman's Thoughts about Women* (1858), Dinah M. Craik displays the concern, characteristic of the era, with the threat of apparently widespread 'deviant' female sexuality:

> Everywhere around us we see women falling, fallen, and we cannot help them; we cannot make them feel the hideousness of sin, the peace and strength of that cleaness of soul which is not afraid of anything in earth or heaven.[2]

The figure of the sinful, fallen woman is evident across a wide range of nineteenth-century cultural forms – in the penny dreadfuls and early stage melodramas for working-class consumption, and in the novels, poetry, opera and art produced by and for the middle and upper classes. Mary Braddon's *Lady Audley's Secret* offers a very particular and potent manifestation of the fallen woman. Published in 1862, this highly popular novel provided a powerful prototype of the 'adventuress', a character whose qualities are wittily celebrated by Jerome K. Jerome in *Stageland* (1889): 'She has grit and go in her. She is alive. She can do something to help herself besides calling for "George".'[3]

In an analysis of mass-produced fantasies for women, Tania Modleski suggests that Braddon created a forerunner of the modern soap-opera villain-ess in her depiction of a character who 'seizes those aspects of a woman's life, which normally render her most helpless and tries to turn them into ways for manipulating other characters'.[4] In effect, the nineteenth-century adventur-ess essentially offers the female reader or audience similar pleasures to the 'Manipulators' ('Dontcha Love Women who Control their Men?') celebrated in a soap fan magazine:

> These are a few of the man-ipulators,
> Those women who control men and often make them look foolish.
> Women who control their men.
> Women who control *all* men.
> Women we wish we could be more like.[5]

Such women were seen to pose a definite threat to the Victorian male estab-lishment: in December 1863 *The New Review* claimed that *Lady Audley's Secret* was 'a forecast of the moral collapse which would inevitably accompany the emancipation of women' and that its heroine was 'a new type of woman, "standing alone, carrying out some strong purpose without an ally or con-fidant, and thus showing herself independent of mankind and superior to those softer passions to which the sex in general succumbs"'.[6] This article will examine the configuration of the adventuress in Braddon's novel and its subsequent stage and film adaptations, and explore the figure's potentially subversive representations of femininity.

The novel

Braddon's novel was published early in a decade notable for an enormous growth in the literary market for women, not only as writers and readers, but also as publishers, editors and printers. *Lady Audley's Secret* in particular enjoyed enormous popularity: it went into eight editions within three months of publication, its sales apparently unaffected (or perhaps rather enhanced) by the moral and critical disapproval it encountered as part of the 'Sensation Mania' that is attacked in a review of Wilkie Collins's *Armadale* in the *Westminster Review* of October 1866:

Sensationalism must be left to be dealt with by time, and the improvement of the public taste. But it is worth while stopping to note, amidst all the boasted improvement of the nineteenth century, that whilst Miss Braddon's and Mr. Wilkie Collins' productions sell by thousands of copies, *Romola* with difficulty reaches a second edition.[7]

Tania Modleski has argued that critical snobbery has continued to characterise attitudes towards popular culture:

Today, the argument runs, only two types of art exist: mass art, which is used by its producers to manipulate the people and to 'colonize' their leisure time – in short, to keep them contented with the 'status quo' – and high art, which is the last preserve of an autonomous, critical spirit.[8]

Modleski's study rejects this view to suggest instead that popular fiction, such as the domestic and sensation novel, can in fact contain 'elements of protest and resistance underneath highly "orthodox" plots'.[9] A similar reading is made in Sally Mitchell's article on 'Sentiment and suffering: Women's recreational reading in the 1860s':

The popular emotional novel gratifies common needs; it provides a mode of distancing which gives repressed emotions a form that is publicly acceptable and makes them a source of pleasure. . . . The particular social situation within which author and reader live at any given time creates specific frustrations which cannot be resolved and must therefore have an outlet in fantasy.[10]

Mitchell's interpretation is clearly relevant to the question of why, in spite of ultimately advocating that 'the woman pays', *Lady Audley's Secret* provoked such a strong moral backlash on its publication. One answer perhaps lies in Francis Paget's parody of the female sensation novelists, *Lucretia, or the Heroine of the Nineteenth Century* (1868):

And the writers of these books, ay, of the foulest of them, – authors who have put forth confessions of the darkest profligacy that an utter reprobate could make, and who have degraded woman's love into an animal propensity so rabid and so exacting, as to profess an opinion that its gratification will be cheaply purchased at the cost of AN ETERNITY IN HELL, – these writers are, some by their own admission, some by internal evidence (where the publication is anonymous), WOMEN; and the worst of them, UNMARRIED WOMEN![11]

The controversy appears to lie not in the contents of the novels, although this in itself is seen as cause for extreme concern, but in the author's gender; Paget's final reference to 'UNMARRIED WOMEN' may be aimed directly at Braddon, whose own life, like that of her heroine, hardly conformed to the Victorian feminine ideal. For three years, from 1857, Braddon worked as an actress to support herself and her mother, and was only able to leave the stage to write through the financial support of an admirer. She later lived with the publisher John Maxwell, unable to marry him until his wife, who was housed in a mental asylum, died in 1874.

The threat of Braddon's heroine lies not in such overt flouting of conventions, but rather in her subversion of the codes of femininity. The concept of the fallen woman necessarily existed in tandem with an image of the feminine ideal – in Victorian terms, the 'Angel in the House'. This figure was central to the nineteenth-century cult of domesticity and motherhood, which celebrated the qualities of piety, purity and submissiveness in woman's vocation as moral guardian of the home. In appearance and behaviour, Braddon initially presents Lady Audley as the incarnation of the 'Angel in the House', with 'the most wonderful curls in the world – soft and feathery, always floating away from her face, and making a pale halo around her head when sunlight shone through them'.[12] However, the compelling description of her pre-Raphaelite portrait already hints at the evil that lies beneath:

> The perfection of feature, the brilliancy of colouring, were there; but it seemed as if the painter had copied mediaeval monstrosity until his brain had grown bewildered, for my lady, in his portrait of her, had the aspect of a beautiful fiend.[13]

At the time of the novel's publication, the critic of *The Times* defined Braddon's moral dilemma as how to 'represent a woman in such a position or with a character capable of such acts; to combine so much beauty with so much deformity: to depict the lovely woman with the fishy extremities',[14] and indeed Braddon can be seen to achieve much sensational effect by delaying the revelation of these 'fishy extremities'. Elaine Showalter has pinpointed how the power of Lady Audley is gradually revealed to lie in her manipulation of the very qualities that embody the feminine ideal:

> Braddon makes her would-be murderess the fragile blond angel of domestic realism. . . . The dangerous woman is not the rebel or the blue-stocking, but the 'pretty little girl' whose indoctrination in the female role has taught her secrecy and deceitfulness, almost as secondary sex characteristics. She is particularly dangerous because she looks so innocent.[15]

This is not to suggest that *Lady Audley's Secret* is a consciously feminist work. Indeed, the novel conforms to a scenario of fall, punishment and death that recurs in nineteenth-century representations of 'deviant' female sexuality. Braddon's heroine, starting as plain Helen Maldon, marries George Talboys to escape the poverty of her home. When he leaves her to earn money for the family in Australia, she walks out on her child and father. Under the false name of Lucy Graham, Helen supports herself as a governess, and bigamously marries the wealthy Sir Michael Audley, believing George to be dead or unlikely to return. When he does re-appear, Helen pushes him down a well, and later attempts to murder Robert Audley, Sir Michael's nephew, when he threatens to reveal her crimes. Robert survives to denounce his aunt, and send her to a mental asylum in Belgium, where she dies unrepentent of her crimes.

While *Lady Audley's Secret* is narrated by an omnipotent, authorial persona, events are largely related from the perspective of Robert Audley. This character becomes a focus for reader identification as he gradually uncovers Lady Audley's past (motivated by the disappearance of his friend George Talboys). Thus at any stage in the novel, the reader knows little more than Robert about his aunt; a forerunner of the film noir *femme fatale*, she is an enigma to be solved by this detective. In the process, Robert develops from an irresponsible dandy and reader of French novels to an ardent advocate of justice, confronting Lady Audley with her past:

> 'No, Lady Audley', answered Robert, with a cold sternness that was so strange to him as to transform him into another creature – a pitiless embodiment of justice, a cruel instrument of retribution – 'no, Lady Audley', he repeated, 'I have told you that womanly prevarication will not help you.'[16]

This shift in character is strongly attributed to the influence of Clara Talboys, George's sister, who is established as a physical and moral inversion of Lady Audley, inspiring Robert's devotion by her fervent loyalty to her brother:

> 'Oh, my God!' she cried, suddenly clasping her hands and looking upward to the cold winter sky, 'lead me to the murderer of my brother, and let me be the hand to avenge his untimely death.'
> Robert Audley stood looking at her with awe stricken admiration. Her beauty was elevated into sublimity by the intensity of her suppressed passion.[17]

The novel concludes with harmony restored in the new family unit of Robert, Clara and their children, and also (in a later edition of the novel) with Braddon's surely ironic wish that 'No-one will take exception to my story because the end of it leaves the good people all happy and at peace'.[18] This closure conforms to the dominant ideology in restoring the domestic ideal of the patriarchal family, and offering to the reader the assurance Peter Brooks has defined as central to the melodramatic aesthetic:

> No shadow dwells, and the universe bathes in the full bright lighting of moral manicheism. Hence the psychic bravado of virtue and its expressive breakthrough serves to assure us, again and again, that the universe is in fact morally legible, that it possesses an ethical identity and significance.[19]

So why, the question remains, was the novel accused of depravity when first published? An attack on the sensation genre in another contemporary review of Wilkie Collins's *Armadale* shows a realisation that a narrative advocating punishment of deviant behaviour does not necessarily cut off the reader's identification with a character's transgression:

Now it is a Count Fosco, now a Lady Audley, now a Miss Guilt: and, however it may be said, that in these tales the Nemesis rarely fails to overtake the guilty, and that the retribution exacted is sometimes very terrible, it must still be felt that even this is insufficient to remove the impression produced by the continual reproduction of such characters. [20]

John Fiske's work on the viewer's response to characters in television drama offers a further illumination of this aspect. Fiske identifies a process of 'implication–extrication' in a female viewer's response to a soap-opera heroine: 'Part of me is inside Linda – it feels rude when she takes off her stockings – it feels lovely when they kiss – but when she gets slapped I'm right back in our sitting room.'[21] While pleasurable identification with transgression is thus withdrawn at the point of punishment, Fiske suggests that such 'extrication' may not be total:

The pleasure of implication with the character when she is exerting power may well be stronger than that of extrication when she is being punished. The difference in what Freud calls 'effect', in the intensity of the experience, may well be great enough to prevent the ideological effectivity of the punishment. [22]

Fiske's theory has clear implications for an 'alternative' reading of Braddon's novel, and is particularly pertinent to Chapter xxxv, entitled 'My Lady tells the truth', in which Robert denounces his aunt. Lady Audley's description of her past life takes over the narrative for ten pages. Her fierce and logical defence of her crimes arguably undermines the subsequent diagnosis of the character as insane:

'I recognized a separate wrong done to me by George Talboys. His father was rich, his sister was living in luxury and respectability; and I, his wife, and the mother of his child, was a slave allied forever to beggary and obscurity. People pitied me and I hated them for their pity. I did not love the child; for he had been left a burden upon my hands.'[23]

The internment of Lady Audley at a mental asylum draws on contemporary psychiatric discourse. Female deviancy from social norms, particularly sexual deviancy, was commonly attributed to mental illness, which was believed to be inherited from mother to daughter. In *The Function and Disorders of the Reproductive Organs* (1865), the author William Acton claims to quote a 'clever married woman' in arguing that 'It seems a hard and unchristian opinion that it is better not to marry the daughter of a divorced woman; but I believe that the sin of unfaithfulness is often inherited, as well as many other family diseases.'[24] In our own age, one can compare the psychiatric discourse used in the media's representation of criminal cases, as analysed by Wendy Holloway:

There is one significant difference in the choice of 'mad' rather than 'bad'. . . .
Whereas 'bad' is a label which requires an understanding of the moral, that is,
the social content of the acts, 'mad' is a label which is used as if it were a self-
sufficient explanation: it is a diagnosis which avoids considering the content of
the acts and thus avoids seeing the link between the individual and society.[25]

In both Victorian and contemporary society, psychiatric discourse is thus
used to present behaviour defined as socially unacceptable as an extreme, an
illness, thereby denying its potential in the norm of femininity and masculinity
respectively. It is on this basis that Helen Talboys defends her actions to
Robert Audley:

'When you say that I killed George Talboys, you say the truth. When you say
that I murdered him treacherously and foully you lie. I killed him because I AM
MAD! because my intellect is a little way upon the wrong side of the narrow
boundary-line between sanity and insanity.'[26]

Yet the question of Lady Audley's sanity remains ambiguous. When Robert
describes her behaviour to the physiologist, Dr Mosgrove, omitting only an
account of her murderous tendencies, the doctor initially fails to find evidence
of madness:

'She ran away from the home, because her home was not a pleasant one, and she
left it in the hope of finding a better. There is no madness there. She committed
the crime of bigamy, because by that crime she obtained fortune and position.
There is no madness in that. When she found herself in a desperate position she
did not grow desperate. She employed intelligent means and she carried out a
conspiracy which required coolness and deliberation for its execution.'[27]

Although Mosgrove (after actually seeing Helen and learning of her attempts
on the lives of Robert and George Talboys) subsequently decides that she
is suffering from 'latent insanity' inherited from her mother, the diagnosis
remains unclear in defining this as the actual cause of her actions: 'She has
the cunning of madness, with the prudence of intelligence. I tell you what she
is, Mr Audley. She is dangerous!'[28] Thus Braddon retains the more
threatening suggestion that a perfectly sane and intelligent woman has, for
very good reasons, rejected the poverty and isolation of the role defined for her
in the home, and has subsequently worked to retain her improved position.
This aspect of the novel is noted by Elaine Showalter, who suggests that 'As
every woman reader must have sensed, Lady Audley's real secret is that she
is *sane* and moreover, representative.'[29]

The play

The extent to which *Lady Audley's Secret* supports this type of 'negotiated'
reading becomes more apparent when the novel is viewed in relation to an

1863 stage adaptation by Colin Hazlewood. In examining the degree to which Hazlewood retains or eschews the subversive tendencies of his source, it is necessary to view his play in the context of the theatre for which he was writing.

Popular fiction provided a major source of material for the drama of the 1860s, and it is unsurprising that, given the huge success of *Lady Audley's Secret*, adaptations of the novel (at least twelve separate versions in all) appeared almost immediately after its publication. Frank Mathews, the actor–manager of St James's Theatre, presented George Robert's adaptation on 28 February 1863: according to MacQueen-Pope, the play enjoyed a record run of 105 nights, 'the critics raved', the production 'held the Victorian playgoers spell-bound', and Louisa Herbert, the actress who played Lady Audley, 'made an enormous hit'.[30] In 1866 Herbert assumed control of St James's, and revived this adaptation of *Lady Audley's Secret*: Bram Stoker records her touring the company with this play (amongst others) to Dublin in 1867, with Henry Irving playing Robert Audley.[31]

The text of George Robert's adaptation was never printed. That of another version, written by Colin Hazlewood, was and still survives today. Hazlewood's play opened in May 1863 at the Royal Victoria Theatre, London, and was subsequently revived at the Britannia in 1866 and the Olympia in 1877. In writing for an East End playhouse, Hazlewood was targeting his work at the working-class audience that had effectively dominated theatre in the first half of the century, the middle and upper classes having largely abandoned the theatre. However, the 1850s and 1860s were marked by a gradual return of a bourgeois audience, and Hazlewood's *Lady Audley's Secret* can be located as part of the new genre of the society melodrama. Dramatists turned from the penny dreadful to the three-volume novel as a source for adaptation, with settings consequently shifting from a working-class environment into the drawing room. New character types, such as the elegant upper-class villain, emerged, and the 1860s also saw the development of the adventuress as a more central figure. For where previously this character had often appeared as an associate of the villain who finally reformed, 1863 saw the arrival of Braddon's Lady Audley with her motto of 'death or victory' in Hazlewood's play.[32]

Yet regardless of shifts in setting and audience, the drama of the era remained rooted in the melodramatic tradition of the earlier nineteenth century. Established conventions in form, language and characterisation clearly influenced Hazlewood's treatment of his source, and the first act of his play gives an indication of how the process of adaptation can alter interpretation of character. The play's narrative begins at virtually the same point in plot time as the novel – two years into the marriage of Sir Michael and Lady Audley. The stability of their ostensibly happy home is swiftly disrupted by the arrival of Robert Audley and George Talboys, the latter recognising his wife in a minia-ture of 'Lady Audley'. A soliloquy by Lady Audley, giving a clear exposition of her past, is overheard by George, and their subsequent confrontation ends when she pushes him down a well: '"Dead men tell no tales! I am free! I am free! I am free! – Ha, ha, ha!" (*Raises her arms in triumph, laughing exultingly – Luke looks on, watching her as the curtain falls.*)'[33]

Much of the menace of Braddon's novel stems from the gradual revelation of violence and crime beneath the ideals of home and womanhood, with Robert's investigation occupying virtually the entire narrative. Hazlewood's decision to reveal instead Lady Audley's secret almost immediately means that the suspense no longer lies in *what* is to be revealed, but in *when* it is to be revealed, the audience awaiting the unmasking and punishment of Helen Talboys. This decision can perhaps be partly attributed to the inevitable loss, in the transition from novel to stage, of Robert Audley's narrative point of view, and also to the melodramatic convention which demanded a swiftly moving plot.

The moral identity of Hazlewood's characters is immediately legible, and conforms to the ethical polarity defined by Peter Brooks as central to the melodramatic aesthetic:

> The peripeties through which they [the characters] pass must be as absolute as they are frequent, bringing alternatively the victory of blackness and whiteness, and in each instance giving a full enunciation of the condition experienced. Polarization is not only a dramatic principal but the very means by which integral ethical conditions are identified and staged, made clear and operative.[34]

Not only does Hazlewood's Lady Audley reveal her 'secret' in Act I, as opposed to two-thirds of the way through the novel, but she does so with a relish that defines the character as the embodiment of extreme evil:

> I live now for ambition and interest, to mould the world and its votaries to my own end. Once I was fool enough to wed for love. Now I have married for wealth. What a change from the wife of George Talboys to the wife of Sir Michael Audley! My fool of a first husband thinks me dead. Oh excellent scheme, oh cunning device, how well you have served me.[35]

The play therefore closes off the ambiguity of the novel, in which Robert's desire to attribute Lady Audley's crimes to insanity is undermined by her own intelligent defence in 'My Lady tells the Truth', and by Dr Mosgrave's diagnosis. In Hazlewood's adaptation, Lady Audley's madness is explicitly presented in the final, public revelation of her guilt:

> (*Laughs wildly*) Mad, mad, that is the word. I feel it here, here! (*places her hand on her temples.*) Do not touch me, do not come near me – let me claim your silence – your pity – and let the grave, the cold grave, close over Lady Audley and her secret. (*Falls – dies – Music – tableaux of sympathy – George Talboys kneels over her.*) CURTAIN.[36]

Hazlewood thus ultimately substitutes Braddon's gloriously unrepentant heroine with a deranged victim to inspire the audience's pity.

The film

Hazelwood's adaptation of *Lady Audley's Secret* clearly operates within the stage conventions of the era in which it is written. An early British film version of the novel, directed by Jack Denton for the Ideal company in 1920, presents an interpretation of the text within a further medium, and demonstrates a changing perception and representation of gender.

Versions of Victorian novels and plays formed a large part of Ideal's output, reflecting a dominant trend in early cinema. The practice was initially motivated by the demand for material, but film-makers, like theatre entrepreneurs before them, increasingly exploited the cultural status of bourgeois texts in a bid to draw their readership to the cinema. Early film technique is thus, unsurprisingly, also influenced by the aesthetic conventions of Victorian cultural media. The earliest shorts, made at the turn of the century, record fragments of live entertainment (e.g. melodrama, music hall, vaudeville) from a static camera position. Film-makers thus reproduced the live performance as closely as possible, rather than adapting the work specifically to their own medium, although the tableaux form was initially dictated by technical limitations. It is only with the gradual developments, over the first two decades of this century, in camera mobility, length of shot, editing and narrative technique, that we see the emergence of a specifically cinematic discourse able to produce the emotional effect outlined by Charles Affron in *Cinema and Sentiment*. For Affron asserts that the viewer's response to a film is shaped not only by content, but equally by:

> the processes of presentation that derive from the dynamics of films and from the specifics of their viewing. . . . While 'conventional' narrative films relish situations which seem to contain sure sentimental appeal – departures, doomed love, mother love, death – it is finally the degree to which these situations conspire with those specifics that ensures a given work's affectivity.[37]

To some degree, Ideal's production demonstrates the development of these 'specifics', for *Lady Audley's Secret* shows the beginnings of the filmic vocabulary that was to dominate British and American cinema. The film adapts the novel's story into a linear narrative structure, although it also employs a number of flash-back sequences. As with Hazelwood's stage version, the film marginalises Robert Audley's role, focusing instead on Lady Audley's story. The narrative opens with her romance with and marriage to George, and follows her progress from the drabness of her home to the splendour of Audley Court. These events occur prior to the point at which Braddon's narrative opens, the novel only gradually revealing Helen's past through George's investigation. The film viewer occupies a more privileged position than the reader in terms of story information, sharing knowledge of the 'secret' denied

to the other characters. This complicity between viewer and character is
further enhanced through a use of close-up in the scenes where Lady Audley
is twinged with guilt, or in danger of discovery. The technique is exemplified
by the sequence in which Robert Audley tells Sir Michael and Lady Audley of
the return of his friend, George Talboys (the dialogue is communicated by
titles). The film cuts from a long-shot of the three characters in conversation
to a close-up of Lady Audley's face expressing concern. This specifically
cinematic use of point of view can be viewed in relation to Affron's analysis of
a scene in the film *Waterloo Bridge* (1940), in which the character Myra
attempts to keep the news of her fiancé's death from her prospective mother-
in-law:

> The view is caught in this simultaneity of revelation and dissimulation. The
> dramatic irony basic to the theatrical process is transformed by the amplifica-
> tory display of cinema where knowledge often is drawn from aspects of the
> visible accessible only through the camera's mediation. Myra can be seen
> better by the camera and the viewer because of their privileged point of view
> and mobility than she can by any eyes closed with her in fiction.[38]

While Denton's film, through its narrative and filmic techniques, can be
seen to foreground Lady Audley's point of view more than Hazelwood's stage
version, the character is by no means the exclusive figure of identification.
Flash-backs and shots from the perspective of George Talboys and Luke also
inform the spectator's response. The adaptation employs a filmic equivalent
of the literary technique outlined by Wolfgang Iser, in his analysis of the
viewpoint in the novel:

> The switch of viewpoint brings about a spot-lighting of textual perspectives,
> and these in turn become reciprocally influenced backgrounds which endow
> each new foreground with a specific shape and form. As the viewpoint changes
> again, this foreground merges into the background, which it had modified and
> which is now to exert its influence on yet another new foreground.[39]

It is necessary to acknowledge the relative sophistication of Denton's film in
its use of such a technique. The advance made is clear when the piece is compared to an adaptation of another Victorian sensation novel, Mrs Henry Wood's
East Lynne, produced seven years earlier by Barker Motion Photography. *East
Lynne's* static, wide-angle shots replicate the form of the theatrical tableaux,
and it is largely left to the performers' gesture and expression to indicate the
emotional focus of each shot. A notable exception occurs in the sequence in
which the villain, Francis Levison, convinces Lady Isabel that her husband,
Archibald Carlyle, is having an affair with Barbara Hare. The film cuts from
a long-shot of Levison and Isabel watching Archibald and Barbara, to a close-
up of Levison supporting Isabel. The close-up intensifies the impact of Isabel's
horror at what she believes to be her husband's adultery, and offers the viewer
the voyeuristic pleasure of sharing private emotion. As early as 1916 Hugo

Münsterberg was developing a theory of the cinema's emotional effect in exactly these terms:

> Our imitation of the emotion which we see expressed brings vividness and effective tone into our grasping of the play's action. We sympathize with the sufferer and that means the pain which he expresses becomes our own pain. [40]

The face is viewed as the focus of emotional 'access' to a character, particularly in silent cinema where the use of verbal language is confined to titles.

The use of titles to mediate this emotional effect can be seen to vary in this era. In Barker's *East Lynne*, they reflect the film's overall treatment of the narrative in aiming at a clear and economic structuring of the plot, in keeping with the advice given to screenwriters in the trade journal *The Pictures* in 1912:

> Carefully study out the needed action for each scene and then describe it briefly, being careful to cut out every act that does not have a direct bearing on the development of the plot. . . . Do not enter too much into details in these descriptions. . . . Use sub-titles or leaders sparingly – only when necessary to the proper understanding of the play. [41]

While *East Lynne's* use of titles is thus mainly limited to description of action that is subsequently shown, *Lady Audley's Secret* exploits their capacity as a vehicle for a form of authorial comment. Eliot Stannard, the screenwriter, uses the opening titles to direct the spectator's view of the character of Lady Audley before she has even appeared:

1. Title: Blind yielding to callous selfishness and brooding discontent.
2. Title: Then the first false deed, that must be helped out by new treacheries, new curses, new wickedness, till the whole edifice of evil tumbles and crashes from its own inherent rottenness.
3. Title: Oh, what a tangled web we weave.
               When first we practice to deceive.
4. Title: Helen Maldon prepares at all costs to have done with shabby gentility.
5. Long shot: Interior, Captain Maldon's House. Helen Maldon paces left to right.

The heightened rhetoric of Stannard's language can be located within the melodramatic tradition. [42] The screenplay continues to use titles to introduce each character and performer as they appear in the narrative; for example Lady Audley's father is presented as: 'Captain Maldon, her reprobate old father, Played by . . . William Burchill.'

The delineation of Lady Audley herself in Ideal's film is noticeably different from that in Hazelwood's play, reflecting the influence of contemporaneous developments in women's history. The *fin de siècle* had seen the emergence of the 'New Woman', a cultural myth circulated in response to an increasingly vociferous rejection by women of their traditional role in the family, politics, education and employment. The cinema, as well as the theatre and literature of the era, produced representations of this character as both heroine and termagant. Material ranged from newsreel footage of suffragette parades and speeches to short dramas lampooning the movement: for example, *Oh! You Suffragette* (1911, USA) and *A Day in the Life of a Suffragette* (1908, France) are two films in which initially unruly women are made to recognise and accept their dependency upon men. And in the United States the National Women's Suffrage Movement collaborated with Reliance to produce *Votes for Women* (1912). Described by *Moving Picture World* as a 'Serious Presentation of Suffrage Propaganda',[43] the film used dramatic narrative to combine fictional characters with prominent members of the suffrage movement.

Clearly, such films, in taking the suffrage movement as their central subject, are easily identifiable in their response and relationship to the 'New Woman'. Yet Ideal's *Lady Audley's Secret*, while not overtly tackling the same issues, can equally be seen to mediate a changing perception of gender. Braddon's novel is updated to a contemporary setting: Lady Audley becomes a lively young wife with blond, bobbed hair, given to proferring Sir Michael a puff of her cigarette. The story is presented predominantly from her perspective, and the film arguably strives, in Margaret Bannerman's naturalistic performance (a style of acting that would come to dominate mainstream cinema in Hollywood and Britain) to explicate the villainess's behaviour in terms of psychological realism. This change in presentation is reflected in a contemporary reviewer's response to Denton's film and its heroine:

> Although the story of her bigamous marriage and callous attempts at murder may be classed as melodrama, she is a character drawn with genuine psychological insight. She has many lovable traits and in different circumstances might have made a model wife and mother; yet her fatal lack of moral sense enables her to commit atrocious deeds, which in a normal person might seem almost incredible.[44]

The development of a critical approach that evaluates in terms of psychological realism, of how 'true to life' the character appears, is further indication both of the shift away from the nineteenth-century melodramatic tradition and its externalisation of conflict,[45] and of the film's more sympathetic depiction of the role of the adventuress.

Yet this modern Lady Audley still retains the distinctive hallmarks of her Victorian counterpart. The editing foregrounds the relish with which she plots to hide her past, cutting from a point-of-view shot of the newspaper announcement of Helen Talboy's 'death', to a long-shot of Lady Audley sprawled in the luxury of her four-poster bed at Audley Court, as she looks up from the paper and laughs. The film also follows its source in playing on the character's masquerade as the 'Angel in the House', for example in the presentation of shots from the point of view of George Talboys, deceived by his wife's appearance. Before George departs for Australia he is shown in long-shot placing a letter by his sleeping wife, the film then cutting to a close-up of Helen that shows his view of her at this stage in the story as the embodiment of innocence, her face softly lit and framed by blonde curls.

The film, beginning its narrative before Helen meets George, allows a greater foregrounding of his perspective on the story than occurs in the novel. Denton cuts the action between George and Helen's stories, which occur simultaneously in narrative time, to emphasise George's role as the victim of a callous wife:

Title: In lone watches by the camp fire George finds comfort in the little book given him by Helen on their honeymoon.
Shot: George by the campfire in Australia.
Shot: Flashback of George and Helen on their honeymoon. Helen gives George the book.
Shot: George by the campfire in Australia.
Title: There she is waiting for my return.
Title: Helen was neither watching nor waiting but had for some time been acting, under her new name, as a governess.

The film's closure also significantly modifies Braddon's character. The internment of Lady Audley in the mental asylum is cut, to be replaced by a sequence which suggests the character dies tormented by guilt. The ghost of George Talboys appears to her in the bedroom at Audley Court, the fact that the character is still alive in the plot defining the apparition as a figment of her imagination. Lady Audley places her hand to her forehead and gulps down some pills from a bottle. The screen fades to black and then up to a scene set the following morning, when the maid finds her mistress dead. The ending rejects the harshness of Lady Audley's punishment in the novel, sentenced to be 'buried alive' in the asylum. The closing shot of the dead woman mourned by her maid bears similarities to the tableau of sympathy that ends Hazelwood's play. In examining the response of female viewers to the victimisation of a female character in the series *Days of Our Lives*, John Fiske suggests:

> The process of revelation builds horror and sympathy which cannot be confined to masochistic identification with the suffering of the woman victim but can overspill into an awareness of the male power that produces the victimization.[46]

The film's presentation of Lady Audley as a victim may negate the threat of the character's rebellion, but, as Fiske's analysis suggests, it possibly also opens up an equally subversive interpretation of the society that destroys her.

In looking at different versions of *Lady Audley's Secret* over a period of sixty

years, it is possible to trace how different eras and systems of representation
have seen changes in the characterisation of the adventuress, while remaining within the same basic narrative structure which advocates the punishment
and death of deviant femininity. Drawing on recent critical works on popular
culture and, more specifically, soap opera, I have suggested that the depiction of Lady Audley may be interpreted as subversive to the ideology of this
structure. Such a reading is closed off in Hazlewood's stage adaptation, while
Ideal's early film version presents a post-New-Woman manifestation of the
adventuress that both perpetuates and modifies the morality of its source.

The representation of women in contemporary society remains rooted in the
dualistic morality of the nineteenth century, defining woman as virgin or
whore, the Lily Maid or the Vamp, Krystle or Alexis. *Lady Audley's Secret* has
remained in circulation as a novel, and in stage, television and radio adaptations. The continuing popularity of the text, and the perpetuation of its female
role of villainess in soap-opera narratives, would suggest that the adventuress
remains a potent figure in contemporary cultural discourse.

Notes

1. G. Cunningham, *The New Woman and the Victorian Novel* (London: Macmillan, 1972), p. 2.
2. D. M. Craik, *A Woman's Thoughts about Women* (London: Hurst and Blackett, 1858), p. 312.
3. J. K. Jerome, *Stageland* (London: Chatto and Windus, 1889), p. 38.
4. T. Modleski, *Loving with a Vengeance: Mass produced fantasies for women* (New York and London: Methuen, 1984), pp. 94–5.
5. *Daytimers*, June 1885, cited by J. Fiske, *Television Culture* (London and New York: Methuen, 1987), p. 188.
6. Cited by J. Uglow, Introduction to Mary Braddon's *Lady Audley's Secret* (London: Virago, 1985), p. x.
7. Unsigned review, *Westminster Review* LXXXXI (n.s. XXX) (October 1866), 1969–71.
8. Modleski, *Loving with a Vengeance, op. cit.* p. 28.
9. *ibid.*, p. 26.
10. S. Mitchell, 'Sentiment and Suffering: Women's recreational reading in the 1860s', *Victorian Studies*, vol. 21, no. 1 (1977), p. 34.
11. Cited by E. Showalter, *A Literature of their Own: British Women Novelists from Brontë to Lessing* (London: Virago, 1978), p. 161.
12. Braddon, *Lady Audley's Secret, op. cit.*, p. 7.
13. *ibid.*, p. 60.
14. Unsigned review, *The Times*, London, 18 November 1862, cited by T. F. Boyle, 'Fishy Extremities: Subversion of orthodoxy in the Victorian sensation novel', *Literature and History*, 9 (1983), p. 93.
15. Showalter, *A Literature of their Own, op. cit.*, p. 165.
16. Braddon, *Lady Audley's Secret, op. cit.*, p. 232.
17. *ibid.*, p. 171.
18. Mary Braddon, *Lady Audley's Secret*, ed. David Skilton (Oxford: Oxford University Press, 1987), pp. 446–7. The Oxford edition is set from the eighth edition of the

novel, which incorporated changes including the additional text in the final chapter from which this quote comes. Any other quotes from *Lady Audley's Secret* in this article are from the Virago edition, which uses the first edition of the novel.

19. P. Brooks, *The Melodramatic Imagination: Balzac, Henry James, melodrama and the mode of excess* (New Haven: Yale University Press, 1976), p. 43.

20. Unsigned review, *London Quarterly Review*, October 1866, quoted in N. Page (ed.), *Wilkie Collins: The critical heritage* (London: Routledge and Kegan Paul, 1974), p. 156.

21. Cited by Fiske, *Television Culture, op. cit.*, p. 188.

22. *ibid.*, p. 189.

23. Braddon, *Lady Audley's Secret, op. cit.*, p. 232.

24. Cited by L. Nead, *Myths of Sexuality* (Oxford: Oxford University Press, 1988), p. 50.

25. W. Holloway, '"I just wanted to kill a woman." Why? The Ripper and male sexuality', in H. Kanter, S. Lefanu, S. Shah and C. Spedding (eds), *Sweeping Statements: Writings from the women's liberation movement 1981–1983* (London: The Women's Press, 1984), p. 17.

26. Braddon, *Lady Audley's Secret, op. cit.*, p. 293.

27. *ibid.*, p. 319.

28. *ibid.*, p. 321.

29. Showalter, *A Literature of their Own, op. cit.*, p. 167.

30. W. Macqueen-Pope, *St James's: Theatre of Distinction* (London: W. H. Allen, 1958), pp. 25–8.

31. B. Stoker, *Personal Reminiscences of Henry Irving* (London: William Heinemann, 1906).

32. C. H. Hazelwood, *Lady Audley's Secret: An original version of Miss Braddon's popular novel in two acts*, in George Rowell (ed.), *Nineteenth Century Plays* (Oxford: Oxford University Press, 1953), Act II, scene i, p. 255.

33. *ibid.* Act I, scene i, p. 248.

34. Brooks, *The Melodramatic Imagination, op. cit.*, p. 36.

35. Hazlewood, *Lady Audley's Secret, op. cit.*, Act I, scene ii, p. 245.

36. *ibid.* Act II, scene v, p. 266.

37. C. Affron, *Cinema and Sentiment* (Chicago and London: University of Chicago Press, 1982), p. 2.

38. *ibid.*, p. 58.

39. Wolfgang Iser, cited by Affron, *Cinema, op. cit.*, p. 11.

40. H. Münsterberg, *The Photoplay: A psychological study* (New York: D. Appleton and Co., 1916), p. 53; cited by Affron, *Cinema, op. cit.*, p. 6.

41. Cited by R. Low, *The History of the British Film*, 1906–1914 (London: Allen and Unwin, 1971), p. 253.

42. Brooks, *The Melodramatic Imagination, op. cit.*, pp. 40–1.

43. *Moving Picture World*, 12, (1 June 1912), p. 811.

44. *The Bioscope*, 4 November 1920, p. 80.

45. Brooks, *The Melodramatic Imagination, op. cit.*, p. 35.

46. Fiske, *Television Culture, op. cit.*, p. 183.

PART V

Women Writing Women

9

Drama as a Trade: Cicely Ḥamilton's *Diana of Dobson's*

SHEILA STOWELL

During the years 1906 to 1914, as a flagging women's movement was revitalised by the controversial Women's Social and Political Union, women of all classes, talents and occupations were galvanised into action. Among them were a number of playwrights who used the overtly 'public' forum of the theatre to argue feminist views. It is the work of one such playwright, Cicely Hamilton, that forms the subject of this paper. Hamilton was a prominent participant in the flourishing suffrage movement of the early twentieth century. As a member of both the Actresses' Franchise League and the Women Writers' Suffrage League (organisations formed in 1908), she was a regular contributor to the agitprop drama of the cause. Her farcical comedy, *How the Vote was Won*, was one of the most popular pieces in the suffrage repertoire, while her historical *Pageant of Great Women*, first produced by Edith Craig at the Scala Theatre in November 1909, was regarded by Ellen Terry as 'the finest practical piece of propaganda written for the movement'.[1] Hamilton chose as well to write for the larger and more broadly based audiences of London's West End, realising a major success with *Diana of Dobson's* (1908), 'a romantic comedy' in four acts in which she manipulates the traditions and conventions of West End theatre according to avowedly feminist lights. Perhaps, however, the place to begin is with a significant passage from Hamilton's autobiography, *Life Errant*; claiming that she was motivated more by feminist than specifically suffragist concerns she insisted:

> I never attempted to disguise the fact that I wasn't wildly interested in votes for anyone, and . . . if I worked for women's enfranchisement (and I did work quite hard) it wasn't because I hoped great things from counting female noses at general

elections, but because the agitation for women's enfranchisement must inevitably shake and weaken the tradition of the 'normal woman'. The 'normal
woman' with her 'destiny' of marriage and motherhood and housekeeping, no
interest outside her home – especially no interest in the man's preserve of
politics! My personal revolt was feminist rather than suffragist.[2]

Such views dominate Hamilton's work, finding their most forceful expression
in *Marriage as a Trade* (1909), a piece of polemical writing which Elaine
Showalter describes as being 'on the brink of the feminist criticism'. Surprisingly, given Hamilton's position on a feminist/suffragist divide, Showalter
claims that 'she bogged down in her efforts to connect women's literature to
the specific goal of the vote.'[3] As its title suggests, *Marriage as a Trade* is an
attempt to debunk the more romantic connotations of that institution through
an examination of its 'trade aspect'. The work focuses upon the extent to
which 'woman' is a social construct, 'the product of the conditions imposed
upon her by her staple industry': 'Vicious or virtuous, matron or outcast, she
was made and not born.'[4] It examines the unhappy consequences for women's
mental and physical well-being of their manipulation into 'the regulation
pattern of wifehood',[5] and confirms the ideology of the suffrage movement in
its assertion that 'the human female is not entirely composed of sex.'[6] The
book launches an attack upon the hysterisation of the female body as Michel
Foucault would come to characterise it, condemning the artificial reduction of
women to sex, and celebrating celibacy and spinsterhood as alternatives to
the subjugation and dependency that marriage and motherhood entailed.

As one specific element in her discussion of *Marriage as a Trade*, Hamilton
considers women's place in art and literature. She argues that:

> Art, as we know it, is a masculine product, wrought by the hands and conceived
> by the brains of men; the works of art that have forced themselves into the
> enduring life of the world have been shaped, written, builded [sic], painted by
> men. They have achieved and we have imitated; on the whole, pitifully.[7]

It is Hamilton's contention that much of women's art is 'artificial',

> not a representation of life or beauty seen by a woman's eyes, but an attempt to
> render life or beauty as man desires that a woman should see and render it. The
> attempt is unconscious, no doubt; but it is there – thwarting, destroying and
> annulling.[8]

Hamilton maintains, however, that a woman can at least attempt to counter
such training, albeit at great cost:

> even in the comparatively few instances where she recognises what her training
> has done for her, when she realises the poor thing it has made of her, and sets
> to work, deliberately and of firm resolve, to counteract its effects upon her life
> and character, it may take her the best part of a lifetime to struggle free of her
> chains.[9]

Diana of Dobson's, one of Hamilton's own deliberate attempts to break free from such chains, was her first full-length play. It is a comedy about a sweated shop-assistant, 'who, on the strength of a small legacy, makes a Cinderella-like appearance in the world that does not toil or spin'.[10] Her unexpected inheritance allows her to live as a woman of means for one brief month at a resort in the Swiss Alps. During this time she is wooed both by the owner of the chain of drapers' shops where she once worked, and by Victor Bretherton, a ne'er do well who, finding it impossible to live 'on a miserable six hundred pounds a year', is encouraged to court Diana on the basis of her supposed fortune. She refuses the former and both rejects and is rejected by the latter when she discloses the true state of her affairs. Her legacy quickly depleted, she returns to England and a life of increasing destitution, one that forces her to haunt the Thames Embankment, where she once more encounters Bretherton. Stung by her taunt that he would 'throw up the sponge in a week' if he had to earn his own living without help from his friends or relations, he has attempted to do just that with a singular lack of success. Convinced now that his income is not 'a miserable pittance' but rather enough for two, he proposes again and Diana accepts.

Upon its completion Hamilton sent the manuscript to the Kingsway Theatre, which, under the management of Lena Ashwell (also an active member of the Actresses' Franchise League), had undergone a pink and white chocolate-box type of refurbishment reminiscent of Madame Vestris's earlier prettification of the Olympic. Like Granville Barker at the Court, Ashwell was determined to establish a theatre that would produce new plays by promising English playwrights. *Diana of Dobson's* was the eleventh play in a pile of twenty-five that Kingsway play-reader, Edward Knoblock, was scouring for possible production. He reacted to the script with an enthusiasm – 'Nothing can compare with the joy of finding a really good, human, crisp, amusing manuscript'[11] – that Ashwell shared, and the play was signed for almost immediate production. It was an astute business decision; this 'delicious comedy', as Ashwell described it, proved a commercial success. Opening on 12 February 1908, it ran for 143 performances and was withdrawn only because Ashwell opted for a period of rest before the commencement of her provincial tour.[12] The play was, however, revived the following year for a further thirty-two performances.[13]

Although Ashwell required few alterations to the script, she did request a change of title.[14] Hamilton had originally called the play *The Adventuress*, in obvious reference to an exchange between Diana and Bretherton in Act III that follows her 'confession':

> *Bretherton*: . . . Oh, hang it all, I know I'm no match for you in an argument. But however much you may sneer and jeer at me, you must know perfectly well that your conduct has been that of an adventuress.
> *Diana (lightly)*: An adventuress! So I'm an adventuress am I? Doesn't this rather remind you of the celebrated interchange of compliments between the pot and kettle?[15]

The rejected title was also, however, a challenge to a dramatic female stereo-type which had its roots in melodrama. In fact, so prevalent was this par-ticular type of female villain that Jerome K. Jerome includes a section on her in *Stageland*, a series of tongue-in-cheek profiles of figures from that genre. According to Jerome, the melodramatic adventuress signifies 'black-hearted and abandoned womanhood',[16] which translated means that she is a clever business woman who dresses well. She almost always has a terrible secret that, when revealed, wreaks havoc with her marital machinations, and she stands in marked contrast to the heroine, a passive figure of nobility and self-sacrifice. She is, in other words, evil step-sister to the victimised but always angelic Cinderella.

The 'mental nausea' suffered by Hamilton in response to 'the utter sloppi-ness of the admired type of heroine'[17] resulted in her endowing Diana with some of the characteristics normally associated with the stage adventuress. According to Ashwell, who played the title-role in the first production,

> Diana is by nature a Bohemian, and, like all Bohemians when they are poor, in a perpetual state of revolt. And when she is thoroughly put out, she says a great many nasty and bitter things about the powers that be.[18]

She is also assertive and willing to initiate action, and as such stands in marked contrast to the prevailing social as well as dramatic ideal of womanly submission.

This is not to suggest that *Diana of Dobson's* launches a full-scale attack upon patriarchal culture. If Elizabeth Robins's feminist society drama, *Votes for Women* (1907), was described by her as a 'dramatic tract', Hamilton's *Diana of Dobson's* presents itself as 'a romantic comedy'. Ashwell described the piece as 'very, very light' and Hamilton maintained that she 'had no serious object in writing [it]'.[19] Yet the play does not lack a critical perspective; Hamilton added in the same interview, 'I am hoping that the story may prove to be interesting to the general public, who do not know as a rule much about the lives of shop-girls, and the want of consideration with which some of them are treated by their employers.' Ashwell noted that 'the authoress can hit hard when she likes, and some of the scenes are written in a spirit that can only be de-scribed as exceedingly sarcastic and satirical.'[20] To borrow Shaw's phrase-ology when talking about his own plays, Hamilton uses devices of romantic comedy to coat the propagandist pill. As the *Era* critic wrote, the play

> is produced quite apropos of the agitation against living in and of the cry for female suffrage. It voices very boldly the revolt of the modern woman against her subjection, her craving for interest in life, her hatred of monotony, and her desire for a 'good time',[21]

In both her redefinition of well-known dramatic female types and her attention to the plight of a group of women workers, Hamilton displays a feminist perspective coloured by issues raised within the growing women's movement. Rejecting what she considered to be the servile and imitative nature of most women's art, she strove instead to produce work that expressed a distinctly female point of view: 'My conception of woman is inevitably the feminine conception; a thing so entirely unlike the masculine conception of woman that it is eminently needful to define the term and make my meaning clear.'[22] *Diana of Dobson's* is just one instance of Hamilton's struggle to define 'woman' apart from the attributes traditionally foisted upon her by a patriarchal ideology. In doing so, she inevitably relies upon dramatic conventions rooted in that ideology: deliberately reconstructing them, however, according to her feminist point of view.

In the case of *Diana of Dobson's*, Hamilton harkens back to a tradition of light comedy initiated by Tom Robertson in a handful of 'cup-and-saucer' plays written for the Bancrofts in the 1860s. Part of a larger-scale reaction to the excesses of much mid-Victorian theatre, Robertson's genteel comedies display 'a cleverness in investing with romantic associations commonplace details of life' (*Athenaeum*, 23 January 1869). His most successful piece, *Caste* (1867), a Cinderella story of cross-class alliance, relies upon delicately rendered romance to side-step the potentially sticky moral and social problems it raises. Unlike the play's other working-class figures, the heroine, Esther, displays a ladylike gentility that justifies the Hon. George D'Alroy's love and desire to raise her to his station. As he says, 'Caste is a good thing if it's not carried too far. It shuts the door on the pretentious and the vulgar: but it should open the door very wide for exceptional merit.'[23] The 'exceptional' Esther, miscast for life among the working class, is rescued through a finely wrought romance, her princely soldier carrying her off to a life of ladylike ease in a very fine house.

Arthur Wing Pinero's *Trelawny of the 'Wells'* (1898) strikes a late-Victorian variation upon *Caste*, enlisting the earlier play's formal structure, romantic plot and genteel tone in a reconsideration of the problem of misalliance and rehabilitation. *Trelawny of the 'Wells'* concerns another working woman's translation into respectability through an impending marriage into the aristocracy. But whereas in the problem plays of the period such cross-class liaisons are doomed by the aggressive social conventions they violate, in *Trelawny of the 'Wells'* the issue is evaded and the marriage sanctioned by means of an aesthetic attitude that unites romance with theatre history. In a 'Robertsonian tribute to Robertson' the reunion of Rose Trelawny and Arthur Gower is engineered to take place during a rehearsal of what in the context of the play is seen as the 'innovative' cup-and-saucer comedy of reforming playwright Tom Wrench/Robertson.[24]

In Hamilton's hands, the romance in such comedy becomes a feminist issue, and *Diana of Dobson's* serves as a practical demonstration of what she calls in *Marriage as a Trade*, 'the business-like aspect of love in woman, the social and commercial necessity for sexual intercourse . . . usually ignored by an imitative feminine art – because it is lacking in man, and is, therefore, not really grasped by him.'[25] According to Hamilton, women are generally less romantic than men by virtue of their commercial interest in matters of sexual attraction, and this effects their reaction to as well as participation in romance:

> It is because her love has always been her livelihood that woman has never been inspired by it as man has been inspired. And it is just because it is so business-like that her interest in love is often so keen. For instance, her customary appreciation of a book or a work of art dealing with love, and nothing but love, is the outcome of something more than sentiment and overpowering conscious-ness of sex. To her a woman in love is not only a woman swayed by emotion, but a human being engaged in carving for herself a career or securing for herself a means of livelihood. Her interest in a love story is, therefore, much more complex than a man's interest therein, and the appreciation which she brings to it is of a very different quality.[26]

Without attempting an exhaustive analysis of Hamilton's achievement in *Diana of Dobson's*, I would like to offer, by way of example, two instances of how this work uses the expectations of its spectators and the conventions of the commercial theatre to seek wider audiences for Hamilton's feminist views. My first example is drawn from the play's much discussed and praised opening act.

The work begins, appropriately enough, in darkness (light itself is a costly commodity at Dobson's drapery establishment and its use regulated by rules and fines), a situation relieved by the fumbling hands of a female shop assistant. Locating the gas jet, she turns the light up on 'a bare room of the dormitory type . . . [with] everything plain and comfortless to the last degree'.[27] It was described by the socialist newspaper, *The Clarion*, as 'a unique blend of barrack, Dotheboys Hall, and workhouse.'[28] As the many illustrations of the set show, five small beds are ranged against the up-stage wall to which, during the course of the act, five tired and worn women repair, talking as they undress. Such potentially titillating stage business might be thought curious from a feminist writer who expressed her rage 'that character, worth, intellect were held valueless in woman, that nothing counted in her but the one capacity – the power of awaking desire.'[29] And certainly some reviewers considered the scene 'a little daring' or potentially 'shocking'. The critic for the *Stage* objected that 'it was an obviously make-believe going to bed, an insincere business with no bearing on the play, introduced merely for whatever sensational appeal it may have in itself.'[30]

Bearing in mind, however, Hamilton's contention that women specialise in personal adornment as a matter of business and not from 'overflowing sexuality', such stage action should be judged as a public disassembling of the female sex-object, a visual dismantling of her various parts. We are meant to witness women's professionalism in the quick and efficient manner in which they discard the puffs and switches, ribbons and collars, waists and skirts that translate them into suitable representatives of attractive womanhood. This may be what motivated the *Stage* reviewer's objection since he goes on to complain that 'these different stages of undress do not happen to be made pretty.' Other critics appreciated the scene's 'professional' aspect. One characterised the women's movements as 'mechanical',[31] while another commented that

> There is nothing approaching the improper in this episode, though we see half a dozen tired shop assistants getting into their bed clothes after revealing secrets of the unmaking of various forms of coiffure, which only a woman would have the audacity to attack.[32]

In the words of H. M. Walbrook, 'if any flippant reader imagines that by booking a seat at the Kingsway Theatre he will get a view of something rather scandalous and improper – well, all we shall say is, Let him book his seat! He will deserve his disappointment.'[33] This process of de-eroticisation is also encouraged by the absence of any male viewers on stage. Women, at least within the context of the play's initial scene, cease to be objects of a dramatised male gaze. In fact, men are completely excluded from the action of the first act, allowing Hamilton to establish a female perspective safe from male inter-ruption. The argument thus introduced is an indication of how far Hamilton has taken the stage undressings used by her male contemporaries for mere titillation.

As the play proceeds, Hamilton allows herself scope to examine in detail the issue of marriage as a trade. Through Diana's experiences as well as those of other peripheral characters, we are made to recognise the overwhelming pressure, financial as well as social, upon women to marry. The conclusion to Diana's own marital negotiations occupies the close of the play, and provides my second example of the manner in which Hamilton both builds upon and subverts the work of her predecessors. The curtain rises on Act IV to reveal 'that place of ill-omen, the Thames Embankment'.[34] We have, it would appear, followed Diana's theatrical odyssey from naturalistic drama through the society comedy of Acts II and III to arrive in the realm of what one reviewer characterised as 'transpontine melodrama'. And certainly, the sight of 'the Thames Embankment in the small hours of a November morning'[35] conjured up an extensive tradition (literary and pictorial as well as theatrical) which coupled that locale with grim scenes of desperation and suicide 'which dis-turbed the imagination of the age'.[36] It is not, however, a helpless, homeless and hopeless Diana we first detect amid that ragged pile of human misery asleep on an Embankment bench. It is Victor Bretherton, only recently descended to 'the hopelessly unemployed class', who is being prodded along by a police constable. The very Robertsonian meeting of old soldiers that follows (the police officer was in Victor's company of the Welsh Guards) provides Victor with an opportunity to explain why he is 'masquerading on this Embankment in these delectable clothes'.[37] He has not, as the constable immediately assumes, suffered ''eavy financial losses'; rather, he has taken Diana up on her Act III challenge to earn his own living.[38]

With the aid of the long arm of coincidence, Diana herself soon enters, her appearance, too, strangely altered. The attractive Paris frocks of the second and third acts, financed by the soon-squandered inheritance, are replaced by the costume of the habitually unemployed: 'a shabby hat and coat, a short skirt, muddy boots and woollen gloves with holes in several of the finger-tips'.[39] One is reminded of Vida Levering's cry in Robins's *Votes for Women*: 'Some girls think it hardship to have to earn their living. The horror is not to be allowed to.'[40] Given such a scenario, one could be forgiven for anticipating a sensational melodramatic conclusion in which a despairing woman resolves to end it all with a grim leap off the Embankment.[41] But Hamilton, like her predecessor Robertson, rejects sensationalism in favour of more restrained comedy. We see not abject poverty but Cinderella after the stroke of twelve. This does not mean that Hamilton's protagonist adopts the passive and acquiescent manner of Robertson's more conventional stage heroines; even in the face of adversity Diana maintains an energetic and confrontational 'sub-acid' style. Nor does the 'invertebrate' Victor, whose chronic weakness drew a mutter of disapproval from critics, suddenly develop the stature of the heroic manly man. The play does not end with a melodramatic windfall; neither Diana nor Victor realise a sum vast enough to finance the life-style they enjoyed in the Swiss Alps. Victor simply takes another look at his circumstances and realises that, far from being 'a miserable pittance, hardly enough . . . to live upon', his £600 a year is 'not only enough for *one* to live upon – it's ample for *two*'.[42] Diana is also invited to take a second look at Victor when, in an inversion of attitudes, he offers her 'proprietary rights in a poor backboneless creature who never did a useful thing in his life'.[43]

Given that *Diana of Dobson's* is the work of a playwright consciously attempting to write from a woman's perspective, it is not surprising that the protagonist then demonstrates a 'business-like' attitude which, Hamilton argues in *Marriage as a Trade*, is an aspect of love for women generally ignored in that bulk of women's writing that merely mimics men's work. Accordingly, when Victor proposes Diana responds in a way that exposes what in *Marriage as a Trade* Hamilton refers to as women's 'double motived' interest in matrimony:

> *Diana* (*turning on him almost fiercely*): Captain Bretherton – I'm homeless and penniless – I haven't – tasted food for nearly twelve hours – I've been half starved for days. And now, if I understand you alright – you offer to make me your wife.
> *Bretherton*: You do understand me aright.
> *Diana*: That is to say, you offer me a home and what is to me a fortune.
> *Bretherton*: And myself.
> *Diana* (*laughing harshly*): And yourself – please don't imagine I forget that important item.[44]

With no other trade readily available to her, Diana accepts marriage, although in deference to the demands of the genre (as well as the box-office?) Hamilton's

'Cinderella' apparently enters 'the housekeeping trade' in order to love as well
as to live. I qualify the latter statement because in the eyes of one reviewer at
least, Diana's love for Victor is not self-evident:

> It is not Miss Ashwell's fault that the audience does not know exactly what to
> think of the girl and her masquerade. . . . The position would be simplified if
> it had been brought out that Diana is in love with Bretherton. The author does
> not free Diana from the suggestion that she is a selfish, hard, and not over-
> scrupulous young woman.[45]

As far as this critic is concerned, Diana might well be an adventuress after all.

The play, which enjoyed a generally favourable critical reception, nevertheless engendered a debate over its purpose and genre. Many reviewers
praised what they considered to be Hamilton's 'ingenious blend' of social
criticism and romance to produce a 'thinking-man's' comedy. The *Illustrated
London News* urged play-goers to attend a work that would make them 'think
and laugh'[46] while the *World*, adopting a more condescending tone to London
audiences, insisted:

> It is a complete success in that it holds the unsophisticated with its 'roe-mance',
> while the more hardened playgoer is amused and interested by the clever
> touches which serve to hide the framework: by the humour, the satire, the study
> of character, the criticism of life.[47]

Others suspected the veracity of the play's conclusion but condoned it as part
and parcel of Hamilton's fairy-tale format. The redoubtable critic for the *Stage*,
on the other hand, insisted upon seeing the play by the light of naturalist
theatre and looked forward to a bleak future: 'The audience, at the back of its
mind, must have a vague uneasiness about the suitableness of the match and
the likelihood of happiness. The married pair, too, will have to reckon with
Bretherton's family, especially with the aunt.'[48] A more intriguing complaint
was lodged by two reviewers who argued that Hamilton's play had in essence
betrayed the labour cause. According to Walbrook, until the end of the third
act *Diana of Dobson's* 'is a rather roughly composed tract on the harsh
conditions of labour and ignominy of pampered laziness', but the fourth act
'arbitrarily as well as sentimentally' dismisses these issues and their ramifica-
tions by opting to save Diana through marriage to a man and his adequate
unearned income. The critic for the *Illustrated Sporting and Dramatic News*
goes further: he maintains that, although the play is intended to argue the
rights of labour against the abuses of capital, it actually makes the opposite
case by failing to portray 'capital . . . [as] unreasonable and labour sensible
and worthy'.[49]

To insist, however, that the play suffers because it *does not*, in melodramatic fashion, divide labour and capital into clearly demarked camps of
good and evil or because it *does*, in melodramatic fashion, side-step such issues
by means of a limited and specific solution, is to ignore Hamilton's choice of

genre as well as the play's feminist component. For *Diana of Dobson's* is not so much an attack upon class or capitalism as a comedic demonstration of Hamilton's claim, most completely articulated in *Marriage as a Trade*, 'that the narrowing down of woman's hopes and ambitions to the sole pursuit and sphere of marriage is one of the principal causes of the various disabilities, economic and otherwise, under which she labours.'[50] Hamilton is concerned with depicting the consequences for women of a patriarchal hierarchy which treated them as mere adjuncts to men and, by insisting that their proper role was marriage and proper place the home, saw no reason to educate them to earn their own livelihood. If, however, a woman failed to secure said husband and home and was forced to support herself, immediately rendering her social position uncertain, she found that virtually all work available to her was intellectually and emotionally unrewarding, low in status and notoriously ill-paid, 'the custom of considering her work as worthless (from an economic point of view) [which] originated in the home, . . . [having] followed her into the world.'[51] Hamilton argued that women as a class were both socially and economically handicapped in a culture that privileged men. Within such a culture money gave power, as Hamilton is at pains to demonstrate in *Diana of Dobson's*, providing women with an independence from men otherwise un-realisable. Unfortunately, most women lacked such moneyed power and were, by various strategies of a patriarchal system, largely prevented from realising it (one is reminded in this regard of the discriminatory inheritance legislation of the period). With most of the work available to them absolutely unrewarding and many better occupations barred to them through custom, regulation or lack of education, women had little choice but to consider 'marriage as a trade'.

It is a credit to Hamilton's craftsmanship that in the last act of *Diana of Dobson's* she is able to exploit the conventions of romantic comedy (which dictate some form of marital resolution) to offer a feminist critique on marriage itself. In a final tribute to her predecessor, Tom Robertson, Hamilton concludes her play with a literal cup-and-saucer tableau of the happy couple enjoying sandwiches and coffee perched on a bench on the Thames Embankment. Yet even this final image is problematic. Are we meant to view it with optimism (after all, it is Victor who fetches the coffee) or read it ironically? One could certainly argue that in the manner of Robertson, the values of the home have simply followed Diana to the river's edge.[52]

Notes

1. E. Terry in *Votes for Women*, 19 November 1909, p. 117.
2. C. Hamilton, *Life Errant* (London: J. M. Dent, 1935) p. 65.
3. E. Showalter, *A Literature of their Own* (Princeton: Princeton University Press, 1977), p. 225.
4. C. Hamilton, *Marriage as a Trade* (1909; London: Women's Press, 1981), pp. 17, 44.
5. *ibid.*, p. 45.

6. *ibid.*, p. 102.
7. *ibid.*, p. 107.
8. *ibid.*, p. 112.
9. *ibid.*, p. 110.
10. Hamilton, *Life Errant, op. cit.*, p. 61.
11. E. Knoblock, *Round the Room* (London: Chapman and Hall, 1939), p. 91.
12. *Era*, 16 January 1909, p. 17.
13. *Diana of Dobson's* was revived by the Department of Drama and Theatre Studies, University of London, 11–14 March 1987.
14. According to Knoblock, '*Diana of Dobson's* had originally a somewhat misleading title. We searched for another one. The heroine being called Diana, we thought it might be good to join it up with the name of the shop at which she worked' (*Round the Room, op. cit.*, p. 91).
15. Hamilton. *Diana of Dobson's* (London: French, 1925), p. 51.
16. J. K. Jerome, *Stageland* (London: Chatto and Windus, 1893), p. 35.
17. Hamilton, *Life Errant, op. cit.*, p. 57.
18. *Pall Mall*, 8 February 1908.
19. *ibid.*
20. *ibid.*
21. *Era*, 15 February 1908, p. 17.
22. Hamilton, *Marriage as a Trade, op. cit.*, p. 19.
23. T. Robertson, *Caste*, in *Plays by Tom Robertson*, ed. William Tydeman (Cambridge: Cambridge University Press, 1982), p. 183.
24. J. Kaplan, 'Have we no Chairs?', *Essays in Theatre*, vol. 4, no. 2, (1986), pp. 119–33.
25. Hamilton, *Marriage as a Trade, op. cit.*, p. 113.
26. *ibid.*, pp. 117–18.
27. Hamilton, *Diana of Dobson's, op. cit.*, p. 7.
28. *Clarion*, 16 February 1912, p. 7.
29. Hamilton, *Marriage as a Trade, op. cit.*, p. 131.
30. *Stage*, 13 February 1908, p. 23.
31. *Illustrated London News*, 22 February 1908. p. 266.
32. *Illustrated Sporting and Dramatic News*, 7 March 1908, p. 19.
33. *Pall Mall*, 13 February 1908, p. 4.
34. *Illustrated London News*, 22 February 1908, p. 266.
35. Hamilton, *Diana of Dobson's, op. cit.*, p. 55.
36. *World*, 19 January 1909, p. 97.
37. *ibid.*, p. 56.
38. In fact, it was not unknown in the period for members of other classes to 'experience' poverty. According to Pember Reeves in her study of the London poor, various middle-class people chose to live on 3d a day in order to demonstrate that it was possible for a working man to do so as well. Reeves is rightly critical of such 'experiments', which did not require the well-to-do person to actually live among the poor, or to cut down expenses, other than for food, to the lowest possible level. See *Round About a Pound a Week* (London: G. Bell, 1913), pp. 143–4. Apropos of this point, Ashwell refers to three young women actors who decided to experience starving on the Thames Embankment so they could depict it more realistically on stage. Accordingly, 'after a good supper at the Carlton and having provided themselves with a bag of buns, they sat through the summer night, enduring the pangs of hunger, gazing at the Thames' (*Myself a Player* (London: Michael Joseph, 1936), p. 120).
39. Hamilton, *Diana of Dobson's, op. cit.*, p. 58. Diana's various changes of dress (and address) serve as a comic demonstration of Vida Levering's account, in Elizabeth Robins's *Votes for Women* (London: Mills and Boon, 1907; reprinted in Spender and

Hayman (eds) *How the Vote was Won and Other Suffragette Plays*), of how she exchanged her fine dresses for 'an old gown and a tawdry hat' in order to really experience the plight of poor, homeless women: 'You'll never know how many things are hidden from a woman in good clothes. The bold, free look of a man at a woman he believes to be destitute – you must feel that look on you before you can understand – a good half of history' (in D. Spender and C. Hayman (eds), *How the Vote was Won and Other Suffragette Plays* (London: Methuen, 1985), p. 50.

40. Robins, *Votes for Women*, *op. cit.*, p. 51.

41. In fact, in an interview before the play opened Ashwell was asked, 'I see that the Thames Embankment is chosen as the scene of the last act. That has rather a grim suggestiveness, taken in connection with the fact that Mr. Norman McKinnel plays the part of a policeman. I hope Diana is not driven to attempt suicide and is rescued only by the strong arm of the law?' (*Pall Mall*, 8 February 1908).

42. Hamilton, *Diana of Dobson's*, *op. cit.*, p. 62. Such an income would place Victor and Diana squarely in the realm of the middle class. According to G. Best in *Mid-Victorian Britain 1851–75* (London: Weidenfeld and Nicolson, 1971), p. 90, statistics for the last quarter of the nineteenth century placed a 'professional man or tradesman' earning £500 a year into the 'upper middle class'.

43. Hamilton, *Diana of Dobson's*, *op. cit.*, p. 62.

44. *ibid.*, p. 62.

45. *Stage*, 13 February 1908, p. 23.

46. *Illustrated London News*, 22 February 1908. p. 266.

47. *World*, 19 January 1909, p. 97.

48. *Stage*, 13 February 1908, p. 23.

49. *Illustrated Sporting and Dramatic News*, 7 March 1908, p. 19.

50. Hamilton, *Marriage as a Trade*, *op. cit.*, p. 22.

51. *ibid.*, p. 96.

52. 'Drama as a Trade' is a partial version of Chapter 3 of my book, *A Stage of their Own* (Manchester: Manchester University Press, 1992). Hamilton's handling of stage undressing is also examined in my essay, 'Re(pre)senting Eroticism', *Theatre History Studies*, vol. XI (1991), pp. 51–62.

Typewriters Enchained: The work of Elizabeth Baker

LINDA FITZSIMMONS

You can't expect him to marry a typewriter.[1]

Elizabeth Baker's plays, especially *Chains* (1909), were praised by her contemporaries. Reviews of *Chains* were mostly favourable, although often somewhat grudging and patronising; those of Baker's subsequent plays often refer back admiringly to *Chains*.[2] For example, the reviewer of *Bert's Girl* in *The Nation and Athenaeum*, 9 April 1927, who liked the play, regretted that 'Miss Elizabeth Baker, the eminent authoress of *Chains*, solicits all too rarely the favour of the public.'[3] She came to be used as a yardstick for measuring the success of other women writers. In reviewing Githa Sowerby's *Rutherford and Son* for *The Saturday Review*, 30 March 1912, John Palmer compares the play at length with *Chains*; welcoming *Rutherford and Son* as 'the best first play since *Chains*', he goes on:

> The conscientiousness and hard logic of a woman applied to the theatre are able to go surprising lengths. These plays of Miss Elizabeth Baker and Miss Sowerby are really astonishing examples of what can be done in a modern theatre by keeping strictly to the point.[4]

Histories of Edwardian theatre have proceeded, mostly, to bury her, apart from brief recognition of her skill as a realist. Histories written early this century usually refer to Baker somewhat admiringly. For example, P. P. Howe (1910) acclaims *Chains* as 'the first realistic play of satisfying achievement in this country'; A. E. Morgan (1924) deals with *Chains* and *The Price of Thomas Scott* and *Miss Robinson* as examples of 'the drama of revolt'; and Camillo Pellizzi (1935) includes *Chains* ('a solitary little masterpiece') and *The Price of Thomas Scott* as examples of 'aristocratic realism'.[5] In 1951 J. C. Trewin refers to *Chains* dismissively as 'a chilling little achievement' and describes it, as he does again in 1976, as 'a wire-and-sandpaper study of a suburban clerk'.[6] And although he refers to Baker by name in 1951, by 1976 she is not even named: he attributes the play merely to 'a woman dramatist'. In two recent books on Edwardian theatre, by Julie Holledge (1981) and Ian Clarke (1989), no mention is made of Baker's work, and Jan McDonald (1986) merely includes *Chains* in a list of plays in Frohman's 1910 season.[7] Baker fades from being recognised as a skilful realist, to being 'a woman dramatist', to being invisible. But even when her work was known and appreciated, the feminist arguments she put forward were ignored by critics. She is, certainly, a skilled realist but, more importantly, she used her skills to participate in the feminist debate around the issues, crucial for women, of work and marriage. Perhaps she has been made all but invisible in standard histories because her work focuses on feminist issues. I shall examine Baker's feminist stance most fully in *Chains*, but first I want to show how several of her other plays, which have been completely neglected, also participate in this debate.

Baker wrote at least fifteen plays, more than half of them one-acters, between 1909 and 1931.[8] Several of them were taken up by the early repertory–theatre movement, and were performed by the independent theatre societies in London, Manchester and Birmingham, and were published by Sidgwick and Jackson, alongside Githa Sowerby, Granville Barker, Stanley Houghton and John Masefield. The progressive theatre movement provided a platform for the work of other feminist writers, too, and a context in which their concerns would be seen sympathetically. Debates current in the feminist movement about the need for the empowerment of women in the areas of the franchise, sexuality, abortion, motherhood, economic independence, work and marriage were explored in the independent theatres. For example, as early as 1893, the Independent Theatre Society presented Florence Bell's and Elizabeth Robins's *Alan's Wife*, debating maternal responsibility; in 1907 Robins's *Votes for Women!*, focusing on the suffrage but also arguing for women's self-determination, was staged at the Court Theatre; Cicely Hamilton's *Just to Get Married*, attacking women's enforced economic dependency on men, was produced in 1911 at the Little Theatre by feminist and suffragist Gertrude Kingston; Githa Sowerby's *Rutherford and Son*, attacking patriarchal tyranny and suggesting a better, female-determined, future was first performed in 1912 at the Court Theatre in John Leigh's matinée season. Baker's particular concern is with examining the ways the central question of the relationship between work and marriage is posed in the lives of lower-middle-class families. Even in some of her postwar plays, when some critics have discerned in women's writing a lessening of the attack and a softening of the focus, she continues to show an awareness of the problems for women both in work – low pay, low status, no protection and little choice of occupation – and in marriage.

Baker's plays reflect the recognition in the early women's movement of the importance of the role of work in establishing women's independence and self-determination. Her focus is constantly the lower-middle class, so the women's work she shows is not glamorous, exciting and intrinsically liberating but, rather, is hard, boring and, often, demeaning. In focusing on these sorts of job, she both explores the exploitation women are subject to in the workplace and exposes the lack of choice available for women, while at the same time insisting on the need for women to have a decent alternative to selling themselves into marriage. In common with many other playwrights of the period, she structures her plays around moral dilemmas which the central characters have to confront; in Baker, the moral dilemmas are often related to the conflicts for women in these areas of work and marriage. She is, of course, by no means a feminist visionary. As Jane Lewis points out:

> Most nineteenth-century feminists accepted women's responsibilities for home and children and believed that women had to make a choice between work, and marriage and motherhood. Their claim was for equality with men in the public world on men's terms, with no special consideration or provision for women as mothers and no suggestion that men might share the work of caring and domestic labour in the home.[9]

Baker shows no married working women (although she does recognise and show domestic work as labour). In this, in keeping with the theatrical style she adopted, she was being realistic rather than utopian. It was mostly the case that unofficial marriage bars operated in the sorts of jobs her women characters do.[10] Further, her young women see paid employment as a prelude to marriage. Often marriage is presented as the conventional dramatic resolution, although it might be that the patness and conventionality of these endings raise subversive questions about the appropriateness of marriage as the solution to the characters' dilemmas.

Baker often presents the workplace, and women working, on stage. The range of jobs her women do is limited, and in this, too, she was being realistic. The jobs she shows are mostly low-paid, of low status and often related to domestic and servicing skills. Her characters work as typists, secretaries and clerks (Angela in *Miss Robinson*; Lois, Constance, Evelyn and Nora in *Lois*), as shop assistants (Maggie in *Chains*; all of the characters in *Miss Tassey*); Annie is a milliner in *The Price of Thomas Scott* and Stella works as a domestic servant in *Bert's Girl*. In *Edith* (1912), written for the Women Writers' Suffrage League, and in *Partnership* (1917) her central women characters are both successful business women but, again, within a defined area: they own dress shops.

Her one-act play, *Miss Tassey* (1910), is set, like the first act of Cicely

Hamilton's *Diana of Dobson's* (1908), in the dormitory attached to a shop. As well as the restrictions imposed on shop workers in their working hours, many of them had to live in, a system which was attractive to parents who could thus allow their daughters to live away from home because of the *in loco parentis* role played by the employers. Baker's dormitory has three beds in it, no comfort, only two photographs by way of personalising the space, and a card of rules on the wall. The action demonstrates the restrictions on the young women's social lives as they try to sneak out to a dance without permission. But it also reflects on the hardship of the work and the lack of control over their own lives that the characters have. Miss Tassey, who is forty-five, is now 'getting too old for counter-work' and is sacked.[11] Unmarried, she is truly a redundant woman. With no pension rights, no future, she kills herself. This is all done in a very unemphatic manner. She is on stage, in bed, for the whole of the play's one act, but everything we know of her we learn through her two young colleagues. In terms of the work/ marriage debate, Miss Tassey's problem is that she ends up with neither. Her lack of self-determination is beautifully expressed in the play by the fact that we never see her and she speaks only once, at the opening of the play. Her failure is seen by Miss Clifton and Miss Postlethwaite to be in her failure to attract a man. She is now a hopeless case as she is so old that 'she hobbles about the shop, and she wears mittens.'[12] The play explores the bleakness of their knowledge that their only possible course is to find a man and keep him: 'My advice is, take him while you can get him. . . . There are plenty of 'em, but they don't always ask you. . . . You be Mrs. Percy . . . when you can'.[13]

In *Lois*, which seems to have been neither performed nor published, and reads as somewhat unfinished, marriage is used as the solution to Lois's problem – unmarried pregnancy – but not, I think, uncritically. Again, work is foregrounded. The play opens in a typing pool where four women work. The emphasis in the first act is on the social freedom that work has brought to the young women (the play probably dates from the early 1920s) and part of the freedom comes from the fact that they work together. Earlier in the period, this had been one of the distinct advantages to young women of office work over the isolation of domestic service or, if your family could afford it, simply staying at home. It did not, though, on the whole, lead to unionisation, except in the Civil Service.[14] Lois's social freedom, encouraged by her mother, who feels herself to have been too restricted when she was a girl, leads to her pregnancy after a week-end away with a friend and two higher-class young men. There is no suggestion of the father marrying her. The play questions the notion of sexual freedom for women: not, I think, suggesting that sexual freedom is wrong, but worrying at the question of who gains from this freedom and who pays for it. It ends abruptly with Lois agreeing to marry her suitor, Alan, who knows about the pregnancy, and the two planning to emigrate to South Africa. And although the ending provides a conventional solution, and seems to approve marriage, it can be read as a not unproblematic solution.

Partly its very abruptness raises questions about its satisfactoriness. And the solution has to be seen in the context of the debate in Act IV, where the feminist Constance Pearse has pleaded with Lois not to be ashamed of her pregnancy and child but to take pride in them and her single state: 'While women will be ashamed of their sex in these things we shall never get real equality between men and women.'[15] The possibility of single motherhood is raised, as it is in Elizabeth Robins's *Votes for Women!* (1907), and so becomes part of a final reading of the play, in which the audience may well come to see Lois's marriage as an unacceptable solution.

Another play in which the central character is a typist is *Miss Robinson* (1918), although here she has the somewhat elevated position of personal secretary to an eminent member of Parliament. We see Angela Robinson working in her employer's home throughout the first act, and see that her role as secretary is extended by the family to that of general household assistant: her office skills are made easily to slide into domestic ones. Her work exposes her sexually, too, when she is seen by one of the sons of the Vintage family as sexually available to him.[16] His harassment of her is turned by the family into a proposal of marriage as a way of buying her silence to protect the family's reputation, after she has learnt that her employer is a bigamist. The Vintages' class snobbery ('What will Sir Eustace and Lady Agatha say when they know my brother has married the typewriter?'[17]) and patronising attitude to Miss Robinson's mother and sister are shown as embedded in the work relationship where Angela's work, at which she is very skilled, is perceived as a form of personal servicing. The play can be read as a reversal of the 'woman with a past' society dramas; in this case it is the man, not the woman, who has a murky past, and the woman who rejects the invitation of the upper class to join it, rather than her being rejected by that class. The play is constrained by its moralistic pattern, in that Baker has Miss Robinson reject the family not because of her recognition that they are exploiting her but because she does not approve of their deceiving themselves and others. The difficulties for women in this sort of personal servicing work are raised, but the solution presented, when Miss Robinson leaves her job to go to her true, and same-class lover, Billy Arden, seems not to be questioned.

Baker's best-known play, *Chains*, deals with the ways in which marriage and restricted work opportunities for lower-middle-class women and men lessen their possibility for personal and economic development. The original reviews of the play saw the chains of the title as binding only Charley, but all three of the central characters, Lily, Charley and Maggie, are shown as being enchained. The plot is slight: Lily and Charley's lodger, Tennant, announces that he is to emigrate to Australia to farm, even though he does not have a job there to go to. Lily and the majority of characters in the play condemn him as foolish and irresponsible, but Charley and Lily's sister, Maggie, are envious. Maggie secretly encourages Charley to emigrate, too. In the final moments of the play he reveals to Maggie that he is about to leave for Australia,

whereupon Lily tells him that she is pregnant. Charley stays. The very slight-
ness of the plot, and the thwarted urge within it to seize freedom, reflect the
play's central concern: the monotonous grind and lack of opportunity faced by
her characters, who are restricted by class and by gender.

The lower-middle-class position of Lily and Charley Wilson is suggested to
the audience through the detail of set and dialogue. The off-stage area and off-
stage action are invoked to reinforce the claustrophobia forced on the family
by their economic circumstances. Their low income is a constant theme.
Despite his patriarchal role as bread-winner, Charley's wages as clerk are not
enough, and he has no prospect of promotion. Lily has taken in a lodger to
supplement their income, it being part of her contribution to do the extra
domestic work this demands. Making married women's economic work invisible by siting it in the home was a practice well-established by this period
and, as Leonore Davidoff suggests: 'Although in one sense taking in of lodgers
was seen as being incompatible with middle-class gentility, on the other hand
it was a way of supplementing income without the women in the household
having to work in public'.[18] Part of Lily's concern at Tennant's announcing
that he is to leave to go to Australia has to do with the potential loss of income
that this will mean, and she is eager to respond immediately to an advertisement asking for lodgings. At the end of Act I, Lily tells Charley that their rent
is to be increased and it is clear to her that the only way they can increase their
income is by taking in a second lodger. Charley will thus be deprived of 'that
little room at the back, over the scullery' where he keeps his cuttings for his
garden – which he complains about – and Lily's workload will be increased –
to which she is reconciled: 'I never said I wanted them. I'm only doing my best
to make things smooth.'[19]

The economies they have to make are evidenced in the details of the set: the
furniture is 'a little mixed in style', a sewing machine is in the sitting room, as
are pots of cuttings.[20] This is reinforced in the dialogue: Charley likes to read
the *Daily Telegraph* but, because it costs a penny, shares the cost with
someone else; Lily wants to keep chickens in the garden because 'they would
be so useful';[21] Charley is sure they are safe from burglars because they
have nothing worth stealing; Lily is envious of Maggie's being able, once she
has married Foster, to send out the washing; their garden is a 'two-penny-
halfpenny back yard' with 'filthy soil', where it is difficult to get anything to
grow.[22] The garden's smallness is emphasised by Charley's frequently being
visible through the garden window when he is working there, and by Leslie's
getting into it from next door by climbing on the dustbin, in the process
standing on Charley's bean plants and smashing a box of tomato plants
because the space is so confined. And from outside they are overlooked and
hemmed in:

> Charley: The man who built that road (*pointing out of the window*) ought to be
> hanged.
> Lily: They're not very pretty, those houses.[23]

All of this is put for the audience in a very particular context, because they may well guess that Lily is pregnant, signalled by her being 'much worried' when we first see her, and by her coyly but insistently talking about 'the baby across the road'.[24] As Lily and the audience know, the new baby will mean extra financial demands.

Their economic difficulties having been suggested in Act I, in Act II we learn that Charley is to have a wage cut. He and Fenwick, who brings the news, know themselves to be helpless agains the cut:

> *Fenwick:* They're offering you the same alternative they offered me – stay on at less – or go.[25]

Charley, unlike Fenwick, does not accept the firm's argument that the wage cuts have been forced on them because of their reduced profits:

> *Charley:* It's all rot about a bad year. Don't expect we've been exactly piling it up, but it's nothing to complain about.[26]

But the work force has no bargaining power because the labour market is saturated:

> *Leslie:* Last week our firm wanted a man to do overtime work, and they don't pay too high a rate – I can tell you. And they had five hundred and fifteen applications.[27]

And the need for solidarity is emphasised by Baker when, following Charley's conversation with Leslie, Percy explains that he has got a new job by under-cutting the man who previously did it:

> *Percy:* Foster's given me Beckett's job.
> *Charley:* And Beckett?
> *Percy:* Well, he's got the sack, you know. It's a bit rough on him, but I couldn't help it, could I?
> *Charley:* I suppose you're doing it cheaper?
> *Percy:* That's about the line.[28]

The men are shown as trapped by the demands of capitalism. Their work is tedious and ill-paid; they have no channels of resistance; their urges to challenge and to escape are worn down. The class system determines the sort of work they will do, and the specific jobs the young men do are chosen for them by their fathers, as both Charley's and Mr Massey's were:

> *Massey:* Do you suppose I like plumbing? Do you think I ever did? No, but I stuck to it. . . . Of course, I hated it, just as you do. . . . I was taught plumbing. We don't have choice. Your grandfather put me to it, and of course I stuck to it. . . . Father was a plumber, and if it was good enough for him, it was good enough for me.[29]

The acceptance of the alienation of labour is complete in Mr and Mrs Massey:

> *Mrs Massey:* Do you expect work to be pleasant? Does anybody ever like work? The idea is absurd. Anyone would think work was to be pleasant.[30]

The opposition to all this is suggested by Baker in two ways: there is the individual action of the men who get out: Tennant, who succeeds, and Charley, who tries but fails. And there is, too, the possibility of socialism, which the play does not explore, but which is raised twice so as to provide a context for the audience's consideration of the issues. The first time it is mentioned is very early in Act I:

> *Charley:* A chap came into the office today in a red tie. Old Raffles had him up, and pitched into him. Asked him if the was a Socialist. Chap said he wasn't, but liked red.[31]

The detail of personal rebellion is very carefully chosen – an orange tie would have been just as flamboyant, but would not have signified in the same way – and links the notion of socialism with those of freedom and rebellion. The second mention, again negatively raised in that the speaker denies that he is a socialist, is during the row between Massey and Charley, and here it is suggested that the people with ideas about freedom and self-respect are the socialists:

> *Massey:* I suppose you're a Socialist.
> *Charley:* Doesn't anybody but a Socialist ever have an idea?
> *Massey:* They're mostly mad, if that's what you mean. And they're always talking about the wickedness of the boss and the sweetness of the working man.
> *Charley:* I never said anything about either and I'm not a Socialist.[32]

The text thus is sited within the capitalist–socialist debate: we see workers without power, alienated from their labour, having their wages cut, losing their jobs to men who will take less pay, having their living standards lowered, having to serve capitalism in tedious, repetitive jobs, and having their creativity stifled.

And if it is bad for the men, it is worse for the women, whose opportunities are limited not only by capitalism but also by patriarchy. Tennant can emigrate. He might not do particularly well once in Australia, but at least he can try. Charley can contemplate going. Lily and Maggie cannot even do that. Maggie recognises that it is her gender that stops her: 'If I were a man, I wouldn't stay in England another week. I wouldn't be a quill-driver all my life. If I were a man.'[33] She can only experience vicariously the excitement of emigrating: this is why she is so keen that Charley should go and why she supports him against her parents and Lily. But in opposing Lily, she overlooks Lily's economic position. As a respectable woman of her class, Lily feels unable to emigrate with Charley; she would have to follow, once he had 'made a home for her'.[34] Without his income, her only option would be to return to her parents' home, for she would have no way of paying her own rent. Furthermore, she is pregnant, as the audience probably knows, but Charley and Maggie do not. She therefore, because of the restrictions placed on her by her class and because of the resistance to employing pregnant women, would be unable to go out to work, and so would have no way, other than relying on her parents, respectably to support herself and her child. Lily's telling Charley at the last moment about her pregnancy is not to be read, as Maggie does, as her scheming to keep her man but, rather, as an economic and maternal imperative: she has to have him there as the bread-winner for herself and her child. This is a situation not of her making. The social division into separate spheres, underpinned by class-specific notions of respectability, forces her hand.

Lily is restricted by her position as married woman to domestic work: we see her carrying out domestic chores in the first act, we hear of her doing the washing, we know that she provides domestic services for Tennant and will, shortly, for a second lodger. Maggie is not similarly restricted by marriage, but is, none the less, limited in her job opportunities by her gender and her class.

Maggie works as a shop assistant, a representative of the many lower-middle-class young women who moved into shop work as a respectable alternative to factory work or domestic service:

> There was . . . an increase in the number of women employed in shops. This was largely because of the growth of the retail trade which paralleled the contemporary trend in industry towards large-scale organisation. The quantity and variety of goods available burgeoned, which led to a massive expansion of the retail trades and the decline of the small independent shop. These businesses, often family run where women helped informally, were replaced by large units with shop assistants whose unskilled status opened the position to women. The occupation involved long hours, often living above the shop, pay was low and union organisation was difficult.[35]

The work was considered respectable because workers had to wear smart clothes and most employers demanded a high standard of personal behaviour. It was, then, seen by parents – it seems that it was mostly mothers who chose their daughters' jobs for them – as a suitably protected place of work.[36] On the other hand, it was seen by some as not as respectable as the hugely expanding area of women's work in offices.[37] In offices, unlike in shops, women and men workers were often segregated into separate work areas, sometimes with separate entrances into the building, or in some cases working in separate buildings. In shops, too, there was exposure to male customers, and personal attractiveness was a criterion for selection used by numbers of employers. Shop work was hard, with long hours and the requirement that staff stand throughout the day – to sit was to show disrespect to customers – and with low pay (in the 1880s, in London, between 7s. and £1 a week). Maggie hates her shop work, but when she fantasises about leaving it, she regrets not having the necessary skills to enable her to find alternative work: the only possibilities are in domestic work, cooking or housekeeping. She knows of one woman who emigrated to Canada: Lily is sure that she would have worked as a servant when she got there, 'and then in the end she'll marry some farmer man and have to work fearfully hard'.[38] The only way for Maggie to escape her hated job is to marry.

The play focuses on the choices made by the characters: Tennant's and Mr Massey's, made before the play starts (Maggie attacks her father with, 'But why didn't you ask for a choice?'), Lily's (when to tell Charley she is pregnant), Charley's (whether or not to emigrate) and Maggie's (whether or not to marry Foster).[39] Until Act IV, the play's main interest is in Charley's choice. Maggie is the only one who encourages him to go, and it is made clear that she wants him to go as a substitute for her going. She is shown with a clear perception that opportunities, choices, are gender-defined. She recognises that the positive thing Tennant has done is that 'he's stirred us all up. He's made us dissatisfied'.[40] Out of that dissatisfaction comes progress; the dissatisfaction represents rejection of the system and the desire to take control of one's own life. In Act IV the focus shifts strongly to Maggie, as she becomes the only one of the three central characters who does take control.

Through Maggie the play examines the issue discussed by Cicely Hamilton in *Marriage as a Trade* (1909) and in several of her plays, particularly *Diana of Dobson's* (1908) and *Just to Get Married* (1911): that marriage for women becomes a question of economics. Baker has Maggie openly admit and discuss the fact that she is marrying Foster, even though she is 'not particularly' fond of him, because he provides an escape from shop work, and quite a comfortable escape, too, in that he is rich enough for Maggie to be able to hire a servant to help her with the worst of the domestic work.[41] Her choice, then, is between tedious, ill-paid work and marriage. But she can only choose within the constrictions of her gendered existence. Because she is a woman, she cannot choose to emigrate, but she can decide not to marry. She has accepted marriage as a trade: the only way she can respectably survive economically, outside shop work, is to give up attempts to support herself, and accept economic dependence. This is what she rejects at the end of the play. She recognises that she was seeing Foster as a meal ticket – 'I found I was just marrying – to get away from the shop! . . . I don't love Walter, only his house' – and in rejecting marriage opts for the only form of risk and uncertainty she can.[42] It is, importantly, not a glamorous choice that she makes. She chooses to stay in her boring shop job because, boring though it is, it does represent a form of freedom: 'I thought what a fool I was to throw up one sort of – cage – for another. . . . I can leave the shop any day, when I've saved enough – and run away. But I couldn't run away from Walter.'[43] She opts not for freedom rather than enchainment, but for a less permanent form of chains and, crucially, a form that she actively *chooses*. Maggie, moving in the final act into the centre of the play, provides an image of women taking control of their lives and empowering themselves, as Baker asserts the importance of the concept of work in the self-determination of women.

Notes

1. E. Baker, *Miss Robinson* (London: Sidgwick and Jackson, 1920), p. 58.
2. Page references to Baker's plays refer to the first edition, except in the case of *Chains*, where references are to the edition of the play in *New Woman Plays* (Florence Bell and Elizabeth Robins, *Alan's Wife*; Cicely Hamilton, *Diana of Dobson's*; Elizabeth Baker, *Chains*; and Githa Sowerby, *Rutherford and Son*), ed. L. Fitzsimmons and V. Gardner (London: Methuen, 1991).
3. *The Nation and Athenaeum*, 9 April 1927, p. 16.
4. *The Saturday Review*, 30 March 1912, p. 391.
5. P. P. Howe, *The Repertory Theatre: A record and a criticism* (London: Martin Secker, 1910); A. E. Morgan, *Tendencies of Modern English Drama* (London: Constable, 1924); C. Pellizzi, *English Drama: The last great phase*, trans. R. Williams (London: Macmillan, 1935).
6. J. C. Trewin, *The Theatre since 1900* (London: Andrew Dakers, 1951); *The Edwardian Theatre* (Oxford: Blackwell, 1976).
7. J. Holledge, *Innocent Flowers: Women in the Edwardian theatre* (London: Virago, 1981); I. Clarke, *Edwardian Drama* (London: Faber, 1989); J. McDonald, *The New Drama, 1900–1914* (Basingstoke: Macmillan, 1986).
8. Baker's published plays include *Chains* (London: Sidgwick and Jackson, 1911; repr. in *New Woman Plays*, 1991); *Miss Tassey* (London: Sidgwick and Jackson, 1913); *The Price of Thomas Scott* (London: Sidgwick and Jackson, 1913); *Miss Robinson* (London: Sidgwick and Jackson, 1920); *Partnership* (London: French, 1912); *Bert's Girl* (London: Ernest Benn, 1927); *Edith* (London: Sidgwick and Jackson, 1927); *Umbrellas* (London: Sidgwick and Jackson, 1927); *One of the Spicers* (London and Edinburgh: Gowans and Gray, 1933).
9. J. Lewis, 'Reconstructing women's experience', in J. Lewis (ed.), *Labour and Love: Women's experience of home and family, 1850–1940* (Oxford: Blackwell, 1986), p. 2.
10. In almost all occupations the public acknowledgement of marriage means for a woman dismissal from her post and diminished economic resources. This is the case in practically all the Government posts . . . and although the same rule is not so strict in private business, there, too, it is rare for married women to be employed. Most women, that is to say, can only continue to preserve that economic independence, so keenly appreciated and won by such fierce struggles, on condition of compulsory celibacy and, what to many women is far worse, compulsory childlessness.

   M. A. Atkinson, 'The economic foundations of the women's movement', Fabian Tract no. 175 (London: Geo. Standring, 1914), pp. 17–18, cited in C. Dyhouse, *Feminism and the Family in England, 1880–1939* (Oxford: Blackwell, 1989), p. 78.
11. Baker, *Miss Tassey, op. cit.*, p. 10.
12. *ibid.*, p. 15.
13. *ibid.*, p. 20.
14. See A. Davin, 'Telegraphists and clerks', *Bulletin of the Society for the Study of Labour History*, 26 (1973), pp. 7–9; M. Zimmeck, 'Strategies and stratagems for the employment of women in the British Civil Service, 1919–1939', *Historical Journal*, 27 (1984), pp. 901–24 and 'Jobs for the girls: The expansion of clerical work for women, 1850–1914', in A. John (ed.), *Unequal Opportunities: Women's employment in England, 1800–1914* (Oxford: Blackwell, 1986), pp. 153–99; and T. Davy, '"A cissy

job for men; a nice job for girls": Women shorthand typists in London, 1900–1939',
in L. Davidoff and B. Westover (eds), *Our Work, Our Lives, Our Words: Women's
history and women's work* (Basingstoke: Macmillan, 1986), pp. 124–44.

15. Baker, *Lois*, Typescript (British Theatre Association Collection at the Theatre Museum), Act ɪᴠ, p. 16.

16. Issues of sexual harassment at work are specifically raised and challenged in *Lois*, by
one of Baker's only women's rights activists, Constance Pearse. They are raised in the
structure of the plot, too, when Miss Paterson is sacked because Mr Stephens kissed
her. He, of course, is not sacked. But the women's reaction to the incident is am-
bivalently presented: Miss Pearse, in making her statement that if women 'are to take
their proper place they must always be fighting men' (Act ɪ, p. 7), has to shout to be
heard over a telephone conversation, and her final statement that she never has
problems with sexual harassment is clearly meant to ridicule her. But the fact remains
that Miss Paterson is sacked and Mr Stephens is not.

17. Baker, *Miss Robinson*, *op. cit.*, p. 60.

18. L. Davidoff, 'The separation of home and work? Landladies and lodgers in nineteenth-
and twentieth-century England', in S. Burman (ed.), *Fit Work for Women* (London:
Croom Helm, 1979), pp. 84–5.

19. Baker, *Chains*, *op. cit.*, p. 97.

20. *ibid.*, p. 87.

21. *ibid.*, p. 88.

22. *ibid.*, p. 89.

23. *ibid.*, p. 97.

24. *ibid.*, pp. 87, 89.

25. *ibid.*, p. 101.

26. *ibid.*

27. *ibid.*, p. 103. 'Clerical work was transformed in the years 1850 to 1914. From 1851 to
1911 the number of clerks increased from 95,000 to 843,000 ($\times$ 9) and the proportion
of clerks to all occupied persons from 1.2 per cent to 4.6 per cent ($\times$ 4).' Zimmeck,
'Jobs for the girls', *op. cit.*, p. 154.

28. Baker, *Chains*, *op. cit.*, p. 104.

29. *ibid.*, p. 119.

30. *ibid.*, p. 112.

31. *ibid.*, p. 87.

32. *ibid.*, p. 121. A similar technique is used by Shaw in Act ɪɪ of *Widowers' Houses*
(1893), when Sartorius's 'I assume, to begin with, Dr Trench, that you are not a
Socialist, or anything of that sort' and Trench's emphatic denial provide the political
context for the audience for the ensuing debate about capitalist ethics.

33. Baker, *Chains*, *op. cit.*, p. 100.

34. *ibid.*, p. 93.

35. L. Davidoff and B. Westover, '"From Queen Victoria to the jazz age": Women's world
in England, 1880–1939', in Davidson and Westover (eds), *Our Work, Our Lives, Our
Words*, *op. cit.*, p. 11.

36. See Davy, '"A cissy job for men; a nice job for girls"', *op. cit.*, pp. 132 and 140: and
E. Roberts, *A Woman's Place: An oral history of working-class women, 1890–1940*
(Oxford: Blackwell, 1984), p. 11.

37. 'From 1851 to 1911 . . . the gender mix of clerical workers changed, as women made
even more spectacular gains than men. While the number of men rose from 93,000 to
677,000 ($\times$ 7), that of women rocketed from a mere 2,000 to 166,000 ($\times$ 83); or from
2 per cent to 20 per cent of the total.' Zimmeck, 'Jobs for the girls', *op. cit.*, p. 154.

38. Baker, *Chains*, *op. cit.*, p. 94.

39. *ibid.*, p. 119.

40. *ibid.*, p. 123.
41. *ibid.*, p. 94.
42. *ibid.*, p. 124.
43. *ibid.*

PART VI

Women in Control

The 'New Woman' at Manchester's Gaiety Theatre

ELAINE ASTON

In the wave of alternative theatrical ventures at the turn of this century, Manchester's Gaiety Theatre, under the management of Annie Horniman, holds a pioneering position in the history of Britain's repertory movement. While this position is duly acknowledged by theatre historians,[1] the contribution which the Gaiety made, both to the professional lives of the actresses involved in the theatre and to the dramatic debate on women's issues offered in the repertoire of new plays, has received scant attention. Although it is not my intention to give a detailed history of the Manchester theatre,[2] and its place in the development of the repertory movement, a brief introduction is offered in order to contextualise the subsequent analysis of the actresses and the plays.

The Manchester enterprise would probably not have occurred at all but for the enthusiasm, drive and financial backing of Annie Horniman. She was born in 1860 into the famous tea-merchant family, and in 1893, following the death of her grandfather, benefited from a legacy which enabled her both to establish her independence from her family and to invest in the arts. In 1894 Annie Horniman provided the financial backing for the Ibsen actress Florence Farr's season of 'new drama' at the Avenue Theatre, London. Although this venture was a financial disaster, it fuelled Annie Horniman's determination to support the development of the 'New Drama' in Britain. Julie Holledge points out that Annie Horniman had taken an active interest in the Ibsen movement after having seen the Norwegian dramatist's plays performed in Germany and that 'together with Florence Farr, she shared Elizabeth Robins' vision of an actress–manager's theatre that could develop the new drama'.[3]

Annie Horniman's next major contribution to the theatre was her backing of Yeats's Abbey Theatre in Dublin. She withdrew from that venture in 1907 as the Abbey moved towards financial independence, and transferred her interests to Manchester.[4] Where the Abbey experiment had proved frustrating for Annie Horniman because it became increasingly obvious that her role was to be limited to that of benefactress, in Manchester her managerial position allowed her to make an artistic as well as a financial contribution. 'Although she was not a performer', writes Julie Holledge, 'her career as a manager is worth pursuing because she shared the ideals of the Ibsen actresses.'[5]

The policies which Annie Horniman sought to implement at the Gaiety were heavily influenced by the Barker–Vedrenne management of London's Royal Court Theatre (1904–7). Her aim was to build a resident company committed to the promotion of young, unknown playwrights, the development of a naturalist style of acting, the abolition of the star system and the introduction of short runs. For the players, this necessitated an equalising of status, re-inforced by a ban on individual curtain calls, the narrowing of the gap between the highest- and lowest-paid members of the group, and an absence of star billing on programmes and posters. While Gaiety audiences still had their favourite performers, they learnt to appreciate a player's versatility in performing major and minor roles. In addition, the stability of the work (Annie Horniman offered her players contracts of forty weeks ending on 31 May each year, thereby leaving players free for summer engagements), and the excitement of participating in a radical challenge to the 'Theatre Theatrical' which 'continued to rule the London stage and its provincial dependencies',[6] compensated for the lower rates of pay and billing.

The policy of encouraging new playwrights gave rise to a body of local writers who became known as the 'Manchester School'. The success of the local dramatists was due in no small measure to the way in which they shared the culture, dialect and social concerns of their audiences. It was due to the progressive attitude of new writers such as these that topical issues like women's suffrage were dramatised. Furthermore, as Miss Horniman read all the scripts submitted to the theatre, women playwrights did not, as was frequently the case elsewhere, find their work dismissed because of their sex:

> She [Annie Horniman] encouraged new playwrights, women as well as men, read all their scripts and advised as to possible production. Although she was not actively involved in the women's rights movement, the Gaiety had a bias towards plays concerned with the position of women and which provided actresses with satisfying roles.[7]

In all probability, Annie Horniman's own disapproval of sex discrimination[8] would have been a significant factor in creating this rare outlet for new women playwrights and for establishing a repertoire of plays in which women were represented as subjects in their own right.

Where so much of Edwardian theatre concerned itself exclusively with middle-class issues and middle-class audiences, one of Annie Horniman's managerial aims was to extend class boundaries in terms of the plays and the play-goers. In an interview for Manchester's *Evening Chronicle* in October 1952,[9] Dame Sybil Thorndike recalled the audiences of the Gaiety in her early working years at the theatre as 'working people' rather than a 'dressy' public. Although the Gaiety did have its share of young, enthusiastic, 'engaged' intellectuals,[10] Annie Horniman's policy of seats at 'popular prices' (a policy which was retrospectively cited as a significant factor in the theatre's ultimate financial collapse) also brought in a working-class section of non-theatre-goers. This, in conjunction with her artistic policies which she strove not to compromise in the interests of financial successes, was finally to put the permanent company out of business in 1917. Rex Pogson summarises these gains (in terms of audience composition) and losses (financial) as follows:

> The empty seats at the Gaiety were the most expensive ones. There was no need to consider one's social dignity there, and Miss Horniman was constantly protesting that people who paid for expensive seats at other theatres sat in the cheaper seats at the Gaiety. It is elementary economics that however full and enthusiastic the Pit and Gallery may be, it is the Stalls which form the chief source of income and keep the doors of the theatre open. . . . One of the heartening things about the Gaiety was that it created, from the working classes, a new body of people interested in the drama. There is abundant evidence of this. In the years after she left the Gaiety, Miss Horniman kept up correspondence with many of these people, and even to-day Sybil Thorndike hears from several women who, as millgirls, were regular galleryites at the Gaiety and whose interest in the drama began then and has never flagged.[11]

Though Manchester's dramatic output included foreign plays in translation, revivals of classic pieces and contemporary lyrical drama, it was chiefly amongst the 'New Drama' that 'the Woman Question' was represented. Unlike so much of the nineteenth-century social drama which explored the marital inequalities of women, but had only one major female role to vocalise the debate, the 'New Drama' at Manchester moved away from star-vehicle writing. For the female performer this meant a wider choice of roles than was generally on offer in mainstream theatre, where the emphasis for the actress was on youth and beauty. Under Annie Horniman's management 'the ideals of the Ibsen actresses' were realised: actresses were given the opportunity of playing a more diverse and demanding range of roles. What follows is an examination of those plays and parts in the Manchester repertoire which contributed to the discussion of woman's position in society, and of the actresses who played in them.

In the opening season of 1907 at the Midland Hotel Theatre, Annie Horniman demonstrated her commitment to the 'New Drama' by including *David Ballard* by Charles McEvoy (a newly discovered Irish dramatist) and Shaw's *Widowers' Houses*.[12] Her support of women playwrights was also evidenced in the production of two plays by female dramatists: Emily Symonds's *Clothes and the Woman* and Antonia Williams's *The Street*.

Clothes and the Woman is a light comedy which highlights how a woman's value is assessed according to her looks. The play's heroine, Robina, is a literary woman, a 'bachelor-girl' nicknamed 'Bobbins' who has spent her life writing of love without ever having experienced it. When her friends instruct her in the 'philosophy of clothes' and she adds beauty to brains, suitors flock to her side. To test their loyalty she resumes her former drab attire and relegates her beautiful costume, hat and wig of curls to a mannequin's dummy. One by one her suitors fade away feeling indignant and cheated. She challenges their hypocrisy:

> I was the same woman before I began to masquerade. But did any man admire me then – much less love me? I might have had a heart of gold, but what do you care for hearts? You only love with your eyes – you never look beyond the pretty frocks, the rosy cheeks, the shining hair.[13]

Eventually, only one faithful Romeo remains. Robina agrees to marriage and announces her intention to temper her literary career with a modicum of interest in dress. Though crudely crafted and compromising in its resolution, the play offers an interesting angle on the objectification of the female body.

The play's author, Emily Symonds, disguised her sex by writing under the pseudonym of George Paston. The reviewer for the local *Daily Dispatch* commented scathingly on the use of the pseudonym which, in his opinion, did not disguise the sex of the dramatist because there was too much 'feminine intuition' in the play's content for it to have been written by a man.[14] The critic and commentator Max Beerbohm, writing on another of Emily Symonds's plays, *The Pharisee's Wife*, suggested that using George as a first name was a sure sign (in the wake of George Sand *et al.*) of female authorship. He goes on to characterise the 'Georgian play' as 'unfeminine in so far that its author has tackled a large subject in a serious spirit' and 'feminine in every other respect'.[15] Beerbohm criticises women's dramatic authorship for its lack of 'fairplay', for its well-drawn female characters and male 'dummies'. However, this assumes that the imbalance in the representation of the sexes transgresses a 'fair' distribution of male and female parts. Beerbohm therefore fails to grasp that concentration on women's issues and roles is an attempt to redress the imbalance created by male stereotyping of women in dominant theatrical forms (which actresses either accepted or attempted to work against in a performance context).

Whatever its artistic failings, the play's success ultimately rested on the choice of its principal interpreter, Margaret Halstan. Pogson explains that she was engaged for the part because of her popularity with Manchester audiences and therefore as a means of guaranteeing the financial success of the opening season, even though this ran contrary to the Gaiety's policy of moving away from the star system.[16] The Gaiety director, Ben Iden Payne, confesses in his memoirs that this 'was a slight – a very slight – concession to box-office considerations. I made it with many qualms, and subsequently resolved never again to compromise for financial reasons in the least degree.'[17]

The natural beauty of Margaret Halstan and the conflicting exigencies of her role were the subject of critical attention (as had been the case with Wynne-Matthison when she performed the role of the 'blue-stocking' in Elizabeth Robins's *Votes for Women* at the Royal Court in April of the same year). 'It is extremely difficult to handicap Miss Halstan in the way that the play suggests', wrote the *Manchester Guardian*, 'and though she wore goggles and what we were to understand as an unbecoming gown, the slights of her men friends are not convincing and their manners are grotesque even in a farce.'[18] The purpose of the play in its exposition of the value placed on a woman's beauty is therefore also mirrored in the image of the actress. What price her talent without beauty?

The Street, by Antonia Williams, returns to the somewhat dated question of the definition of a 'pure' woman. (It was a play that was subsequently pro-duced by Edy Craig's Pioneer Players in November 1913 at the Little Theatre.) The central argument of the drama is that a woman who has been wronged may in fact find love and happiness with a man who has full knowledge of that wrong. The case was pleaded by the victim–heroine, Margaret Martin, played by Mona Limerick, the off-stage wife of Ben Iden Payne. Her sultry dark looks and the vivacity and emotionality which characterised her playing style drew high praise from the critics. The *Era* lavishly described her performance as 'exceptional as genius itself';[19] the *Daily Dispatch* wrote of her 'exceptional talent';[20] and the *Manchester Guardian* enthused over her emotionality:

> Of Miss Mona Limerick, in a most difficult and exacting part, one can hardly find adequate praise. The play leapt into life with her sudden apprehension of her sister's danger when the interchange of ideas gave way to the facts of the case. With all manner of subtle modulations she never relaxed the tension. Her outbursts were splendid, and there were pitiful little gusts of vexation that were most moving.[21]

Mona Limerick was strongly supported in this production by two actresses who had been recruited by Payne from experimental ventures: Hilda Bruce Potter (who came from Poel's Elizabethan Stage Society) and Clare Greet (from Barker–Verdrenne's Court Theatre). Their backgrounds were suited to the ensemble style Annie Horniman was seeking for the Gaiety. Hilda Bruce Potter played the rather dull part of the virtuous sister Violet, whose chastity is only superficially threatened, but the actress did not fall into the trap of equating insipid virtue with dull acting. The part of the selfish, short-sighted, ineffectual mother was played by Clare Greet. It afforded her the opportunity of creating one of the cockney characterisations in which she specialised.

In the autumn season of 1908 Annie Horniman's players moved to their permanent home at the Gaiety Theatre, where they continued to develop their repertory policy. In this season they were joined by another actress of 'emotional' power who made an immediate impact on Manchester audiences: Letitia Darragh. Pogson describes her as a 'well-endowed and finely intelligent actress, particularly effective in the portrayal of cultured and sophisticated modern women'.[22] Having impressed audiences as a wife tempted to leave her husband for her lover in *The Vale of Content* (a translation of Hermann Sudermann's *Das Glück im Winkel*), she went on to play a wife who succumbs to temptation in the one-act piece, *Reaping the Whirlwind*, by local writer Allan Monkhouse. The play centres on the tensions and actions which arise when a husband neglects his wife in favour of his work. When the wife repents of taking a lover, the husband is willing to forgive her action since it was triggered by resentment rather than passion. The short piece has a novel conclusion as the lover shoots himself on the couple's doorstep at the moment of the wife's return. The couple retire to bed with the dead man laid out in their house, a haunting presence which poses a threat to the reconciliation. Reviews of the production indicate an appreciation of Letitia Darragh's acting and recognition of her particular talent for the role of 'anguished wife'.

The revival of one-act plays was a particular feature of the Gaiety and they were more than just 'curtain raisers'. After Letitia Darragh's successes came a series of five short plays in the first week of October. Among these was the first production of *Makeshifts* by playwright and actress Gertrude Robins, who wrote several one-act plays and was also identified with the 'Manchester School' of writers.

Makeshifts is a woman-centred 'mistresspiece' which focuses on the lives of two lonely spinster sisters. Quietly and subtly the text delineates the desperate loneliness of two women who have neither beauty nor money to secure homes and families of their own, and who struggle to hide their disappointments. Pathos blends with comedy as neither sister wishes to be caught 'man-catching', though secretly it is their mutual aspiration. The two sisters were played by Ada King, who took the part of the elder sister Caroline, burdened with domestic duties, and by Louise Holbrook, who played Dolly, doomed to a life of infant-school teaching. Ada King was the most popular character actress at the Gaiety and delighted audiences over the years with her local, comic characterisations. In *Makeshifts* she played her part 'with quiet, dignified pathos and a complete absence of sentimentality.'[23] Pogson, in addition to describing the off-stage rivalry of these two performers, comments on Louise Holbrook's range as narrower than Ada King's, but points out that 'she was unsurpassed in spinsterish characterisations, particularly those requiring dialect.'[24] Together, these two actresses made an excellent duo for depicting the tragic waste of single women who were bound by the limitations of their sex to domestic drudgery or pedagogic penury.

In March of the 1909 season, Mona Limerick and Hilda Bruce Potter were again playing alongside each other in *The Three Barrows*, another full-length play by Charles McEvoy. The pattern of Limerick as heroic victim and Bruce

Potter as the centre of far less attractive female interest was repeated. The play, a rather confused study of a lover who courts both an heiress and a penniless country girl and ultimately chooses the heiress, was incoherent in both its composition and its criticism of middle-class marriages. Though audiences were bewildered by its vacillating hero (or, rather, anti-hero), his hopeless lack of backbone and weakness of character were designed as symptomatic and indicative of the hollowness of bourgeois values. Rustic simplicity and emotional honesty among the agricultural classes were contrasted favourably with the emotional dishonesty and hypocrisy of the land-owning middle classes.

The dark beauty and passionate on-stage temperament of Mona Limerick resulted in a highly praised rendition of the penniless Anna, 'by turns a Madonna of the early Italians and the Venus of Beardsley'.[25] Hilda Bruce Potter was further credited for her portrait of the unsympathetic, small-minded Clara Ossler.

Mona Limerick was again to prove the saving grace the following month in *Trespassers will be Prosecuted*, the first play by Manchester's M. A. Arabian. The play offers a satirical view of marriage. The heroine, Christophera (Mona Limerick), is in love with a married man, Oscar Eckersley. Despairing of her own hapless marriage, Christophera compromises her position in society by taking a lover for comfort, but this relationship turns out to be an even greater disappointment. Oscar's wife then dies, but Christophera now feels unworthy of Oscar's love and, under pressure from conservative familial forces, is about to return to her marriage when Oscar insists on claiming her and referring her idiotic husband to the divorce courts. The trespass against bourgeois marriage, and the suggestion that a woman may have an option other than an unhappy marriage or the social degradation of a love affair, strikes a radical and refreshing note. Mona Limerick excelled in her performance and demonstrated a flair for the tragic. As C. E. Montague's account in the *Manchester Guardian* stated, she performed:

> with a genius that kept the house breathless for every word she had to utter. . . . Miss Limerick's power can bend anything tragic to its own uses; or rather, perhaps, it has a boundless faculty of surrender to the emotion of the tragic character. . . . She conceives the desolation and abasement of Christophera with the fierceness of imaginative energy that the playgoer's mind cannot withstand; anything that matters enormously to the performer matters enormously to the spectator, and whatever Miss Limerick does on the stage she diffuses a sense of its tragic importance, as of a whole sky darkened.[26]

This description offers a clear indication of Mona Limerick's power over the emotional sympathies of her audience.

Opposite the talents of Mona Limerick in *Trespassers will be Prosecuted* were cast those of an aspiring young actress, Sybil Thorndike. She appeared on the side of those trespassed against when she played the thoroughly middle-class Gertrude Eckersley, whose main object in life consisted in the keeping up of social appearances. This undertaking was summarised by the *Era* as a worthy performance 'in one of the acerbous rôles that seem to suit her gifts, and must be accounted one of the successes of the evening'.[27]

An attempt to draw upon the background of the suffrage movement as a dramatic source was made in local playwright Stanley Houghton's *Independent Means*, performed in August 1909. Houghton's comedy is disappointingly conventional despite expectations to the contrary hinted at in the title. Sidney, the modern woman of ideas, defies the conservative family she has married into, sets about joining the WSPU and insists on earning her own living when the family fortune is lost. Re-alignment with the conservative defence of the family unit is affirmed, however, by ultimate reconciliation between husband and wife, and the disclosure of Sidney's pregnancy.

The *Manchester Guardian* lamented the limited treatment of ideas in the play and the contradictions within its heroine which resulted in the 'imperfect sympathy' of the audience rather than admiration for a 'woman of spirit and character' which ought to have been elicited.[28] The local *Daily Dispatch* was critical of the play's construction, which it described as a 'small bundle of sociological pamphlets done up as a comedy', and which consequently minimalised its appeal to the politicians in the audience wishing to jeer at one another.[29]

Sidney Forsyth was played by a newcomer to the Gaiety, Edyth Goodall, who interpreted the part with a little too much 'vehemence' for some critics, but nevertheless with the positive hint that she would prove an asset to the company. Due partly to the erratic foregrounding of the woman of 'independent means' in the crafting of the play and to the greater renown of Letitia Darragh amongst Manchester audiences, it was the latter, in the rôle of Sidney's mother-in-law, who attracted more critical attention and acclaim. The part itself is a more finely developed study of traditional wifely forebearance, rather than the delineation of Sidney as a 'New Woman'. Drawing upon her reputation and talent for playing the anguished wife, Letitia Darragh added a poignant study of a woman's silent suffering in an unhappy marriage. She instilled the older Mrs Forsyth with an unspoken sense of grievance as powerful as the volubility of the most emotional *révoltée* from the younger, modern generation:

> Her suppressive intensity, her quickness and mobility of mood, the receding background of unspoken trouble that seems to brood in her gestures and intonations, her voice in which tears flow as they never flowed from eyes – all these things are not quite of our dramatic world, but they are very fine for all that.[30]

These sad, sombre notes were interspersed with humorous interjections from Ada King in her part as the Forsyths' old and faithful servant.

Performed with Houghton's *Independent Means* was the one-act play

Unemployed by Margaret M. Mack, dismissed by the *Daily Dispatch* as 'another essay "after Galsworthy"', in which the 'trail of the pamphleteer was horribly obvious'.[31] Its bald statement on capitalist inequality between rich and poor was indeed a crude, oversimplified, socialist tract, which made for poor theatre and poor propaganda. When the Stage Society produced the play in the spring of 1909, Beerbohm suggested that the society's committee had 'fallen into the habit of believing that any play written with a socialistic bias must be a masterpiece'.[32] Perhaps, in the case of the Gaiety, Annie Horniman's zeal for establishing new and, where possible, local writers was not always matched by a talent for authorship. It is indeed curious that some of the 'New Drama' at Manchester – a city sympathetic to reformist policies – should have amounted to the semi-rehearsed ideas of plays such as *Independent Means*, the incompetent socialist satire of J. Sackville Martin's *A Question of Property* (October 1908) (which takes a satirical look at the socialist who abandons his principles when he comes into property and turns capitalist), or the ill-conceived *Unemployed*. These plays failed in terms of both their political and entertainment value.[33] One understands critical concern for a more serious, competent attitude towards dramatisation of the new, though in fairness, this was not to be levelled indiscriminately at the Gaiety's overall output.

More successful was Shaw's one-act play, *Press Cuttings*, which was given its first public performance on 27 September 1909. The play had previously been censored because of the barely disguised naming of the characters of the prime minister and the general as Balsquith and Mitchenor, and had consequently only been performed privately at the Royal Court in July 1909. The ban was lifted when an agreement that the names be changed to Johnson and Bones, respectively, was reached. Like Houghton's *Independent Means*, *Press Cuttings* used the suffrage movement as its backdrop to create a highly entertaining farce with a pro-suffrage theme. Pogson describes it as a piece of 'uproarious nonsense', the humour of which derived from 'the idea of a Prime Minister disguising himself as a Suffragette in order to leave Downing Street in safety', and from the 'satire on men and military matters'.[34] The leaders of the anti-suffrage campaign, Mrs Banger and Lady Corinthia, were played by Emily Patterson and Edyth Goodall. The *Manchester Guardian* sympathised with the actresses for taking on roles that were 'hardly actable', but praised them both for essaying them 'valiantly'.[35] Ada King as the Irish charwoman had a better, comic role, though despite the laughter she generated the *Manchester Guardian*'s reviewer felt that her Irish accent was not well done and that 'no one could well have known, from this one performance, that she is an artist of genius.'[36]

The new productions of the following 1910–11 season included a full-length drama, *Chains*, by playwright Elizabeth Baker. This had first been performed by the Play Actors at the Court Theatre April 1909, had then been revived at the Frohman Repertory Theatre in May 1910, and was well

received by the Manchester audiences in the May of 1911. Unlike the previously cited semi-successful dramas, *Chains* is a finely crafted, realistic
work and original in its treatment of the detrimental restrictions imposed by
the condition of matrimony. The play's originality lies in its demonstration of
the way in which marriage may be as constricting for men as for women, a
balance of viewpoints in a woman's drama that might even have satisfied
Beerbohm's criticisms. It avoids the Parisian, high drama of husbands leaving wives or wives taking lovers, and shows that for men and women who have
no economic means to buy themselves out of a humdrum existence, there is
little chance of escape.

The play dramatises the situation of the poorly paid clerk, Charley Wilson,
who has a constant struggle to make ends meet and to support his pathetically
clinging wife, Lily. The dreariness of his lot is suddenly underlined by
his lodger who decides to try to make his fortune in Australia. However,
Charley's surge of *Wanderlust* is squashed by the chains of his marriage and
in-laws, who misinterpret his longing for new horizons as the intention to
desert his wife. His only support comes from his sister-in-law Maggie, who
shares his longing for a greater freedom and in her own way achieves this by
backing out of a marriage of convenience. Charley's last and secret attempt to
find a 'brave new world' is dashed by Lily's announcement of her pregnancy,
a chain which binds him more tightly than ever to a domestic and clerical
destiny.

Edyth Goodall gave another performance as a woman of ideas in the part of
Maggie and Hilda Bruce Potter took the comparatively dull part of Lily, but
again infused the role with life and interest, uncommon to studies in insipid
virtue, and 'cleverly' captured 'the manner and the humour of an average
suburban housewife'.[37] Ada King created another successful character piece
in the part of Lily's mother:

> Miss Ada King as Mrs Massey was a Gorgon of the highest perfection. The way
> she awoke joyless from an uneasy Sunday afternoon sleep in the parlour and
> glared round, like a bilious basilisk, seeking matter for offence and wrath,
> convulsed every judicious spectator.[38]

In the week following the production of *Chains*, the first production of P. R.
Bennett's one-act play, *Mary Edwards*, was given. Set in the eighteenth
century, the play centres on the wealthy heiress, Mary Edwards, married to
Lord Hamilton, who then assumes control of her fortune. When she realises
how he is squandering her money, she destroys her marriage lines: the proof
required to legalise the deed giving him access to her money. She exits
declaring her intention to live a separate life with her two sons.

The *Manchester Guardian* considered it strange that an author should
choose to base a play on outdated marriage laws,[39] but nevertheless regarded
the enterprise as a success. The part of Mary Edwards was played by Irene
Rooke with 'clarity', 'serenity' and 'easy mastery of the stage'.[40] It was her first

season at the Gaiety, which she had joined at the same time as the actor Milton Rosmer. They had both come from a repertory background in Glasgow. Now that Mona Limerick made fewer appearances at the Gaiety owing to poor health, Irene Rooke had opportunities to play the emotional, tragic victims. She actively invited comparisons between herself and Mona Limerick by playing the title role of *Nan* in John Masefield's tragedy: a part which Mona had made famous when she first performed it at Manchester in May 1909.

A more successful one-act piece, both in terms of composition and critical reception was Harold Brighouse's *Lonesome Like*, which was performed by the Gaiety's summer company in August 1911 and was then included in the autumn repertoire of the 1911–12 season. *Lonesome Like* takes the case of Sarah Ormerod (successfully played by Ada King) who is on the point of being forced to go into the workhouse, as she has had to give up her job as a weaver owing to the paralysis of her hands. A neighbour, Emma Brierly, stops by to help and is proposed to by the 'idiot', Sam Horrocks, whose mother has recently died, leaving him alone in the world. Emma refuses him as she is already engaged, but Sarah agrees to act as a substitute mother for Sam, thereby providing a solution to their mutual difficulties.

This dialect play therefore reflects Annie Horniman's concern to extend class boundaries in her choice of repertoire. The play highlights the hardships in store for working, working-class women.[41] No doubt, Emma, as a young weaver, has the same fate in store for her as Sarah, if her husband dies early or she is left unprovided for. The tone of the play is critical of society (and the church in particular) for its failure to care for people once they become a burden on the system. Pathos and pessimism are, however, countered by the play's advocation of working-class solidarity as a means of combating poverty and loneliness.

Working-class interests were also central to the new full-length drama, *Mary Broome*, by Allan Monkhouse, performed in October 1911 with Irene Rooke playing the role of the eponymous heroine. *Mary Broome* is a novel reworking of a familiar situation. A servant becomes pregnant by the young, dilettante son of a wealthy family, but instead of being cast out by the family she is married to her seducer. Just as the play is unusual in terms of its action, the role of Mary also moves away from the passionate tones of a victim and is characterised instead by the hallmark of common sense, highlighted by the totally impractical disposition of her lover and husband to-be. Her common sense prevails throughout all of her misfortunes and when her baby dies, a tragedy which she is left to bear on her own, she leaves her hopeless husband in order to emigrate to Canada with a man of her own kind. At last her husband understands the middle-class charade which passes as marriage, and, as in McEvoy's *The Three Barrows*, it is working-class honesty and common sense which are seen as having value. The dramatic device of highlighting middle-class shortcomings by contrast with working-class virtues, would no doubt have been popular with the working-class section of the Gaiety audiences. A domestic servant's common sense proving more substantial than the narrow-mindedness of her employers could not have failed to please, though middle-class criticism still quibbled over the 'purity' issue. Pogson comments on the way in which critics resented Monkhouse's choice of an 'unmitigated cad' for a hero, pointing out that it is Mary who ought to have been 'read' as the focus of interest. [42] Implicitly, this reinforces the prejudicial blindness, a willingness not to see or hear the centrality of the female argument.

Given Mary Broome's plain speaking, Irene Rooke had a harder task of winning sympathy: harder, that is, than if she were a weeping, penitent victim. The *Era* complimented her on having 'realized throughout the simple, half-educated woman, quite passionless and docile, though primed with commonsense'. [43] It is a pity, however, that no one thought to comment on the power of a working-class heroine who not only marries but also leaves her middle-class husband.

Early in the 1912–13 season, Manchester audiences were treated to the most famous production to come out of the Gaiety's work: *Hindle Wakes* by Stanley Houghton, which treats the question of a woman's right to sexual freedom. The play opens with Mr and Mrs Hawthorn anxiously awaiting the return from the 'wakes' of their headstrong daughter, Fanny. When they discover that Fanny has spent her holiday with a young man they insist on her getting married. Fanny, however, refuses, arguing for a woman's right to sexual pleasure outside of marriage.

The play was produced in London in the summer of 1912 prior to its autumn Manchester début. In the capital, controversy over the play's moral issues provided the chief discussion point. A somewhat patronising tone creeps into some reviews, such as comments from *The Times* on the novelty of 'rough-tongued Lancashire ways' for London audiences, [44] though overall the play was clearly enthusiastically received. In the London production by the Stage Society at the Aldwych in the June of 1912, Edyth Goodall added the part of Fanny to her 'New Woman' repertoire. It was a performance which, when the play was given a West End run at the Playhouse, provoked discussion on the relation between the morals of the actress and her role. [45]

After such a tumultuous London reception, Gaiety audiences were eager for the play. In the Manchester production Muriel Pratt, who had under-studied the part of Fanny in London, now made it her own. The *Manchester Guardian* thought her finest moments were those of 'obstinacy and *abandon*' in the first act and her 'pertness and practical commonsense' of the last. [46] The *Daily Dispatch* favoured Ada King's 'vivid actuality' in the part of Mrs Haw-thorn and found Muriel Pratt 'less impressive as Fanny, though still gloriously free of the ordinary tricks of theatre'. [47]

Pogson cites the London production of *Hindle Wakes* as marking a change and decline in the fortunes of the Gaiety. Work for the company was taking the players away from Manchester as productions opened in London and tours were organised in the United States and Canada. While, on the one hand, this promoted the work of the Gaiety on a national and international scale, on the other hand, it decentralised the focus on its home base.

In the remainder of the pre-war repertoire, there is little more that is pertinent to the discussion of the representation of women in the 'New Drama', with the exception of the major success later in the 1912–13 season, St John Ervine's new play, *Jane Clegg*. This production brought one of the future stars of British theatre and film, Sybil Thorndike, to the favourable attention of the critics. Her success is testimony to the importance of Annie Horniman's company as a training ground for actresses and actors.

Jane Clegg is a study of the most unfortunate marriage of the eponymous heroine to a worthless husband, whose crimes against his family – stealing his firm's money, lack of regard for his children's good name, gambling and adultery – finally give Jane the strength to keep him from her door and to encourage him to join his pregnant mistress. She is left to care for the children and his burdensome mother. The usual imbalance of power between the patriarch (as head of the family) and the mother (as powerless comforter and supporter) is reversed by virtue of Jane having money of her own. It is money, the play teaches, which may give a wife and mother the power to leave her marriage and survive without a husband's support. Jane's position at the end of the play is sad but resolute, in contrast to her husband's unchanging weakness and incompetence.

Though in her years at the Gaiety Sybil Thorndike played a variety of parts (in between raising a family with her husband, the director–actor Lewis Casson, who became artistic director at the Gaiety in 1911 after Iden Payne's departure), she does not figure prominently in this selection of the 'New Drama'. *Hindle Wakes* provided her with the role of the unfortunate fiancée, Beatrice, a rather dull lady of unquestionable and uninteresting virtue, but in Jane Clegg she had a part which enabled her to give 'what was then considered the finest performance of her career'.[48] The whole of the play centred on her performance as abused wife. 'She never stressed a note unduly', wrote the *Manchester Guardian*, 'she maintained the type with unfailing fidelity; it would not be easy to recall a piece of acting at the Gaiety more austerely right in its expression.'[49] The *Daily Dispatch* had praise for the 'good acting' of the company in general, and aside from Sybil Thorndike, Clare Greet also got a special mention amongst reviewers for her performance as the querulous mother who can see no wrong in her miscreant son.[50]

This brief and selective documentation of the 'New Drama' at Manchester indicates the ways in which Annie Horniman's company and her new writers attempted to move away from gender stereotyping, thereby widening the scope for the actress in her choice of roles. While some of the 'New Drama' is erratic in composition, it also offers some refreshing insights into certain well-trodden arguments on women's issues of the day. In this context, it is the everyday, mundane, working-class heroines who populated this provincial stage who are perhaps the most interesting feature of all. Women like Fanny

Hawthorne, Jane Clegg and Mary Broome are welcome additions to the stage because they raise class as well as gender issues. They possess none of the 'glamour' which surrounds the romanticised figure of the 'fallen' woman, so popular on the Victorian and Edwardian stages. Yet on behalf of working-class women, such as the millgirls in the gallery, they successfully refute the roles of marital unhappiness and inequality, and demand their own, alternative routes to a greater, personal freedom.

Notes

1. See, for example, G. Rowell and A. Jackson, *The Repertory Movement: A history of regional theatre in Britain* (Cambridge: Cambridge University Press, 1984).
2. This has been adequately sketched by R. Pogson in *Miss Horniman and the Gaiety Theatre, Manchester* (London: Rockliff, 1952), to which I am indebted as a source of background material for this chapter.
3. J. Holledge, *Innocent Flowers: Women in the Edwardian theatre* (London: Virago, 1981).
4. For further details see Rowell and Jackson, *The Repertory Movement, op. cit.*, p. 33.
5. Holledge, *Innocent Flowers, op. cit.*, p. 40.
6. J. C. Trewin, *The Edwardian Theatre* (Oxford: Basil Blackwell, 1976), pp. 2–3.
7. Holledge, *Innocent Flowers, op. cit.*, p. 41.
8. An example which confirms Annie Horniman's antipathy towards sex discrimination is her failure in her negotiations for the Gaiety to obtain an excise licence for the sale of alcohol on the premises; a decision she felt certain was made on the basis of her gender and was one which therefore 'aroused all her fighting instincts' (Pogson, *Miss Horniman and the Gaiety Theatre, op. cit.*, p. 40), as her struggle finally to obtain a licence was to prove.
9. The exact day of publication is unclear, but the interview is to be found in the *Miscellaneous Collection of Horniman News Clippings 1907–78*, Manchester Central Library.
10. H. Lake's article 'That audience', in H. Austin (ed.), *Gaiety Theatre Annual: Supplement 1911–12* (London and Manchester: Sherratt & Hughes, n.d.), pp. 23–5, is an amusing outcry against the young, intellectual converts amongst the Gaiety's followers:

    > I abominate and despise the Gaiety audience. I regard it as the most representative gathering of utterly objectionable people that was ever drawn together outside a vegetarian restaurant . . . everyone who regards himself or herself as an advanced thinker considers it a duty to go to the Gaiety. As a result, you get within those four walls practically every kind of crank that exists, from the nut-eating Fabian freak to the soulfully spoofing spiritualist. You may be jammed between antivivisection incarnate and a hectic suffragist; you may enter the theatre with a sermon on anti-vaccination attacking one ear and a discussion of the single tax assaulting the other.

11. Pogson, *Miss Horniman and the Gaiety Theatre, op. cit.*, p. 192.
12. *ibid.*, p. 33, Pogson explains that *Widowers' Houses* 'had never got beyond its original Independent Theatre production' and goes on to describe the play as 'the type of work sure of a welcome in Manchester, where housing and slum problems were far from old-fashioned, and rent exploiters still active'. This illustrates the way in which Manchester audiences warmed to plays which offered topical, social debate to which they could relate.

13. E. Symonds, *Clothes and the Woman* (London and New York: French, 1922), Act III, pp. 55–6.
14. *Daily Dispatch*, 15 October 1907, p. 6.
15. M. Beerbohm, *Last Theatres* (London: Rupert Hart-Davis, 1970), p. 81.
16. Pogson, *Miss Horniman and The Gaiety Theatre, op. cit.*, p. 35.
17. B. Iden Payne, *A Life in a Wooden O* (Newhaven, Conn., and London: Yale University Press, 1977), p. 82.
18. *Manchester Guardian*, 15 October 1907, p. 9.
19. *Era*, 9 November 1907, p. 14.
20. *Daily Dispatch*, 6 November 1907, p. 4.
21. *Manchester Guardian*, 6 November 1907, p. 7.
22. Pogson, *Miss Horniman and The Gaiety Theatre, op. cit.*, p. 54. He also remarks upon her unexplained refusal to be called by her Christian name, so that throughout her stage career she was always known simply as 'Miss Darragh'.
23. *Manchester Guardian*, 6 October 1908, p. 11.
24. Pogson, *Miss Horniman and The Gaiety Theatre, op. cit.*, p. 58.
25. *Manchester Guardian*, 23 March 1909, p. 6.
26. *ibid.*, 27 April 1909, p. 6.
27. *Era*, 1 May 1909, p. 13.
28. *Manchester Guardian*, 31 August 1909, p. 6.
29. *Daily Dispatch*, 31 August 1909, p. 4.
30. *Manchester Guardian*, 31 August 1909, p. 6.
31. *Daily Dispatch*, 31 August 1909, p. 4.
32. Beerbohm, *Last Theatres, op. cit.*, p. 447.
33. Pogson, *Miss Horniman and The Gaiety Theatre, op. cit.*, p. 84, does defend the entertainment value of *Independent Means*, stating that the play was 'much to the public taste'. However, textual analysis validates not only the critics who complained about the play's lack of didacticism, but also Pogson's own observation with regard to the play's 'shallow characterisation'.
34. *ibid.*, p. 85.
35. *Manchester Guardian*, 28 September 1909, p. 7.
36. *ibid.*
37. *Manchester Evening News*, 2 May 1911.
38. *Manchester Guardian*, 2 May 1911, p. 9.
39. *ibid.*, 9 May 1911, p. 6.
40. *ibid.*
41. The issue of women and work was also treated in J. M. Barrie's one-act play, *The Twelve-Pound Look*, first performed at the Duke of York's in 1910, and in Manchester, April 1911, and in Elizabeth Baker's one-act play *Miss Tassey*, premièred in London in 1910, and performed in Manchester, February 1913. *The Twelve Pound Look* examines the independence women might gain from a career in typing, while *Miss Tassey* takes a critical look at the working conditions of shopgirls. *Miss Tassey* requires an all-female cast of five women, and was performed in Manchester with Macdonald Hasting's full-length drama, *The New Sin*, which, by contrast, required an all-male cast.
42. Pogson, *Miss Horniman and The Gaiety Theatre, op. cit.*, p. 104.
43. *Era*, 14 October 1911, p. 12.
44. *The Times*, 18 June 1912, p. 10.
45. For a summation of the discussions carried on in leading papers, notably the *Pall Mall Gazette*, see Pogson's chapter, 'Hindle wakes', *Miss Horniman and The Gaiety Theatre, op. cit.*, pp. 125–34.
46. *Manchester Guardian*, 29 October 1912, p. 8.

47. *Daily Dispatch*, 29 October 1912, p. 4.
48. Pogson, *Miss Horniman and The Gaiety Theatre, op. cit.*, p. 141.
49. *Manchester Guardian*, 22 April 1913.
50. *Daily Dispatch*, 22 April 1913, p. 4.

Entertaining Ideas: Edy Craig and the Pioneer Players

CHRISTINE DYMKOWSKI

The pun of my title, 'entertaining ideas', neatly encapsulates the twin aims of the Pioneer Players. Edy Craig founded this play-producing society in 1911 to present, in the words of the First Annual Report, 'the type of play which is . . . known as the "play of ideas", and particularly that variety which deals with current ideas, social, political, and moral'.[1] Craig, however, had no intention of offering intellectually worthy but theatrically dull plays; 'an enterprise which stimulates thought and strengthens the action of the heart', the report continues, 'is not at all incompatible with entertaining people'. In setting out to present serious and controversial issues in an entertaining way, Craig hoped to make audiences entertain ideas they might otherwise dismiss.

She aimed to create a truly political theatre, one with a practical as well as an intellectual dimension. The plays presented would not just hearten the committed and enlighten the misguided, but as fund-raisers would also provide material support for various political groups.[2] Underpinning Craig's political aims was a firm and broad feminism that went far beyond a narrowly suffragist viewpoint: gaining the vote would be no miracle remedy for the problems facing women, for those problems were rooted in cultural attitudes that could not be erased by legislation; they were tied to other realities, like class and economics, which cut across sexual boundaries. Perhaps for these reasons, nothing in the written rules of the society indicates its feminist assumptions and preoccupations; to do so might validate the wider perception that such ideas were part of an extremist fringe rather than an essential perspective on contemporary concerns. Indeed, the First Annual Report says as much; to complaints that the Players are not, in fact, interested in all kinds of movements but only in 'Suffragist propaganda', it counters: 'It is obviously quite impossible nowadays to produce thoughtful plays written by thoughtful people which do not bear some traces of the influence of the feminist movement.'[3]

The feminist basis of the Pioneer Players is apparent both in its organisation and in its repertoire. The great majority of its members were women, as were the members of the advisory committee which managed its business. Women carried out the production work, while Edy Craig designed many of the sets and directed most of the sixty-five plays produced in the thirty-seven subscription programmes.[4] The plays the society performed showed a similar commitment: not only did they provide a large number of parts for women, but many were also written by women. Some were the work of practising playwrights; others were commissioned from women who would otherwise probably never have written for the stage. The Pioneers also revived interest in the plays of the tenth-century Benedictine nun, Hroswitha, with Craig's 1914 production of *Paphnutius*, and introduced Britain to the work of many contemporary European dramatists, often in translations by women. Finally, the content of the Players' repertory was also broadly feminist; many of the plays dealt with issues like prostitution, the double standard and power relations, economic and sexual, between women and men.[5]

The Pioneer Players began their public life at the Kingsway Theatre, London, on 8 May 1911. Their first bill consisted of three original one-act plays, all written by women. The first was *Jack and Jill and a Friend*, written and directed by Cicely Hamilton, followed by Margaret Wynne Nevinson's *In the Workhouse* and Christopher St John's *The First Actress*, both directed by Edy Craig.[6] The three plays provided twenty-six parts for actors, only five of them for men, thus reversing the usual unfavourable female:male ratio. As this was a subscription performance, open only to members, friends and the press, the audience was composed predominantly of women; they were, as the reviewer for *The Academy* put it, 'enthusiastic and evidently sympathetic'.[7]

Because the history of the Pioneer Players extends beyond the scope of this book,[8] the focus of this essay will be on the Players' first bill, the one by which they announced their existence and intentions to the world at large. Reactions to this first performance can tell us much about how the New Woman was faring both on the stage and in society. Because references to the Pioneer Players do not often appear in memoirs of the period, newspaper reviews form the chief source of such information and provide a useful spectrum of opinion. While reviewers for the feminist press were, of course, women, critics for the mainstream press were men: their attitudes range from downright misogyny to enlightened liberalism, and they often comment on the partisan nature of the audience. While this spread of opinion does not give a complete picture of how successful or unsuccessful the plays were both as dramatic entertainment and as propaganda, it does at least provide two definite reference points: reception of the plays by the already converted woman and by the highly resistant man. There is also a middle range of response harder to pinpoint exactly: receptive male critics may already have been feminist sympathisers or may have been won over by the plays themselves.

Luckily, the début of the new society received wide press coverage; besides the feminist press, reviews appeared in the London dailies and weeklies, in regional and foreign newspapers and even in religious and sports papers. In researching the contemporary reception of the Players' first programme, I have consulted forty-one domestic newspapers and periodicals and found thirty reviews.[9]

Although the notices are apparently mixed, an overview gives the impression of an immense success. To begin with, the acting was unanimously praised in the highest terms, even by those reviewers alienated by the plays' subject matter. In addition, each of the three plays was singled out by various reviewers as the afternoon's conspicuous success, so they all worked on some level. Significantly, the most negative reviews nail their colours firmly to an anti-feminist mast; their judgements are clearly rooted in attitudes outside a consideration of the plays themselves. Nevertheless, a satisfying number of notices suggest that the Players achieved exactly what they set out to do: to provide well-produced and thought-provoking entertainment.

It is worth noting first of all the critics' general reaction to what they inferred as the Players' aims. Quite a number of the reviews begin ominously, warning the reader that propaganda and drama do not mix easily; for example, the *Daily Telegraph* begins in this way:

> No one will quarrel with the first of [the society's objects], granting, of course, that the plays are as interesting as the movements with which they deal. On the other hand, playgoers as a mass can hardly be expected to wax particularly enthusiastic over stage works of the purely 'propangandist' order.

The reader is now firmly prepared for the reviewer's negative verdict. But, surprisingly, he continues: 'Be that as it may, a very fair start was made yesterday at the Kingsway Theatre. The programme included three little pieces, of which only one belonged to the domain of polemics.' The *Telegraph*'s reviewer is not alone in using this opening tactic; the *Observer*, for example, announces that

> The Pioneer Players . . . are nothing if not propagandist, and . . . they are most of them ladies. The mere male critic, therefore, feels at a disadvantage in discussing the diatribes – some dainty and delicate, others very much the reverse – in which the pretty Pioneers indulged, partly for his confusion and partly for his entertainment.

The critic's patronising vocabulary – the 'pretty Pioneers' indulging in 'dainty' diatribes against the 'mere male critic' – is geared towards discrediting the enterprise, just like the *Telegraph*'s admonition against mixing aesthetics and polemics. But, surprisingly, this critic too continues with positive comments:

'What he may safely say, however, is that he derived considerable enjoyment from two out of the three plays here devoted to the demonstration of man's injustice and inferiority to woman'. This critical tactic is significant, indicating both a resistance which has been overcome and a reluctance to admit it. The half-unwilling praise provides evidence that not only a partisan audience enjoyed the afternoon's offerings, but that 'even the masculine playgoer could relish' two of the plays on the bill, as the *Observer*'s reviewer confesses.

Such a response, however grudging, is generous compared to the more extreme reviews; the following examples, respectively from the *Daily Graphic*, the *Referee*, and *The Times*, show the mixture of flippancy and aggression with which the feminist venture was met by many male critics:

> We went to the theatre all unsuspecting; but it soon dawned on us that we were to be 'Trafalgar Squared', for it would seem that the object of the Pioneer Players is to disseminate Suffragist teaching by means of the stage.

> Statistics show, I believe, that as regards Great Britain's population the females are far in excess of the males. This excess was proportionately observed at the Kingsway last Monday afternoon, when that new histrionic Suffragettic body,
>
> THE PIONEER PLAYERS — or PLAYERESSES
>
> gave their first performance.

> We had walked in so innocently, imagining that the pioneering of the Pioneer Players was to be dramatic, not (if we may be pardoned the ugly word) feministic. . . . Ought not the programme to have been printed in mauve and green on a white ground?

Reviews such as these do not go on to judge the plays in dramatic terms, as will be evident in my discussion of each play.

Cicely Hamilton's *Jack and Jill and a Friend* is a one-act comedy in two scenes which seemingly belies its title. It does not revolve around a love triangle, but is the story of an engaged couple who, unknown to each other, enter their unpublished novels in a competition in the hope of being able to set up home with the prize money. In the first scene, each confides their hope to the friend of the title; in the second, Jill wins and has to deal with Jack's hurt pride, which threatens to end the relationship. The play cleverly points up the gulf between what a woman wants and what a man thinks a woman wants, or should want: in the first scene, Jack berates himself for not 'making enough to support' Jill, while Roger, the friend, counters that 'it doesn't strike me she's the sort of girl who minds working for herself.' Jack *'fiercely'* replies: 'But I mind for her – I mind – I want to tell her she can chuck it all and come to me – to give her a home of her own – so that she can look after it and be happy.'[10] When in the second scene Jack refuses the home of their own that Jill offers him, she points out the arrogance that calls itself love: 'if you think that I'll give up my brains – even for you, and to please you – you are very much mistaken. . . . You wanted me to be your wife; but also, being your wife, you wanted to be able to look down on me . . .'.

Hamilton's play was generally well received by the critics, with Athene Seyler's performance as Jill coming in for unanimous praise: 'the best thing in a really interesting afternoon', according to the *Westminster Gazette*. Attitudes to the play ranged from the same paper's contention that it was 'The only real play of the afternoon' to the *Evening Standard and St James's Gazette*'s complaint that 'if there were lady dramatic critics . . . this [blatant and obvious little] play would be unmercifully "roasted".' The most widely held opinion was that the play was effective, enjoyable and well written, if not particularly original; tellingly, none of the critics who make this complaint explain why they find the play derivative. The more bad-tempered reviews criticise the play outside its own terms: the *Daily News* wants to know 'the sequel, and whether Jack squirmed very much as the years went on'; *The Times* claims sympathy with Jack because the bad news arrives 'After all . . . just before lunch.' While such criticisms are clearly rooted in anti-feminist attitudes, they nevertheless serve to trivialise the play. Similarly, the *Referee* objects to the play's happy ending: Jill says she can fend for herself, but 'Strangely enough . . . she (and . . . the authoress) funked this conclusion'. The reviewer misses the dramatic strategy that Hamilton uses in many of her plays: the use of conventional ingredients to challenge and subvert conventional attitudes. While this strategy may surprise those familiar with Hamilton's devastating analysis of matrimony, called *Marriage as a Trade*,[11] it is effective within the romantic-comedy tradition in which Hamilton is here working. A refusal to grant the conventional 'happy' ending would imply an incompatibility between feminist principles and the possibility of marriage and would therefore undo all the play's probing and questioning of male attitudes and expectations *within* marriage. Hamilton's exposure of sexist norms is, in fact, strengthened by her use of a successfully romantic ending.

Jack and Jill was followed by Nevinson's *In the Workhouse*, the item that provoked the greatest controversy. The play was an attack against the law of coverture, under which, as Nevinson writes in the Preface to the published edition, 'the wife has no separate existence whatever; like an infant, she is entirely under the custody and control of her husband.'[12] The play was based on a real case which around 1908 had come to Nevinson's attention through her work as a Poor Law guardian. Because of drunkenness on duty, a cabdriver had lost his licence and brought his family to live in the workhouse. His wife, a skilled dressmaker, wished to leave in order to earn her own living, but her husband had '"power by his marital authority to detain"' her there. Nevinson and other suffragists publicised the case, which led to its being raised in the House of Commons, and eventually the woman was allowed to leave, but without any change in Glen's Poor Law Orders themselves.[13]

Nevinson had written a sketch, 'Detained by Marital Authority', based on this incident, which was published in the *Westminster Gazette*.[14] As Nevinson relates in her memoirs, Edy Craig asked her to dramatise the story – an important point as it shows Craig actively seeking out certain kinds of material.[15]

The play Nevinson wrote, set in a workhouse ward, has seven female characters, among them Lily, who has just had a baby and is planning to marry its
father the next day; Monica, a mentally handicapped girl of eighteen who has
just had her third child; Mrs Cleaver, who is being detained in the workhouse
by her husband's authority; and Penelope, unmarried with five children, a
free agent who uses the 'quiet and skilled medical attention' available at the
workhouse whenever her babies are due. The play itself consists of lively
conversation between these and the other women, some married, some not,
one of the points of which is the legal anomaly that married women have no
rights over their children, quite contrary to unmarried mothers. Listening to
this discussion, Lily decides not to go ahead with her wedding the next day,
and the curtain falls on Monica's 'ecstatic shriek': 'I do love my biby! [sic]'. As
Nevinson herself points out in her Preface, the play attempts to 'illustrate . . .
some of the hardships of the law to an unrepresented sex', among them the
operation of the double standard, the oppression of married women and the
sexual exploitation of the vulnerable.[16]

Critical reaction to the play swung between two extremes – the *Referee*'s
review refused to name the author, 'as doubtless by now she is ashamed of
herself for having written it', while the critic of the *Pall Mall Gazette* called
the play 'so important that probably no theatrical manager will have anything
to do with it'. Explaining that the play was 'also so outspoken that it will no
doubt be described as "vulgar" and "in bad taste" by critics of extreme
delicacy and refinement', the writer goes on to praise it, comparing it to some
of Brieux's works.

As expected, most of the criticism sidesteps a real appraisal of the play. A
good number complain that it would have made a better article or pamphlet;
the *Academy*'s stated basis for this judgement is that it is too biased, a charge
seldom brought against plays prejudiced in favour of the status quo. The
Westminster Gazette complains that 'The manner of the dialogue was not
natural', simply because 'Persons in the humblest ranks spoke of "lethal
chambers" and other such scientific things'; the gassing of stray cats and dogs
at the Battersea Dogs' Home and other places had in fact put the term into
common use.[17] The *Gazette*'s writer then concludes that 'As a picture of life,
. . . the scene was not a success. As a disquisition it was undoubtedly interesting, though showing too much of a tendency to generalise from occasional
cases.' The criticism contains an inherent contradiction: if the cases were
particular, it is unclear why the play was dismissed as too abstract.

Another, more common, complaint concerned the indelicacy of the subject
matter for representation to a mixed audience; many male reviewers, both
facetiously and genuinely outraged, made clear the offence to their sense of
modesty. The *Daily Mail*'s E. B., for one, found 'The talk . . . painful to listen
to in the presence of a mixed audience, for whom its intimate indiscretions
and its cynical conclusions must have been the reverse of edifying', while the
Referee's Carados wrongly assumes the play was not licensed: 'If it was then

[the censor] ought to be ashamed of himself'. While the *Observer*'s critic 'felt himself a kind of Paul Pry eavesdropping at a bedroom door', the reviewer for the *Evening Standard and St James's Gazette* assumes a mocking tone of moral superiority:

> In one of the intervals . . . some few of us discussed one of the plays we had just seen. 'Hush!' said one, 'there are two ladies close behind you.' How masculine! How stupid! Nothing that had been said came within measurable distance of the frankness of the dialogue, the emancipation of the ideas that had been set forth upon the stage.

All the critics, including the sympathetic ones, mistakenly believe the play is set in a workhouse maternity ward; as Nevinson makes clear in her memoirs, it was in fact set in the 'ordinary "Young Women's Ward", where most of the unmarried mothers had done their seven or eight hours at scrubbing or laundry work'.[18] The mere presence of babies on stage, however, was enough to cause the ill-informed mistake, and in the minds of hostile critics, this supposed setting led to the conclusion that the play was about 'obstetrics' and sex. Nevinson reports in *The Vote*, a suffragist paper, that 'only about five per cent. [of reviewers] have at all understood the point of the play', leading to some 'strange and bewildering criticisms'. She points out the 'air of injured innocence in the tone of some of the critics', calling it 'revolting and hypocritical'; in other words, the very men whose behaviour can lead to such consequences for women are shocked by discussion of those consequences. She continues by quoting one paper's contemptuous comment that '"The piece was loudly applauded by an audience consisting almost entirely of women."' To this Nevinson adds that 'Not a single woman was shocked, so far as I know; . . . ex-Poor Law guardians told me, not only had I not exaggerated, but in many ways the reality was far worse than the play'.[19]

Nevinson cleverly concludes her article by counterpointing critical lambasts with critical praise; her purpose is to point up the arbitrary nature of reviewers' opinions, but it also serves to uphold my contention that each of the plays in the Pioneers' triple bill can be counted a success. For instance, the *Academy*'s judgement that 'the whole thing left an unpleasant taste' is contradicted by the *Sheffield Daily Telegraph*'s view that 'The play is cold and clean and humorous', as well as 'a superb genre-picture'. Similarly, *The Times*'s criticism of her 'Extreme looseness of technique' bears no relation to the *Daily Telegraph*'s crediting of the author 'with a good deal of skill in the manipulation of her material'. In other words, the criticisms levelled at the play reflect individual tastes and prejudices rather than a consensus of opinion.

Besides achieving a partial critical success, *In the Workhouse* also accomplished its political aims: to begin with, it set people thinking and talking. Nevinson comments on the effectiveness of agitprop theatre in the article just quoted. To the critical opinion that she should have written a pamphlet rather than a play, she replies:

I have written pamphlets and have seen them fall to the bottom of the Dead Sea of printed matter. My counsellors are wrong for propaganda purposes. Never before have I had notices pouring in by dozens at a time from [all sorts of papers].

But the debate the play aroused did more than raise consciousness: it led to a change in the law within 'the following year', which Nevinson attributes to the spotlight thrown on the issue by the Pioneer Players' production.[20]

The final play of the Pioneer's bill that afternoon was Chris St John's *The First Actress*, which has been described as more of a pageant than a play. Anyone who has read it, however, can vouch for its lively and pointed wit and dramatic potential. The play is set backstage at the New Theatre, Drury Lane, in 1661, at the end of a performance of *Othello*, in which for the first time a woman has played Desdemona. Margaret Hughes has been pelted off the stage with apples, and she and a fellow actor, Griffin, discuss the reasons for her failure to impersonate a woman successfully. We soon discover, with the entry of Margaret's lover, Sir Charles Sedley, and his friend, Lord Hatton, that Margaret has been a pawn in his grudge against the successful boy-actress, Kynaston; he ignores her to talk to Hatton, treating her much as Henry Higgins and Colonel Pickering will treat Eliza Doolitle in Shaw's *Pygmalion*, written the following year:

MH: Were you pleased with my performance, Charles?
CS: You were radiant, exquisite, charming! The lines were not always intelligible perhaps – but so much the better. Othello is sorry stuff. . . . Where is Kynaston now? . . . You wouldn't believe it, Hatton, but the other day. . .

and so on.[21] St John is able to use the situation to make several points: she shows Margaret being used for male ends rather than fulfilling any personal ambition; however, Margaret understands that not only is she being judged personally for something for which she has received inadequate training, but that, through her, all women might be deemed unsuited to the stage. Griffin, in trying to console her, offers all the rationalisations that women still hear about other activities three centuries later: women have not the skill, have not the mental ability to acquire the skill, should not acquire the skill even if they can because it will rob them of 'womanly delicacy', and in any case, every woman's 'true vocation' is to be a wife and mother.[22]

Left alone and in despair that she has 'made it impossible' for other women to follow her onto the stage, Hughes falls asleep and dreams of the great women actors who will in fact succeed her: the visions of Nell Gwynne, Mrs Barry and Mrs Bracegirdle, Nance Oldfield, Peg Woffington, Kitty Clive, Sarah Siddons, Mrs Abington, Mrs Jordan and Mme Vestris enter by turns, in character, cheering her on. Their entrances and interactions are lively and observations they make salient: contrary to some accounts,[23] the writing does call for acting rather than for mere appearances. For example, Peg Woffington is speaking when '*Kitty Clive dances on*', ignoring her; both try to speak at once, Clive with less success than Woffington, who is in fighting mood against men who 'doubt a woman's intellect [and] . . . grit'. During their struggle for the sleeping Hughes's attention, Siddons enters '*as for the sleep-walking scene*' in *Macbeth*; although she would not do so for 'a Singing Chambermaid', Woffington yields her 'place to the Tragic Muse most gladly'. With her departure, Clive seizes her chance and begins her speech with the following result:

Clive: 'I, Kitty Clive –'
Siddons: Out damned spot. (*Exit Kitty Clive.*)[24]

There is obviously ample room for comic business here; this was no solemn procession of stately figures, as the *Era* reviewer indeed makes clear: May Whitty as Woffington 'calmly stood her ground against the efforts of Miss Dorothy Minto's chic Kitty Clive to dislodge her, Kitty being unceremoniously thrust aside by Miss Saba Raleigh, a stately Mrs. Siddons. . .'.

Many of the visions talk of the parts they played and the kinds of drama they acted in; for example, Dorothy Jordan asks whether she shall 'play tragedy–comedy, high or low, opera or farce? Sure, I'll play 'em all . . .'; Mme Vestris enters as Captain MacHeath, boasting 'I'll not content myself with playing the woman, not I! Since men once put on the petticoats and played all *our* parts – Vestris will put on trousers and play some of theirs for a change! And play them so well too, that man will hardly know himself . . .'.[25] As Vestris recognises, Griffin's argument that acting is an art cuts both ways.

As these examples show, and as one or two reviews noted, the visions represent not just women's success as actors but their success across the whole range of acting possibilities.[26] Furthermore, the parts of the visions were played by popular and legendary actors like Ellen Terry, May Whitty, Dorothy Minto and Auriol Lee,[27] who themselves showed this same range, culminating in the appearance of 'An Actress of To-day'. It is just as accurate to say that she *was* Lena Ashwell as that she was played by her, for in its final moments, the play roams into the area of metatheatre, where reality and illusion coalesce. In steering the play in this direction, St John uses theatre as a vehicle for liberation both literally and metaphorically, and for this reason Ashwell's speech is worth quoting in full:

When I am born, dear Peg, people will quite have forgotten that the stage was ever banned to us. They will laugh at the idea that acting was once considered a man's affair – they will be incredulous that the pioneer actress was bitterly resented – yet they will be as busy as ever deciding what vocations are suitable to our sex. It will be 'Man this' and 'Woman that' as though we had never taught them a lesson.

I see an old map where the world is divided into two by a straight line. The Pope who ruled that line across the world said: 'All territory to the right of the line in future to belong to Spain – all to the left to Portugal'. To my age such a division of the world will seem comical indeed, yet that is how I see them still dividing the world of humanity – 'This half for men', 'That half for women.' If in my day that archaic map is superseded, we shall not forget that it was first made to look foolish when women mounted the stage.[28]

This speech makes an extraordinary fitting climax to the Players' first venue. By using the living greats of the contemporary theatre to impersonate the legends of previous ages, St John effectively discredits male prejudice; no one in the audience could possibly side with Griffin's views. And, as many critics point out, his views are couched in language and were delivered in a manner deliberately reminiscent of current anti-suffrage speeches.[29] Further-more, by blurring the line between the theatrical fiction and the audience's reality – by having Ashwell play herself in the context of this play – St John not only highlights the way theatre has already opened up opportunities to women but also indicates ways it can continue to do so, through ventures like the Pioneer Players; indeed, the remark that people 'will be incredulous that the pioneer actress was bitterly resented' is self-referential as well as historical. Finally, with the colonialist reference, the fight against male supremacism is viewed not in isolation but as part of a wider context of political imperialism re-inforced by religious power.[30] Unsurprisingly, most of the negative reviews of the play either take refuge in learned disputes about whether Margaret Hughes really *was* the first actress or else deny that her treatment has con-temporary resonances.[31] A few critics, like that of the *Daily Mail*, gracefully admit that the author's 'hit is quite adroit in its present-day application, and it strikes home'.

This first production, which included romantic comedy, agitprop drama, and a self-referential play about the power and potential of theatre, shows well the strengths of the Pioneer Players and the varied ways in which they united political ideology with theatrical practice. They built well on their first suc-cess, becoming the only play-producing society, besides the Stage Society, to survive the First World War. According to George Bernard Shaw, they were also the best: '"by singleness of artistic direction and unflagging activity [they] did more for the theatrical vanguard than any of the other coterie theatres"'[32] And yet the plays they produced receive only this mention in a standard reference work like Allardyce Nicoll's *English Drama 1900–1930*: 'The short pieces sponsored by actresses active in the Votes for Women movement can all be dismissed'.[33] Critical reaction to the Pioneer Players' first production in 1911 provides some evidence of the ways in which a feminist enterprise was redefined by male critics and subsequently more easily written out of theatrical history by male theatre historians; fortunately, some of the other critical reactions cited highlight the injustice of their erasure. The final line of St John's play – 'forgotten pioneer – your comrades offer you a crown' – can stand as a sadly apposite salute from modern feminists to the Pioneer Players themselves.

Notes

1. The Pioneer Players: First Annual Report and Balance Sheet with List of Members for 1911–1912 and Rules for 1912–1913, Ellen Terry Memorial Museum, Smallhythe Place, Kent, p. 7. The quotation following is from p. 11 of the same report.

   It is as well to state here that the Pioneer Players are a different society from the Pioneers, which disbanded in 1908.

2. In the First Annual Report, Rule 3 specifies the objects of the society as follows:

   > (a) To produce plays dealing with all kinds of movements of interest at the moment. (b) To assist social, political, and other Societies by providing them with plays as a means of raising funds; and to undertake when desired the organisation of performances for such Societies by professional or amateur players. (p. 13)

   In the Fifth Annual Report 1915–1916, Rule 3(a) was amended to allow the production of 'plays which, although they may be outside the province of the commercial theatre, are sincere manifestations of the dramatic spirit' (p. 3). The change reflects the interest the society has already shown in presenting the work of foreign dramatists and of serious playwrights not engaged with contemporary issues; it also reflects pragmatic considerations and practical difficulties arising from the war, which had delayed the start of the previous season (Fourth Annual Report 1914–1915, p. 8).

3. First Annual Report, p. 7.

4. Of the advisory committee's fourteen members in its first season (1911–1912), Laurence Housman was the only man. Craig directed fifty-five of the plays, fifty on her own and five in conjunction with another person, usually the author. My figures are derived from an examination of the subscription programmes; Christopher St John estimates that Craig produced 150 plays for the society in its ten-year life (in E. Adlard (ed.), *Edy: Recollections of Edith Craig* (London: Frederick Muller, 1949), pp. 10, 25); St John's figures may include Pioneer Players' productions undertaken on behalf of other groups.

5. The Pioneer Players' history and achievements form too broad a subject for the present essay; for further information readers should consult J. Holledge, *Innocent Flowers: Women in the Edwardian theatre* (London: Virago Press, 1981), and J. Melville, *Ellen and Edy: A biography of Ellen Terry and her daughter, Edith Craig, 1847–1947* (London: Pandora Press, 1987). N. Auerbach's *Ellen Terry: Player in her time* (New York: W. W. Norton; London: Dent, 1987) also pays some attention to the group. The present essay is part of an unfinished wider study of Edy Craig's theatre career.

6. Christopher St John was the pseudonym of Christabel Marshall, who lived with Craig from 1899 until the latter's death in 1947 (Christopher St John, 'Close-up,' in Adlard, *Edy, op. cit.*, p. 21).

7. *The Academy*, 2036 (13 May 1911), p. 587.

8. Their last full season was that of 1919–1920, though the society did revive for a final production of Susan Glaspell's *The Verge* in April 1925.

9. Reviews appeared in the following newspapers and periodicals on 9 May 1911, unless otherwise specified: *The Academy*, 2036 (13 May 1911), p. 587; *The Christian Commonwealth*, 17 May 1911, p. 570; *The Common Cause* (published by the NUWSS), 18 May 1911, p. 105; *Daily Express*, p. 2; *Daily Graphic*, p. 14; *Daily Mail*, p. 8; *Daily Mirror*, p. 4 (photo and caption only); *Daily News*, p. 2; *Daily Telegraph*, p. 6; *Era*, 13 May 1911, p. 17; *Evening News*, p. 4; *Evening Standard and St James's Gazette*, p. 5; *Jewish Chronicle*, 12 May 1911, p. 30; *Morning Post*, p. 5; *Observer*, 14 May 1911, p. 9; *Outlook*, 13 May 1911, p. 610; *Pall Mall Gazette*, p. 4; *Referee*, 14 May 1911, p. 2; *Reynolds's Newspaper*, 14 May 1911, p. 4; *Sheffield Daily Telegraph*,

p. 10; *Sketch*, 17 May 1911, p. 172; *Stage*, 11 May 1911, p. 18; *Standard*, p. 9; *Star*, p. 2; *The Times*, p. 13; *The Vote* (The Organ of the Women's Freedom League), ed. C. Despard, 20 May 1911, p. 52; *Votes for Women* (published by the WSPU), ed. F. and E. Pethick Lawrence, vol. 4 (n.s.), no. 166 (12 May 1911), p. 538; *Westminster Gazette*, p. 3; *Winning Post*, 13 May 1911, p. 15 (short mention only); *World*, 16 May 1911, p. 710 (review by H. Farjeon).

I also consulted the following publications without finding any reference to the production: *Athenaeum*, *Globe*, *Graphic*, *Illustrated London News*, *Illustrated Sporting and Dramatic News*, *Nation*, *Play Pictorial*, *Saturday Review*, *Sunday Times* (carried an announcement on 7 May 1911, p. 6, but no review the following week) and *Tatler*. M. W. Nevinson (see note 17) quotes excerpts from reviews in *Morning Advertiser* and *Yorkshire Daily Post* (*sic*); I was, however, unable to find any review in the *Yorkshire Post*. Taking Nevinson's references into account, reviews appeared in thirty-two of the forty-two publications mentioned above. (The *Manchester Evening Chronicle* was unavailable for consultation at Colindale Newspaper Library because of bomb damage.) All reviews mentioned in my text refer to the newspaper issues detailed above.

10. C. Hamilton, *Jack and Jill and a Friend* (London: French, 1911), p. 7. The following quotation is from p. 19.

11. C. Hamilton, *Marriage as a Trade* (1909; rpt London: The Women's Press, 1981).

12. M. W. Nevinson, *In the Workhouse*, The New Era Booklets, 2 (London: The International Suffrage Shop, 1911), p. 13; the text is printed on one side of the page only, the verso side being left blank.

13. Nevinson describes the case in her Preface to the play, p. 15, where she quotes the power by which the woman was detained in the workhouse, and in her memoirs, *Life's Fitful Fever* (London: A. and C. Black, 1926), pp. 223–6. In the latter, when discussing the husband's 'power by his marital authority' (p. 223), she refers the reader to Glen's Poor Law orders.

14. It was reprinted in her collection, *Workhouse Characters and Other Sketches of the Life of the Poor* (London: George Allen and Unwin, 1918), pp. 21–6.

15. Nevinson, *Life's Fitful Fever*, op. cit., p. 224.

16. Penelope's desire for medical attendance comes from *In the Workhouse*, op. cit., p. 57; Monica's shriek from p. 69; Nevinson's remarks from the Preface, p. 21.

17. In a long article called 'A bewildered playwright' in *The Vote*, 3 June 1911, p. 68, Nevinson addresses the baffling critical response her play received. She mentions this particular criticism, commenting on the reviewer's lack of awareness of the effects of 'forty years of compulsory education, free libraries, and free newspaper-rooms, Moreover, every child in Battersea or near the Cats' Home has heard of "the lethal".' Nevinson's self-defence is justified, as the rest of the play's vocabulary is natural and appropriate to the characters.

18. Nevinson, *Life's Fitful Fever*, op. cit., p. 224.

19. Nevinson, 'Bewildered playwright', op. cit., p. 68.

20. In *Life's Fitful Fever*, op. cit., pp. 225–6, Nevinson relates that 'the law was altered . . . on the precedent of the Jackson Case (1891) – "that a husband has no right, where his wife refuses to live with him, to take her person by force and restrain her of her liberty" (60 L.J.Q.B. 346)'. She comments that the reform should really have been 'based on the Habeas Corpus Act: "illegal detention without trial", for in the case of a young couple under sixty, workhouse law forbids them to live together'. Nevinson's objection to the use of the Jackson precedent presumably arises from the loophole that lack of co-habitation could provide.

Nevinson makes clear her belief that Craig's production of the play effected this legal change in *Life's Fitful Fever*, p. 225, and in the frontispiece to *Workhouse Characters*, which advertises *In the Workhouse*: 'Note. – Two years [*sic*] after this piece was given by the Pioneer Players the law was altered.'

21. C. St John, *The First Actress*, TS, 17pp., British Library, Lord Chamberlain's Plays, vol. 14, no. 128 (1911), p. 5. The play was also privately printed by the Utopia Press.

Shaw, a friend of Craig's and St John's and in 1911 their neighbour in Adelphi Terrace, was present at the Pioneer Players' first performance; he may have been influenced by St John's play in the composition of his own.

22. St John, *First Actress, op. cit.*, pp. 8–10. The quotation in the following sentence is from p. 11.

23. This impression is given by Holledge, *Innocent Flowers, op. cit.*, p. 124 ('More of a spectacle than a drama'), and also by several of the reviews (i.e., *Daily News, Daily Telegraph, Morning Post, Stage* and *World*). The unjustified judgement presumably arises from the number of actors and costumes involved and from the shortness of each vision's appearance; a cameo role, while not providing an occasion for a sustained performance, does nevertheless offer particular acting opportunities. Reviews that stress the play's pageant-like quality also tend to equate it with the visions; in fact, the latter occupy only the final third of the play (six of the typescript's seventeen pages). Such an equation, while throwing doubt on the reviewers' acumen, none the less testifies to the visual impact and effectiveness of Craig's staging of the visions.

24. St John, *First Actress, op. cit.*, pp. 14–15.

25. *ibid.*, p. 16.

26. For example, the *Daily Mail* comments 'that Miss St. John's piece forms a convenient vehicle for the introduction on the stage of *all sorts of* famous actresses from Mrs. Siddons to Mme. Vestris as impersonated in characteristic costumes by some of the most popular of their successors' (italics mine).

27. The rest of the cast included Nancy Price, Lily Brayton, Suzanne Sheldon, Henrietta Watson, Saba Raleigh, Mona Harrison, Lillian Braithwaite, Lena Ashwell, Edmund Gwenn, Ben Webster and Tom Heslewood.

28. St John, *First Actress, op. cit.*, p. 21. I have standardised St John's use of quotation marks and related punctuation.

29. This point was made by both the *Sketch* and *Reynolds's Newspaper*.

30. The printed text of the play replaces 'Pope' with 'man', p. 21, cutting the link between imperialism and religion but strengthening the one between colonialism and sexual oppression. It is unclear whether the change was made before or after the play's perfomance.

31. Examples of the former approach can be found in the *Referee, Outlook* and *The Times*; of the latter, in the *Observer* and *Evening Standard* ('Women can act – therefore give them the vote. The argument is irrefutable').

32. Quoted by C. St John in *Ellen Terry and Bernard Shaw: A correspondence* (1931; rpt London: Reinhardt and Evans, 1949), p. 85.

33. A. Nicoll, *English Drama 1900–1930* (Cambridge: Cambridge University Press, 1973), p. 224.

Further Reading

Books referred to in individual essays have been listed in the notes to each paper. The following, whilst including some of the works cited above, is intended as a brief selection of useful texts in three main categories.

The New Woman and her context

Baily, L., *Scrapbook 1900–1914* (London: Frederick Muller, 1957).

Beckett, J. and D. Cherry (eds), *The Edwardian Era* (Oxford: Phaidon, 1987).

Brandon, R., *The New Woman and the Old Men: Love, sex and the Woman Question* (London, Secker and Warburg, 1990).

Crow, D., *The Edwardian Woman* (London: Book Club Associates, 1977).

Cunningham, A. R., 'The "New Woman Fiction" of the 1890s', *Victorian Studies* 17 (December 1973), pp. 177–86.

Cunningham, G., *The New Woman and the Victorian Novel* (London: Macmillan, 1978).

Dijkstra, Bram, *Idols of Perversity: Fantasies of feminine evil in fin-de-siècle culture* (Oxford: Oxford University Press, 1986).

Dowling, L., 'The decadent and the New Woman in the 1890s', *Nineteenth Century Fiction*, 33 (1979), pp. 434–53.

Evans, R. J., *The Feminists* (London: Croom Helm, 1977).

Helsinger, E., R. Lauterbach Sheets and W. Veeder (eds), *The Woman Question*, 3 vols (Manchester: Manchester University Press, 1983).

Hollis. P. (ed.), *Women in Public: The women's movement 1850–1900* (London: Allen and Unwin, 1979).

Jeffries, S., *The Spinster and Her Enemies: Feminism and sexuality 1880–1930* (London: Pandora Press, 1985).

Kent, S. K., *Sex and Suffrage in Britain 1860–1914* (London: Routledge, 1990).

Lewis, J., *Women in England 1870–1950* (Hemel Hempstead: Harvester Wheat-sheaf, 1984).

Nead, L., *Myths of Sexuality: Representations of women in Victorian Britain* (Oxford: Basil Blackwell, 1988).

Rubinstein, D., *Before the Suffragettes: Women's emancipation in the 1890s* (Hemel Hempstead: Harvester Press, 1986).

Showalter, E., *A Literature of their Own: British women novelists from Brontë to Lessing* (London: Virago, 1978).

Showalter, E., *Sexual Anarchy: Gender and culture at the fin de siècle* (London: Bloomsbury, 1991).

Stokes, J., *In the Nineties* (Hemel Hempstead: Harvester Wheatsheaf, 1989).

Stubbs, P., *Women and Fiction: Feminism and the novel 1880–1920* (1979; London: Methuen, 1981).

Vicinus, M., *Independent Women: Work and community for single women 1850–1920* (London: Virago, 1985).

Zatlin, L. G., *Aubrey Beardsley and Victorian Sexual Politics* (Oxford: Oxford University Press, 1990).

Women and theatre 1850–1920

Adlard, E. (ed.), *Edy: Recollections of Edith Craig* (London: Frederick Muller, 1949).

Ashwell, L., *Myself a Player* (London: Michael Joseph, 1936).

Aston, E., *Sarah Bernhardt: A French actress on the English stage* (Oxford: Berg, 1989).

Auerbach, N., *Ellen Terry: Player in her time* (New York: W. W. Norton; London: Dent, 1987).

Baylis, L. and C. Hamilton, *The Old Vic* (London: Cape, 1926).

Christiansen, R., *Prima Donna* (London: Penguin, 1984).

Clément, C. *Opera, or the Undoing of Women*, trans. Betsy Wing, (London: Virago Press, 1989).

Davis, T. C., 'Acting in Ibsen', *Theatre Notebook*, vol. xxxix, no. 3 (1985), pp. 113–23.

Dempsey, D., *The Triumphs and Trials of Lotta Crabtree* (New York: William Morrow, 1968).

Drinker, S., *Music and Women* (New York: Coward McCann, 1948).

Duncan, I., *Isadora; My life* (London: Victor Gollancz, 1928).

Farson, D., *Marie Lloyd and the Music Hall* (London: Tom Stacey, 1972).

Ferris, L., *Acting Women: Images of women in theatre* (London: Macmillan Education, 1990).

Findlater, R., *Lilian Baylis: The lady of the Old Vic* (London: Allen Lane, 1975).

Fitzlyon, A., *The Price of Genius: A life of Pauline Viardot* (London: John Calder, 1964).

Fitzsimmons, L. and V. Gardner (eds), *New Woman Plays* (London: Methuen, 1991).

Garden, M. and L. Biancolli, *Mary Garden's Story* (London: Michael Joseph, 1952).

Gardner, V. (ed.), *Sketches from the Actresses' Franchise League* (Nottingham: Nottingham Drama Texts, 1985).

Gilder, R., *Enter the Actress* (London: Harrap, 1931).

Goodie, S., *Annie Horniman: A pioneer in the theatre* (London: Methuen, 1990).

Guilbert, Y., *The Song Of My Life*, trans. Beatrice de Holthoir (London: George G. Harrap, 1929).

Guilbert, Y. and H. Simpson, *Struggles and Victories* (London: Mills and Boon, 1910).

Hamilton, C., *Life Errant* (London: Dent, 1935).

Holledge, J., *Innocent Flowers: Women in the Edwardian theatre* (London: Virago, 1981).

Howard, K., *Confessions of an Opera Singer* (London: Kegan Paul, 1920).

Kellogg, C. L., *Memoirs of an American Prima Donna* (New York and London: Putnam, 1913).

Kent, C., 'Image and reality: The actress and society' in Martha Vicinus (ed.), *A Widening Sphere: Changing roles of Victorian women* (1977; London: Methuen, 1980).

Kettle, M., *Salome's Last Veil: The libel case of the century* (London: Granada, 1977).

Kingston, G., *Curtsey While You're Thinking . . .* (London: Williams and Norgate, 1937).

Knapp, B., *That Was Yvette: The biography of the great diseuse* (London: Fredreich Muller, 1966).

Johnson, C., *American Actress: Perspective on the nineteenth century* (Chicago: Nelson Hall, 1984).

Johnson, J., *Florence Farr: Bernard Shaw's 'New Woman'* (Totowa: Rowman and Littlefield, 1975).

McCarthy, L., *Myself and My Friends* (London: Thornton Butterworth, 1933).

Maitland, S., *Vesta Tilley* (London: Virago, 1986).

Melville, J., *Ellen and Edy: A biography of Ellen Terry and her daughter, Edith Craig 1847–1947* (London: Pandora Press, 1987).

Moore, E., *Exits and Entrances* (London: Chapman and Hall, 1923).

Nevinson, M. W., *Life's Fitful Fever* (London: A. and C. Black, 1926).

Peters, M., *Mrs Pat: The life of Mrs Patrick Campbell* (London: Hamish Hamilton, 1985).

Peters, M., *Bernard Shaw and the Actresses: A biography* (New York: Doubleday, 1980).

Pogson, R., *Miss Horniman and the Gaiety Theatre, Manchester* (London: Rockliff, 1952).

Raby, P., *Fair Ophelia: Harriet Smithson Berlioz* (Cambridge: Cambridge University Press, 1982).

Robins, E., *Both Sides of the Curtain* (London: Heinemann, 1940).

Robins, E., *Theatre and Friendship* (London: Cape, 1932).

Robins, E., *Ibsen and the Actress* (London: Hogarth Press, 1928).

Spender, D. and C. Hayman (eds), *How the Vote Was Won and Other Suffragette Plays* (London: Methuen, 1985).

Stokes, J., M. R. Booth, S. Bassnett, *Bernhardt, Terry, Duse: The actress in her time* (Cambridge: Cambridge University Press, 1988).

Stowell, S., *A Stage of Their Own: Feminist playwrights in the suffrage era* (Manchester: Manchester University Press, 1991).

Terry, E., *The Story of My Life* (London: Hutchinson, 1907).
'Trim' (ed.), *The Original, Complete, and Only Authentic Story of 'Old Wilds'* (Bradford, London: G. Vickers, 1888).
Vanbrugh, I., *To Tell my Story* (London: Hutchinson, 1948).
Vanbrugh, V., *Dare to be Wise* (London: Hodder and Stoughton, 1925).
Weaver, W., *Duse: A biography* (London: Thames and Hudson, 1984).
Weintraub, R. (ed.), *Fabian Feminist: Bernard Shaw and woman* (Pennsylvania: Pennsylvania State University, 1977).
Whitelaw, L., *The Life and Rebellious Times of Cicely Hamilton: Actress, writer, suffragist* (London: The Women's Press, 1990).

Theatre 1850–1920

Archer, W., *The Old Drama and the New* (London: Heinemann, 1923).
Archer, W., *The Theatrical World of 1893–1897*, 5 vols. (London: Walter Scott, 1894–8).
Baker, M., *The Rise of the Victorian Actor* (London: Croom Helm, 1978).
Beerbohm, M., *Around Theatres*, 2 vols (London: William Heinemann, 1924).
Beerbohm, M., *Last Theatres* (London: Rupert Hart-Davies, 1970).
Booth, M. R., *Victorian Spectacular Theatre 1850–1910* (London: Routledge and Kegan Paul, 1981).
Bratton, J. S. (ed.), *Music Hall: Performance and style* (Stony Stratford: Open University Press, 1986).
Busby, R., *British Music Hall: An illustrated who's who from 1850 to the present day* (London: Paul Elek, 1976).
Chance, N., *Cues and Curtain Calls* (London: Bodley Head, 1927).
Clarke, L., *Edwardian Drama* (London: Faber, 1989).
Donnay, M., *Autour du Chat Noir* (Paris: Arthene Fayard, 1924).
Filon, A., *The English Stage: Being an account of the Victorian drama* (London: John Milne, 1897).
Fyfe, H., *Sir Arthur Pinero's Plays and Players* (London: Ernest Benn, 1930).
Holroyd, M., *Bernard Shaw*, 3 vols. (London: Chatto and Windus, 1988–91).
Jackson, R. (ed.), *Victorian Theatre* (London: A. and C. Black, 1989).
Jerome, J. K., *Stageland* (London: Chatto and Windus, 1893).
Jobe, J. (ed.), *The Romance of Ballooning: The story of the early aeronauts* (London: Patrick Stephens, 1971).
Knoblock, E., *Round the Room* (London: Chapman and Hall, 1939).
Marston, W., *Our Recent Actors* (London: Sampson Low, Marston, Seale and Rivington, 1890).
Meisel, M., *Shaw and the Nineteenth Century Theatre* (Princeton, N.J.: Princeton University Press, 1963).
McDonald, J., *The New Drama, 1900–1914* (Basingstoke: Macmillan, 1986).
McQueen Pope W., *Haymarket: Theatre of perfection* (London: W. H. Allen, 1948).
McQueen Pope, W., *Gaiety: Theatre of enchantment* (London: W. H. Allen, 1949).
McQueen Pope, W., *St James's: Theatre of distinction* (London: W. H. Allen, 1958).

Mullin, D. (ed.), *Victorian Actors and Actresses in Review* (Westport: Greenwood, 1983).

Powell, K., *Oscar Wilde and the Theatre of the 1890s* (Cambridge: Cambridge University Press, 1990).

le Roux, H. and J. Garnier, *Acrobats and Mountebanks*, trans. A. P. Morgan (London: Chapman & Hall, 1890).

Rowell, G., *Victorian Dramatic Criticism* (London: Methuen, 1971).

Rowell, G., *The Victorian Theatre 1792–1914*, 2nd edn (Cambridge: Cambridge University Press, 1978).

Rowell, G. and A. Jackson, *The Repertory Movement: A history of regional theatres* (Cambridge: Cambridge University Press, 1984).

Sanderson, M., *From Irving to Olivier* (London: Athlone Press, 1984).

Scott, C., *Some Notable Hamlets* (London: 1905; repr. New York and London: Benjamin Blom, 1969).

Scott, C., *Drama of Yesterday and Today*, Vols I and II (London: Macmillan, 1899).

Segal, H. B., *Turn of the Century Cabaret* (New York: Columbia University Press, 1987).

Shaw, G. B., *Our Theatre in the Nineties*, 3 vols (London: Constable, 1932).

Stokes, J., *Resistible Theatres* (London: Paul Elek, 1972).

Taylor, G., *Players and Performance in the Victorian Theatre* (Manchester: Manchester University Press, 1990).

Thetard, H., *La Merveilleuse du histoire du cirque* (Paris: Prisma, 1947).

Toole-Scott, R., *Circus and Allied Arts: A world bibliography* (Derby: Harpur, 1958–71).

Trewin, J. C., *The Edwardian Theatre* (Oxford: Basil Blackwell, 1976).

Woodfield, J., *English Theatre in Transition 1881–1914* (London: Croom Helm, 1984).